Endless Enemies

Endless Enemies

Inside FBI Counterterrorism

Raymond W. Holcomb
with Lillian S. Weiss

Potomac Books
Washington, D.C.

Library of Congress Cataloging-in-Publication Data
Holcomb, Raymond W.
  Endless enemies : inside FBI counterterrorism / Raymond W. Holcomb, with Lillian S. Weiss. — 1st ed.
      p. cm.
   Includes index.
   ISBN 978-1-59797-361-8 (hbk.)
   1. Holcomb, Raymond W. 2. United States. Federal Bureau of Investigation—Officials and employees—Biography. 3. Terrorism—Prevention. I. Weiss, Lillian S. II. Title.
   HV7911.H57A3 2011
   363.325'1630973—dc22

                                                    2011005057

Printed in the United States of America on acid-free paper that meets the American National Standards Institute Z39-48 Standard.

Potomac Books, Inc.
22841 Quicksilver Drive
Dulles, Virginia 20166

First Edition

10 9 8 7 6 5 4 3 2 1

To Kim and Michael

Contents

Acknowledgments

In many cases, I have changed names or used only first ones to protect privacy and to avoid endangering some of the individuals I worked with during my career with the Federal Bureau of Investigation. I have also not identified sites when to do so could compromise national security.

The following individuals allowed me to use their names and generously contributed some of their recollections to this story: Dave Bernal, one of my partners in Athens; my close SWAT team members, Bob Aldridge, Tom Lagatol, Clint Guenther, Kirby Scott, Paul Sutherland, Dan Fethiere, and Tom Bara; George Piro, one of my Fly Team stars; and Mike Dorris, the amazing legal attaché whom I first met in Istanbul.

Thank you, Geoff and Squad C-25, for a great, memorable ten years. There were countless days on the job when I wondered out loud, "And they pay me to do this?"

I am indebted to many others who stood with me, covered my back, and taught me to be a better agent. Time did not allow me to seek each of you out and request permission to use your names.

All photos are from my personal collection unless otherwise noted.

I am grateful to my wife, Wendy, for her unparalleled support, encouragement, and commitment to me and to the telling of my story. It has been many years in the making, and she has been generous in affording me the space and time to complete it.

I would also like to thank my coauthor, Lillian Weiss, for her endless patience and quiet determination. If there is some literary value in this book, it is a result of her subtle ability to oftentimes dissuade me from engaging in the "locker room" diatribe so common to the business I was in. She was able to take my endless ramblings and create a cogent and compelling narrative of my twenty-two-year career.

I wrote this book for many reasons, but first and foremost I wanted to honor the men and women of the FBI for their heroic work. I salute them all.

▪   ▪   ▪

Several government agencies reviewed this book prior to clearing it for publication. In some instances, names, places, and activities have been redacted on the basis that inclusion could adversely impact national security.

Preface

"Terrorism is the unlawful use of force and violence against persons or
property to intimidate or coerce a government, the civilian population,
or any segment thereof, in furtherance of political or social objectives."
—28 Code of Federal Regulations, section 0.85

The events of September 11, 2001, rocked the core of the institutions
charged with protecting America, inviting recriminations and accusations
from every quarter of the government and society. Some of the organizations
that deserved a share of the blame lay low, cosseted by the screen of secrecy.
Some used the failings and weaknesses to seize bigger budgets and more authority, neither of which were necessarily justifiable or of value. The Federal
Bureau of Investigation, meanwhile, could not hide by asserting that matters
were classified and therefore not for public consumption.

FBI Director Robert S. Mueller III delivered straightforward answers,
calmly and professionally, to a long string of congressional subcommittees.
Mueller was the right man at one of the thorniest periods in FBI history. With
his leadership, the FBI looked at what went wrong and resolved to fix it. All
bureau elements cooperated with every official inquiry and investigation. The
institutional self-analysis was brutally honest.

By their nature, government institutions resist change, and the FBI is no
exception. Nevertheless, the FBI, a hundred years old in 2008, made a radi-

cal shift in record time. Director Mueller understood that the FBI's existence depended on a new antiterrorism strategy and made it clear that developing it was now the bureau's first priority. He would address the identified organizational deficiencies and transform the FBI into an entity that could combat terrorism.

The outcome of the government's 9/11 probe was an acknowledgment of the government-wide need to consolidate and streamline the collection, analysis, and dissemination of information about threats to America and its interests. It revealed that there was no one place where all the evidence relating to terrorist threats could be sifted to look for the connections among the various leads.

With respect to the FBI in particular, we recognized that the bureau needed not just more personnel assigned to counterterrorism but also that the FBI's decentralized structure contributed to its inability to correlate the knowledge its components possessed. How could any agency make so radical a change in short order without sacrificing its principles? The FBI managed to do it. Meanwhile, it did not resort to harsh interrogation measures. It did not engage in unofficial covert propaganda campaigns to impugn other organizations or snatch power for the sake of having it. The bureau also continued to be admirably restrained, skilled, and sensitive in dealing with the Muslim community, pursuing every hate crime allegation that hinted at anti-Muslim paranoia.

Some of the information-sharing quandaries that 9/11 exposed would require massive recalibration among all the agencies involved and even legislative change. The FBI has to abide by many rules and regulations in preparing cases for trial to make sure their evidence stands up in court. Intelligence agencies don't have those concerns. The need to prepare for trials had always made it difficult for the FBI to cooperate with other agencies. Our intelligence-gathering organizations struggle daily with the idea of sharing information with another law enforcement agency that has to play by difficult rules. With few exceptions, successful prosecutions cannot be built on intelligence that is collected through sensitive techniques that cannot be disclosed to the enemy and that involve valuable human sources, people who have exposed themselves to extreme danger to acquire critical information and who cannot be identified and presented for cross-examination in civilian courts.

Individual privacy concerns referee every FBI investigation. Although the infamous pre-9/11 "wall" that barred the sharing of information collected under the Foreign Intelligence Surveillance Act (FISA) with criminal investigators has been largely dismantled, the bureau must still tread cautiously and observe the constitutional rights of every American citizen. No other U.S. intelligence-gathering or national security organization deals with the challenge that the FBI faces. Some other organizations still don't fully understand it. However, every day since the events of September 11, 2001, the FBI has gotten better at the job of tackling international terrorism while staying within the rules.

Of course, human frailties will always figure in the failure of law enforcement and intelligence agencies to work together. The drive for recognition and the egotism that is part of our nature continue to play a role in the hoarding of data. In nearly every position I held I saw the competition among law enforcement agencies, the resistance to change, and the jealous retention of information. The competition that put us at cross-purposes was under a microscope after 9/11, but it was an obvious yet unacknowledged problem well before that day.

▪   ▪   ▪

I was with the bureau for almost twenty-three years. During that period, I witnessed a metamorphosis from the J. Edgar Hoover days of six-shooter-toting, fedora-wearing G-Men hell-bent on catching bank robbers and top-ten most wanted fugitives to an organization committed to stopping terrorist attacks of a scope and nature unlike anything America had ever seen.

My career started in Athens, Georgia, where I experienced the culture shock of the Ku Klux Klan on parade, poverty and incest, moonshiners turned drug dealers, voting fraud, and police corruption. Moving to the bureau's New York City office, I conducted counterintelligence against the Soviet Union while the Cold War was still pretty hot and arrested organized crime figures. I became a counter-narcotics agent, working with a squad that racked up the biggest stateside heroin seizure in the history of U.S. drug enforcement. I also worked national security matters, responsible for the management, or "handling," of a high-level asset with access to the inner workings of some of our most dangerous enemies at the time. During this same period I spent fourteen years with the New York division's special weapons and tactics (SWAT) team and eventually, toward the end of my time in New York, became the first full-time SWAT team leader and coordinator.

When FBI SWAT first deployed overseas in response to the embassy bombings in Tanzania and Kenya in 1998, I was one of the first members of the New York team on the scene, walking the devastation that had been embassy sites. Although I had seen the damage caused by the first World Trade Center bombing in 1993, nothing impacted me as much as the destruction wrought by these homemade, truck-borne bombs. I deployed to Yemen after the USS *Cole* attack in October 2000 and was there on 9/11, when our mission abruptly changed to targeting the people who had played a role in the worst terrorist attack ever to take place on the U.S. mainland. I returned from Yemen, two months after 9/11, to a changed Manhattan and with a changed perspective.

After trying to resume my duties as the New York SWAT team leader, I elected to join the federal trial team preparing for the prosecution of Zacarias Moussaoui. A former attorney, I was assigned to the assistant U.S. attorney responsible for preparing the death penalty argument. As part of this assignment, I reviewed all the emergency phone calls from the World Trade Center victims, the cockpit recordings from the hijacked aircraft, and every private video taken of the Twin Towers by passersby on that terrible day.

In 2002, on the orders of the director of the FBI and with the able support of one or two others, I created the FBI's Fly Away Team (eventually referred to as the Fly Team). A first of its kind, it was intended to be a headquarters-based, elite counterterrorism unit. The *Washington Post* heralded the event with a headline, "FBI Director to Propose 'Super Squad' for Terror." My new assignment took me to facilities and places in Guantánamo Bay, Cuba; areas throughout Afghanistan; Istanbul, Turkey; Jakarta, Indonesia; West Africa; Yemen; and some other not-to-be-named locations.

I have been knuckle to knuckle with fanatical jihadists; Taliban members; young, radicalized Americans; and shrewd terrorism facilitators who are making a buck off of murder. And I have worked side by side with some of the most dedicated, decent people in the world. Whether in the United States or in some far corner of the world, most cops have an unwritten understanding, a bond. Many of them are driven by an overwhelming desire to improve things, to give their families and their countrymen a chance for a better life. Possibly the most rewarding part of my career was working with men and women who share this sentiment all over the world.

At the same time that the current was pulling me around each bend in my career, the FBI as an institution was undergoing the most tumultuous changes in its hundred-year history. Many times I found myself in the midst of some of the biggest FBI investigations in the last thirty years. Sometimes I was the captain of the team, and other times I was just the water boy with a sideline view of the action. But with unusual consistency I seemed to be at the right place at the right time.

During the span of my career, from the war against moonshiners to the one against terrorists, the vast majority of the agents I have known got up every day with a singular goal—to arrest criminals and put them behind bars. Their only medals are the successful convictions of these criminals and the confidence and respect of their peers. Americans know little about this battle. What they hear about in the headlines are the overblown errors or outright misrepresentations. My stories are about what good people, men and women, do every day—from the back streets of American cities to the mountains of Afghanistan.

One

Men in White Sheets

Often roused from bed in the middle of the night to arrest felons or to head for third world nations on extended missions, I worked long days and weekends for nearly twenty-three years. I did not become a rich man, and the toll on my personal life was immeasurable. However, I convinced myself that as a committed, hard-working agent, I was a positive role model for my children. In my mind, the example I set equated to being a good father. Duty to country, respect for the rule of law, and protecting the weak from those who prey on them are all good qualities for children to emulate.

However, it wore on my family. After years of my sudden departures and extended stays away, they stopped counting on my being there for them. My passion for the job kept me from seeing that the FBI family had, in some ways, supplanted my own. Even if I had recognized the imbalance, I doubt I would have done anything to right it. Being an FBI agent was not simply a means to feed my family and put a roof over our heads. It was as vital to me as the air that I breathed.

My first assignment city as a freshly minted FBI special agent was Athens, Georgia. It was a small town about sixty miles northeast of Atlanta, a two-man satellite office in dire need of damage control because, I was told, of an agent who had "entered his midlife crazies with a vengeance." I did not ask for Athens. I wanted New York since I lived in New Jersey, but agents rarely get a first assignment to a city near their home. J. Edgar Hoover set a policy early

1

on that sent agents as far away from home as possible, believing they were less susceptible to corruption in an unfamiliar environment. He also thought that transferring young agents to remote spots would encourage them to substitute the FBI for their traditional nuclear family and friends and that this close-knit circle would forge loyalties that benefited the bureau.

It was August 1984. I drove down to Athens to find a place to live and meet my new partner. After crossing Lake Hartwell, which separates South Carolina from Georgia, I exited the interstate onto a two-lane road that skirted the hometown of Joel Chandler Harris, the journalist of post-Reconstruction Atlanta who wrote the Uncle Remus series. The setting was bucolic, as I had expected; *Gone with the Wind*'s Tara was a replica of a plantation just south of Athens.

The setting became gloomier. Although New Jersey gets ridiculed for its turnpike refineries and rude, loud people, Georgia is marketed to the rest of the country as warm and friendly, the land of civility and Southern courtesy. No one tells you about the insidious fields of kudzu, the Asian weed import that is gradually overtaking a vast expanse of the Southern countryside; the ramshackle tenant farmer shacks where the descendants of original plantation slaves still lived below the poverty level; or the interminable acres of auto salvage yards that blight the landscape. It was remarkable. That day, on a protracted stretch of backcountry road, I met the underbelly of the Peach State. I made a wrong turn through an impoverished neighborhood where chickens had claimed the streets and poor families sat clustered on stoops fronting shuttered, crumbling homes. Very conscious of my New Jersey plates, I hurried toward the town's center. It featured the ubiquitous statue of a Confederate soldier, saber held high in defiance and his back toward the North. Then the Ku Klux Klan (KKK) in full regalia, carrying Confederate flags, came marching down Main Street. For a Yankee, the entire scene was surreal.

An old, marble-encased federal building framed by huge magnolia trees housed the FBI's Athens resident agency. As I walked up the steps, an elderly black man, a little ahead of me, stepped aside and held the door open. Maybe he did so because of my suit, or he could have thought I was the postmaster or the circuit court judge. My footsteps echoed through the hollow stairwell as I climbed the three floors to the FBI office. A giant figure answered my knock. He sported a full beard, a Greek fisherman's cap, sneakers, a tight T-shirt, and shorts much too small for his immense frame. He reminded me of Popeye's archenemy, Bluto.

"Welcome!" His booming voice matched his frame. "The name's Wayne. Your new partner, Ed, is not here. He's home helping his wife unpack." As a huge hand enveloped mine, I glanced around the ragged walls of the minuscule, two-room office. The sole adornments were the FBI seal and two ancient pictures of J. Edgar in his classic bulldog posture.

Wayne sat down behind the standard, battleship-gray, metal government desk, motioning me to do the same next to a wall with shards of peeling paint curling downward like Howard Hughes's fingernails. Wayne had been a Chicago cop before he joined the FBI, and he'd only been with the bureau a short while. "When I got the job, they wanted me to go undercover with the Hells Angels. I ride a Harley, and I'll be the first to admit that I do look like one of them." He had said no because he had two young kids and the assignment carried too much risk. He did not want his family to get involved and could not let the Angels know his wife and kids even existed. That situation would have meant living two separate lives. He had landed in Athens, and now the bureau wanted him in New York City. Although accustomed to working in a big city, Wayne said no to New York. "They wanted to assign me to a Chinese counterintelligence squad. I couldn't see it. And you can barely eke out a living on an agent's salary there." He gave me the rundown about Athens and then relayed a message from my partner. "Ed would like you to stop over his house later."

I called my new partner for directions from my motel and drove to his modest rental. Inside we sat on folding chairs in the cramped living room, boxes stacked up to the ceiling. Ed was seventeen years my senior, a veteran agent with a relaxed, confident demeanor. He had met his wife, Cathy, when he was with the FBI's Boston office. Cathy was part of the steno pool found in every major bureau office of that time, staffed with skilled, educated, and highly motivated women who were proud to be working for J. Edgar. Hers was a respectable job, which often had the added benefit of enabling her to meet a good man to marry. In Ed and Cathy's case, the relationship had worked out according to script.

I felt good about Ed; our conversation was easy. We discussed my history, and I could tell he was sizing me up, wondering whether I was going to carry my weight. Although Ed said little about himself, I sensed I was about to work with a professional. He explained that this transfer was his fourth and that they only got harder. On orders from the bureau, he and Cathy had once again moved from the town where they had tried to settle in, arriving in Athens and struggling to find the energy to start all over.

I had to find a place to live. The sergeant in charge of the Athens post of the Georgia State Police, good friends of the local FBI, offered me a private room in their barracks until I could find a house. The first morning I awoke and shuffled down the hall to the common shower, I returned to find my bed made military style, and my shoes polished and neatly positioned on the floor. Minutes later, men in white jumpsuits with a large black stripe running down each pant leg walked up and down the hall, taking out trash and pushing mops. Prisoners from the county jail, they had earned the right through good behavior to wash cars, mop floors, and make beds.

Within a matter of three days, I plunged into a way of life I thought no longer existed and for which I had no frame of reference. From tobacco fields to "Welcome to the Home of Song of the South" signs, sharecroppers, the Ku Klux Klan, the Confederate flag flying in the town square, prison trustees polishing my shoes, and deferential older blacks still bearing the scars of fear and oppression, I'd have to adapt to do my job. On top of it all, my new partner and I had to rebuild the tarnished reputation of the FBI in northeast Georgia, thanks to one of our predecessors.

Ed became my mentor, teaching me countless lessons that were important for this northern boy to learn, including how to deal with southern folk. Ed grew up in the South but had spent time in the U.S. Navy and then traversed the country for the bureau. He took the time to understand the people and the local culture. He told me, "When you are out in the country trying to find a location, first find a local gas station, not some modern 'pump and go' but an old mom-and-pop operation. There'll be a little old man in a rocker on the porch. Go into the store and buy an RC Cola and a MoonPie or a Little Debbie, then sit on the front step next to that little old man. Never talk fast. That will mark you as a Yankee straight away. Ask about the weather; say it's a nice day and just converse for a while. Then, when it's comfortable, pose your question in a very polite way. Nine times out of ten you will get an honest and friendly answer." That kind of intuitive sense made Ed one great investigator.

Within weeks, Ed was developing several good criminal cases. One involved a former deputy sheriff turned private investigator who was also dealing drugs. He was running wiretaps for his drug clients and exchanging money and dope with his friends inside the sheriff's department for protected information on local people. With the help of an informant, Ed developed an airtight case. The night of the arrest, Ed had arranged for a hidden camera and mike in a local motel room where the informant was to meet with the subject. Ed's team, consisting of Georgia Bureau of Investigation (GBI) agents and Clarke County detectives, watched as the subject completed a drug deal and then took a big hit of cocaine. Conspicuous in his waistband was a semi-automatic pistol. When he rose to leave the motel, Ed gave the radio signal to arrest him.

I had just gotten into town that night from Atlanta and arrived at the location as Ed gave the signal. Not wanting to miss out, I radioed for instructions, and Ed told me to help with the arrest. Inexperience and eagerness can be dangerous. As I turned the corner of the motel, a door flew open and a plainclothes officer screamed out, "Freeze, motherfucker!" as he drew down on me with his weapon. The look in his eyes told me that he was a split second away from shooting me.

I stopped on a dime and bolted behind a column. "Don't shoot! I'm FBI!"

He instantly lowered his weapon and without a word we intuitively moved on together to help with the arrest. Just at that moment, another officer confronted our subject in the parking lot and ordered him to halt and raise his hands. The subject, high on drugs, smiled and continued walking. Without any verbal communication, the two officers and I tackled him from three directions. The effect of all of us hitting the subject simultaneously was similar to striking a telephone pole. All we did was stand him up straight. The one cop, still grasping his pistol, wrapped his arm around the subject's neck. Seconds into the melee, his gun discharged. In Keystone Kop fashion, we all froze, including our big, drugged-up, former deputy sheriff. Everyone was patting himself down, expecting to find blood spurting from some part of his body. The gun had discharged next to the subject's ear, obliterating his hearing and leaving a powder burn on his cheek. Incredibly, the bullet missed everyone, managing to pass vertically down through a Gordian knot of human limbs and implant itself in the pavement.

This bust was my first arrest, the first time I had drawn my weapon for real. Later that evening, after the adrenaline rush had subsided, alone and having a beer on my back porch, I realized how easily this job could get me killed.

As the junior agent in the office, I had to do some mundane background investigation work in addition to my caseload. It related to people who had lived or gone to school in Athens and were being appointed to top government positions or under consideration for an FBI job. Of course, I liked it better when I could work my own criminal cases or was assigned to a "special," where our headquarters in Atlanta authorized a surge of manpower to help with a major investigation or case about to be taken down. One of these specials involved a corruption case in Atlanta, where a senior police officer was among those arrested by the joint FBI and GBI task force. Another involved voting fraud allegations in a northern Georgia county smack in the middle of Appalachia.

As it turned out, I was fortunate that the local sheriffs accepted me, a Yankee G-Man. Through sheer luck (my surname is extremely common in northern Georgia), hard work, and the regular sharing of modest amounts of confiscated moonshine, I could work effectively in an environment that didn't usually respond well to outsiders.

Our territory encompassed most of northeastern Georgia, and it took hours to make our way across those big counties. Once a month, I would head out on a road trip as a public relations gesture, visiting some of the local sheriffs. Inevitably, they would pull out a little mason jar full of clear liquid from a desk drawer. It was seized moonshine, high-octane stuff that could blind you if it wasn't made right. It even could kill you if the still was made of the wrong kind of metal, but I could rely on the quality of the sheriff's take. These men knew all the moonshiners in their region, so they were privy to who made the best liquor and always saved a sample for "evidence." I would have a couple of shots with one sheriff and more with the others. It was challenging making it home after these stopovers, but it was essential to working rural Georgia in those days. The locals—sheriffs and cops—could get by without the FBI, but the reverse was not true. Young agents learned early that if they were going to be successful they needed the locals.

The moonshiners were a tough bunch. Most of the successful ones transitioned into the cocaine business. Their money-laundering and transport systems worked almost as well for cocaine as they did for moonshine. They adapted to new criminal opportunities; with smuggling routes already in place, they developed systems for concealing their cash profits. Relying on longtime, trusted employees, many of them relatives, the moonshiners usually had a few members of local law enforcement and some politicians in their back pockets. That made the shift to narcotics, primarily cocaine, relatively easy. They flew it in from southern Florida and transported it farther north and west by car. The planes touched down on landing strips carved out of farm fields, and crooked sheriffs ensured that no honest law enforcement was in the general vicinity when they expected incoming flights. This era was cocaine's heyday, when southern Florida was awash in drugs and *Miami Vice* was the most popular show on television. Routinely, we received anonymous tips about drug dealers who were flying their product to northern Georgia on private planes, paying off the local deputies, and off-loading their cargo on someone's farm or dropping packages from the air to waiting boats on one of the lakes. Even though we knew there were corrupt sheriffs and deputies, these were hard cases to crack since a G-Man could not step into a Georgia county without someone tipping off the sheriff. It was the most effective early warning system I have ever seen, in the pre–cell phone era, when pay phones were far apart and party telephone lines still serviced most of the countryside.

With most of these good old boys turning into cocaine cowboys, van conversion companies were springing up all over the region. A lavish lifestyle needed authentication with a legitimate income source. Van conversion was as good as any trade for laundering drug cash. You only needed money and a rudimentary knowledge of auto mechanics to get into the business. Tough and shrewd, these boys sported a veneer of civility, hobnobbing with politicians and playing golf at the local country club. They owned the bars, the prostitutes, and the drug distribution rings. They branched into city and county contracts; bought vacation homes in the Florida Panhandle, more commonly known as the Redneck Riviera; and sent their children to the better southern colleges. They lived just as the Italian mobsters up North did.

These boys had a unique way of disposing of people who threatened them. If the annoyance didn't roast in a trailer home fire, he was tossed down one of the many defunct wells that spotted the Georgia countryside, with a stick or two of dynamite chucked in after him. We called it a Dixie Mafia send-off.

Ed and I were developing one local boy who had snorted, gambled, and drunk himself into debt and needed an informant's paycheck. Just as he was beginning to provide some reasonably good information on a dishonest sheriff we had been after, he burned himself up in his double-wide. There was firm evidence that someone had blocked the trailer door from the outside and little question that the fire was arson. These southern dons were no less serious about protecting their lucrative businesses than the Colombo or Lucchese crime bosses in the North and were every bit as vicious.

FBI agents out of the Atlanta office built major corruption and narcotics cases against a number of people, including "respectable" businesspersons, politicians, and a deputy chief of the Atlanta Police Department. I led one of the arrest teams. Our location was a house where narcotics were stored, processed, and distributed. My three teammates were GBI agents, talented and seasoned people with more experience than I had. It was a rainy night, and in the fashion of the day, I was wearing my suit and tie even as I carried a twelve-gauge shotgun. The only item missing was a fedora. We knocked and waited the requisite seconds for a response. When we heard none, we took the door down with a sledgehammer and went inside to begin our methodical search. Buried in the freezer were several kilos of cocaine, scales, and all the usual drug paraphernalia.

Our search had taken over two hours, it was late, and I was tired and wondering why two of my men were taking so long to search the bedroom. When I walked in, I saw a stack of videocassette recorder tapes on the bed and the two agents on the edge of the mattress, glued to the television set, playing home videos of cocaine queens that our subject had seduced with drugs. Some of these women could have walked away with the crown in any beauty pageant, yet they were submitting to everything conceivable so they could get their dope. "OK, guys, what's going on here? We've got to wrap this up some time tonight!"

"Agent Holcomb, these tapes could contain vital clues, important information that could lead us to other members of this drug operation."

"Well, guys, how would you identify those 'other criminals' in a lineup? From what I'm seeing the only thing you'd have to go by would be the shape of their butts, but it may be that y'all are good at that."

▓   ▓   ▓

Many of my investigations took me deep into the mountains of Appalachia. Searching for a bank robbery fugitive in one dilapidated home, I almost toppled into a hole in the middle of the floor. The stench of feces was strong, but it still took a few seconds to realize that I was staring down into a makeshift privy. Only fifty feet out the back door was a wooded area where anyone with just a little ambition or concern for basic hygiene could have dug a latrine. Years later, doing counterintelligence work in the worst parts of Harlem and the Bronx, where crack cocaine vials crunched underfoot everywhere I stepped and I thought the roaches would carry me away, I would never see anything remotely similar to the primitive conditions I came across in parts of Appalachia.

One day our headquarters in Atlanta received a complaint that one political party was buying just enough votes to sway the county commission election. This county had only twenty thousand registered voters, and the margin of victory was two hundred votes. The FBI has always taken political corruption and voting fraud cases seriously, so a dozen agents headed for the northwestern mountains of Georgia, right up against the Tennessee–North Carolina border.

We started with verifying all the write-in ballots. Two-agent teams, each accompanied by a local deputy, took a stack of ballots daily and then set out to find the folks who had signed them. Whenever I felt I could trust local law enforcement to some degree, I would sit down with the chief or sheriff and politely ask for his assistance. He always appreciated it. Even if I was targeting his department or the man I was talking to, I could devise a convincing story about why I was in town and why I needed help finding a particular person or place.

So every day for a week, we picked up our packet of ballots and struck out with our deputy to track down and interview voters. Once we drove down a rutted dirt road to find a shack built, in part, from billboard signs. I learned early to watch for chicken manure, since few things smell worse, especially once it was tracked into the car. After carefully stepping around the minefields, we approached the hovel, the clapboard door swinging open eerily. A horrible blast of rank air hit us. The obligatory mongrel junkyard dog was beside the man who stood on the threshold. His age was hard to determine.

He could have been as young as twenty-two or somewhere around fifty, but he reminded me of a disheveled Anthony Perkins in *Psycho*. He greeted us with standard southern politeness, probably in response to the suit, tie, white shirt, and wingtips we wore. We would always dress that way whenever we were on duty, whether we were going to a court of law or a trailer park. When folks in the country saw us, they had a good idea we were one of Hoover's boys. More often than not, in spite of an ingrained suspicion of government and outsiders, they trusted us. To many there was a clear difference between the FBI and local law enforcement. While most of the sheriffs and deputies were good, honest men, too often their departments, just as most of the local government in general, harbored a bias against those folks who had campaigned or voted against the party in power, and somehow everyone always seemed to know who those folks were. There were few secrets in rural Georgia. During my time in Athens, I spoke with a number of Georgians who told me that they had had to move to another county after their candidate lost.

Yet we, the FBI, were the one connection rural folks had to a world where there was some justice, where men swore an oath and stuck to it. One anonymous caller to our office explained how strange, low-flying planes were dropping parcels into Lake Hartwell late at night. He concluded the message by saying, "You are the only people around here I can trust." Early on in my Athens assignment I recognized this fact, and I doubled my commitment to my job, realizing that Ed and I were in many cases these people's last line of hope.

Just as Ed explained to me early on, I had to make small talk with these people, and a northern pace would not do if I wanted them to trust me. After identifying myself as a special agent of the FBI to the man in the shack's doorway, I started a conversation about generalities. I chatted about the area and asked him what a stranger might consider unique about the terrain. He responded, "These hills are filled with Indian arrowheads. I've been collecting them all my life."

I expressed an interest, only in part self-serving, and he invited us inside to see his artifacts. One wall displayed Indian arrowheads, spearheads, and tomahawk heads that he had pulled from mountain streams. I have been to museums all over the world and have never seen so extensive and varied a collection as the one this humble man had meticulously mounted on his walls. The stunning array stood out among the squalor.

The shack had mostly dirt floors except a couple of rooms had old sections of scavenged linoleum covering the ground. Little light entered inside, and bare bulbs glared from the ceiling. I asked who had signed the ballot we held. He said he had signed it for his parents because they were both too feeble to write. At my request to meet his folks, he motioned us into another room, which was the darkest yet. It took a few seconds for my vision to adjust, and I sensed the beginning of a throbbing headache. It was becoming a minor distraction.

My eyes focused on the flame of a gas heater in the center of the room. Then I got it. The smell, the headache—I was being poisoned by gas, slowly, as surely as this ashen gray man was gradually killing himself. He motioned to something on an old sofa against the wall. "There's Mommy and Daddy," he said in that typical southern way that grown, rugged men refer to their parents. The two ancients on the couch looked like cadavers, sitting side by side and staring out with almost lifeless eyes, filthy blankets pulled up under their chins. I stared at the couple, looking for a sign of life, and noticed a flicker of movement from the father. Neither was in any condition to answer questions.

"Mr. Parsons, why don't we step outside," I said. "And by the way, Mr. Parsons, I think you've got yourself a faulty heater there. It could be endangering your health and your parents' health, too."

"I surely will look into that, sir, I surely will," Parsons said politely. I could see that my advice hadn't registered.

Too much dead in there already, I thought, before speaking to him again. "So, Mr. Parsons, I have only a couple of questions. Please remember that you are speaking to a sworn law enforcement officer who has authority to investigate violations of the federal voting laws."

"I surely understand, sir." He nodded.

The fresh mountain air was starting to ease my pounding head. "So you signed these forms on behalf of your mother and father. When you signed these forms and dated them, was the rest of the form completed?"

"Naw, sir, the form was blank."

"So you returned it incomplete?"

"I reckon that is correct, sir."

"Have you always completed write-in ballots that way, Mr. Parsons?"

"As far back as I can remember. I've been getting twenty dollars for them for a long time now."

As we walked back up the hill, my partner shot me a stare of disbelief. We knew not to discuss this development in front of the local deputy, since the sheriff handpicked all his men. I did comment loud enough for the deputy to hear, "It's got to be that propane heater that's killing them all."

The deputy, chewing on a toothpick, nodded, "I'll get the county welfare folks out here to take a look." I seriously doubted that it was going to happen anytime soon.

Most of our forays into the mountains were in search of fugitives. Appalachian folk had polite and cordial exteriors that sometimes belied an unsavory side. They would lie to protect kin, and I had no doubt that a few would resort to violence under the right circumstances.

In the main, we looked for bank robbers and thieves who specialized in stolen motor vehicles or heavy construction equipment. For some reason these southern boys had perfected the art of stealing bulldozers, earthmovers, dump trucks, tractor trailers—anything big and yellow. They would jump-start them at construction sites and transport the machinery into the mountains, where they would bury them in pre-dug holes until the heat died down. Then they would dig them up, grind off their serial numbers, repaint them, and sell them to unscrupulous contractors. This activity was big business in the South.

We also had to deal with an undercurrent of racism still prevailing in Athens, a town infamous for the murder of a black U.S. Army Reserve officer in the early 1960s. During that period of heightened racial tensions when the civil rights movement was just starting to gain strength, three black officers were driving to Washington, D.C., after completing summer reserve duty at one of the military bases in Georgia. Since the interstate highway did not exist, they had to pass through Athens, stopping for gas. Members of the local KKK spotted these black men in a car with D.C. plates and presumed that they were civil rights activists bringing trouble to town. The Klan members got some friends to join them, followed the reservists out of town, and killed one of the three, Lemuel Penn, with shotgun blasts. Getting a fair jury in the state superior court trial became an obvious problem. Some of the jurors were secretly KKK members, and certainly most of the others were sympathetic to their cause. The verdict was not guilty.

The Civil Rights Act of 1964, passed nine days before the killing, gave the federal government jurisdiction over murders that occurred in the context of a civil rights violation. For the first time, the FBI could move in on such a case, taking it out of the hands of state and local prosecutors. Instructed by Attorney General Bobby Kennedy, Hoover sent an enormous amount of manpower to Athens, approximately sixty-five agents headed by a special agent in charge (SAC) who would oversee a massive investigation into the murders that would test the new civil rights law.

Overnight, agents were everywhere. They knocked on doors and developed informants, convincing one of the participants in the murder to testify against the others. Every evening they cabled a detailed progress report to Washington for Hoover's eyes only. Within months, they had a solid case, filed charges, and got a conviction in federal court. The verdict sent a message that blacks would no longer be harassed, attacked, tortured, and murdered without redress and that a big hammer would come down on you no matter where you were or what your cronies' political connections were. Kennedy delivered on the promise he had made with his brother, the late president John F. Kennedy, and Hoover, ever the shrewd survivor, threw the FBI into the fray with fervor.

Even in 1984, however, a racist overtone was still palpable within the ranks of state and local law enforcement. Because of the amount of work Ed and I were turning in and the volume by which we had increased the arrest and conviction stats, the FBI gave us a third body a year after I got to Athens. David Jesus Bernal was straight out of the academy. Big and handsome, the son of first-generation Mexican Americans and a former Kansas City, Missouri, police officer, he had the polished voice of a radio disc jockey. While Dave had to be cognizant of the lingering tinge of racism, he always handled himself as a professional, and those who dealt with him—even the good old boys—learned to respect him.

At a state police barbecue late one afternoon, some of those good old boys were drinking heavily in one corner as Ed, Dave, and I made light conversation nearby. When the only African American law enforcement officer assigned to Athens, State Trooper Johnson, entered the room, one of the white troopers started throwing around the term "nigger" loud enough for Johnson to hear. When the loudmouthed white trooper noticed Dave glaring at him, he started in with an Indian chant. The room was electric with tension by the time some of his less inebriated buddies escorted him out of the room.

Ed told one of the veteran troopers, "Sarge, it's getting a little late, and we're going to excuse ourselves." The sergeant was Ed's friend and a man of character. He called Ed the next day to apologize for the incident and told him that certain men of his would be working the night shift for some time to come.

A few days later, the offending trooper personally apologized to Dave. After that, he made himself scarce whenever Dave came around.

FBI Headquarters in Washington made civil rights cases a priority. The staffers assigned people to review every major national newspaper, scrolling for stories that smacked of civil rights abuses. They circumvented the standard process of sending investigative leads to the field offices for forwarding to the local resident agencies. If a headquarters staffer found something of concern in our territory, we would get a teletype message with marching orders directly from the Hoover Building in D.C., and a quick response was expected. As the new kid in the office, at least until Dave joined us, I handled most of the civil rights investigations. They were important, but chasing after people for sending hate letters, painting graffiti, or burning crosses—while these things were despicable—was not as glamorous as capturing bank robbers or Mafia killers. Civil rights investigations required some special skills, especially in areas of the Deep South where a northern-raised federal agent was clearly operating in semi-hostile territory. On top of that, an agent can never forget that a friend on the task force, or the local detective who provides the help an agent can get nowhere else, may one day be the target of a federal case. Civil rights and corruption cases are the divides that will always stand between the FBI and other law enforcement agencies. It is that responsibility that will always keep the FBI agent from being a complete "brother in arms" with most police officers. Good cops understand that distinction and respect it.

Only a short time after I arrived in Athens, we received word that a prisoner appeared to have committed suicide in an outlying facility. A young black man, he was found hanging by a bedsheet in his cell in the Elbert County jail. I was handed the case and called for a meeting with the sheriff. Ed knew I was nervous. Because he had done a good job of sizing me up, he told me in his understated but wise way, "Ray, if you have any questions or concerns, just ask. I know you can handle it." On my long drive out to Elberton, I wondered how I, a northerner and an FBI agent investigating a possible civil rights crime, was going to barge into a town in the Deep South and stick my nose into the sheriff's business. If his men did not slam the door in my face, they would undoubtedly lie, hindering my investigation in any way they could. I was in their world, with only a semi-reliable bureau radio connecting me to mine.

I pulled into Elberton where, just as in many other southern towns of that era, stray dogs slept in the street and a statue of good old Colonel Buford stood defiantly in the middle of the town square. I walked into the sheriff's office and, although as obvious as a billboard, identified myself. Hardly looking up, his secretary responded, "Sheriff's busy. Have a seat."

As I waited, I noticed that everyone coming and going into the building was black. I thought that a little curious. Finally, the black secretary summoned me into the sheriff's inner sanctum. I steeled myself so I could look confident and in charge. I walked into the office, hesitating slightly when I saw a large black man wearing the sheriff's uniform sitting behind a desk cluttered with all the insignia of rank and authority. Then I got it.

Elberton was one of those old sharecropper towns populated largely by blacks. If a crime had really occurred here, it was not racially motivated. Had this been a white-versus-black situation, it would have been a tough investigation. I was relieved that the FBI lacked clear jurisdiction and glad to pass the case on to be somebody else's headache. Murder is generally a state offense unless it falls within one of the federal categories. Misuse of police power to deprive someone of his life can be construed as a federal offense, but U.S. attorneys, typically overwhelmed with work, rarely directed resources at a problem that did not scream out "federal violation."

After some small talk and questions, I asked, "So, Sheriff, what is your opinion regarding what actually happened?"

The big man pondered the question. Scanning the office ceiling, he said, "Well, Agent Holcomb, in my opinion this here is a clear-cut case of self-inflicted suicide."

I made a conscious effort not to show any expression. I thought, Hmmm, other than "suicide by cop," isn't all suicide self-inflicted?

"Thank you, Sheriff," I answered. "If I could, I'd like to talk to the folks on duty in the jail that night, and then I'll be on my way. Also, I'd like to thank you for your cooperation."

I spent a few more hours conducting interviews and learned that the victim's cell had been the only one with a bedsheet and that the deceased was considered by most to be the town's troublemaker. The coroner's report was absolutely no help. Days later, I prepared my preliminary report and delivered it to the U.S. attorney in Macon. That same day his office declined the matter, turning it over to the county prosecutor for further investigation.

After two and a half years in the Peach State, family reasons pushed me to ask for a transfer to the Northeast. My boss at that time was SAC Weldon Kennedy, who was well regarded throughout the bureau. A short time after my departure, he would successfully negotiate the end of a thirteen-day violent takeover at the Atlanta penitentiary. Even later, he would oversee the investigation and arrest of Oklahoma City bombers Timothy McVeigh and Terry Nichols.

Kennedy pondered my request. "Your situation wouldn't qualify as a hardship case, Ray, but I might be able to arrange a transfer to one place up there—New York City."

Two

Becoming a G-Man

I was almost thirty-four years old when the FBI accepted me. I had gone to law school and had practiced for seven years, making a nice living. I knew that being an agent meant a government salary instead of the substantial dollars I could have been making practicing corporate law. I recognized the risks in dealing with hard-core criminals. I knew some older FBI agents and was aware of the transfers and disruption inherent in being in the bureau. It didn't matter. I couldn't think of anything else I'd rather do for a living.

It started when I was a kid. When other boys were outside playing stickball, I was on the living room sofa, watching cop shows and envisioning myself, Raymond W. Holcomb, in uniform, carrying a pistol, and saving the day. I grew up in an era when the FBI was on a pedestal, romanticized in television shows and movies, and when the media and public held J. Edgar Hoover in high esteem. Thanks to the genuine success of many agents, the bureau had gained the repute of a vital American institution, a bulwark against the criminal underworld and the insidious spread of godless communism.

Hoover was a public relations genius. The man was one of the first spin doctors, befriending the powerful to promote an image that still holds up today. Unlike most agency heads who come and go, Hoover was married to the FBI. It was his family, and just as many a demanding, obsessive parent, he insisted on his children's success.

※　※　※

In April 1984, I began the sixteen-week, new agent training program at Quantico, the sprawling U.S. Marine Corps base that housed the new FBI Academy. Hoover's crown jewel had already assumed a fabled reputation as a state-of-the-art facility in every aspect of law enforcement training. The place resembled a modern university, covering acres of picturesque Northern Virginia countryside with tiered classrooms, laboratories, gymnasiums, helicopter landing pads, firearms training ranges, running tracks, and special obstacle courses designed to test decision-making and leadership skills. Whatever the academy lacked, the Marines gladly provided. The relationship is symbiotic and unique to anything else in the federal government. The special agent ranks have always been flush with former Marines, and the bureau has its own Marine Corps Association.

I lugged my bags through the lobby, struck by the bustle and energy of agents moving in groups from lessons to lunch, to the firearms training range and the gun-cleaning room, and back to class. New recruits were channeling through the academy every month during 1984, with each class assuming a unique identity. The anticipation and excitement I felt reminded me of my college football days, but I was not a kid anymore, and this place looked as if it might be one hell of a ride for a grown-up.

After settling in, my class of thirty-five recruits gathered in the gym for physicals. I was a little concerned about how I would measure up against my peers, since I was one of the older people in the group, but I was pretty fit for a codger and did fine. After a simple stress test, two of our classmates had to pack up and head home. It was a bitter pill for them, one of whom had flown in from Honolulu only the previous day. I was unsympathetic, though, and surprised that anyone offered a chance to be a special agent would show up in less than top shape.

A former All-American football player led our first fitness class. He took out a bunch of old-fashioned leather medicine balls and made us jog in circles while we held them over our heads, then out to our sides or in front, as he barked instructions like an army drill sergeant. We ran until two of my classmates fell to their knees and vomited. This exercise was the acid test. Somebody had to throw up before he would let us shower.

The training reminded me of preseason football practice. I had played strong-side linebacker at the University of Delaware, a medium-size college powerhouse. Linebackers are the lunatics of the game, as their primary mission is to find the football and obliterate the carrier. I was used to getting beat up and dishing out punishment. The pain, the sweat burning the eyes, the coaches screaming—I had missed it all during the years I sat behind a desk practicing corporate law.

In the '60s, coaches would deny players water to make them tough. Twice daily, we would practice in the sweltering heat, pummeling each other for hours without a sip of liquid, and develop headaches so fierce we could not see straight. Our trainer would pour aspirin in our hands and practically sneer as he told us to swallow them dry. When somebody collapsed from dehydration, the coach, annoyed by the interruption, had us put the exhausted player on the tackling dummy trailer. Once practice was over, we would cart the player into the locker room with all the rest of the equipment.

When I boxed at the academy, taking shots to my body and head, I felt as if I was back on the gridiron. Boxing was new for many and hated by most, but a law enforcement officer has to be ready for the day he takes a sucker punch to the face. If he has never experienced a hard blow to the head, he will likely lose critical time recovering his senses. We also practiced handcuffing techniques and weapon retention so often that some of us woke in the middle of the night trying to disarm an imaginary assailant. Veteran instructors pounded home the point that if someone went for our weapons, we had to do whatever was necessary to save ourselves. That included gouging eyes, crushing a larynx, biting off ears—anything to keep from losing our guns.

We studied basic martial arts techniques from an ethnic Korean who had served in the Republic of Korea Marine Corps, one of the toughest military organizations in the world. Although small in stature, he could put the biggest recruit on his back with one blinding move. After accidentally injuring a succession of students, he was "transferred" to the firearms range, where he would have limited opportunities to manhandle recruits. In the process, we had learned never to underestimate a small man.

It was not any easier on the firearms training range. I could always feel my stomach begin to knot up before the drills. Some recruits became quiet and introspective while others became comedians. Good jokes usually alleviated the tension. The former cops and military veterans in the group wanted to show who was top dog, and we all worried about how we would perform in

The author on the FBI Academy's firearms training range, with six-shooters and speed loaders.

front of our peers. We could not graduate unless we shot ninety or better out of a maximum score of a hundred with the revolver, a Remington 870 shotgun, and an M16 rifle. A recruit could get through if he or she failed once or twice, but the recruit was considered suspect and watched closely from that point. Today, agent recruits can extend their time at the academy until they manage to qualify, even if it takes months at taxpayers' expense. The kinder, gentler world is producing kinder and gentler agents. I am not so sure that kind of agent is what the public needs or wants.

I knew how to shoot before I got to Quantico. My family hunted and my dad was on the local police pistol team. He once shot two fighting bucks almost simultaneously. I was waiting at the hunting camp the evening he dragged in both carcasses, turning one over to an older hunter who had failed to bag his own on the last day of the season. Dad taught me how to use a gun and made me respect it. On our first hunt together he scared me straight, whispering, "If I ever see your hand on the trigger when it shouldn't be, or if I catch you pointing a gun where it shouldn't be pointed, I'll knock your head off." I knew he was serious and more than capable of doing it. The tough son of a farmer, he had gone to law school after World War II. Here was a man who could stalk game for hours in the driving snow and field dress a deer as easily as today's couch potato spreads cheese on his crackers. I listened to Dad.

We agents all carried revolvers. Bureau issue was the trusty Smith & Wesson Model 13, .357 Magnum six-shooter. The small, leather bullet pouch on our belts held six rounds, and we packed the balance of fifty rounds in our pants pockets. We had to learn how to reload quickly without losing sight of the threat. By the time my stint at the academy was almost over, the bureau had adopted a new device known as a speed loader, which dropped six bullets into the cylinder in one move. At the time, this mechanism was a staggering technological advance.

The Remington 870 12-gauge pump-action shotgun and the M16A1 standard military issue automatic rifle made up the rest of the bureau's arsenal. The shotgun, packing the greater wallop, was the most intimidating choice for the majority of the recruits. I had hunted small game for years with a shotgun, often training on clay birds, so the 870 was familiar. When we shot it, we had to brace the weapon tightly against our shoulders or it would smack us like a hammer. Many people learned the hard way. The first time one female recruit, a Hispanic woman who was barely over five feet tall, shot the 870, she forgot to stagger her feet and snug the butt of the weapon into her shoulder. The kick knocked her over onto her back. But I gave her a lot of credit. As much as she hated that shotgun and as much as it beat her up, she kept at it until she qualified.

The M16 was new to me, but it is shooter friendly, designed for accuracy in the hands of the unskilled. Lightweight and with little kick, it resembles a toy and pops like a firecracker, but it is a serious weapon.

The academy was academically demanding as well. If anyone failed one of the principal courses, he or she had to pack his or her bags. Instructors, many of whom were former teachers and lawyers, drove home our responsibility to obey and defend the Constitution and follow the letter of the law. Other than packing a whole lot more into a shorter period, the academy's law classes compared in almost every respect to what I had been through at Seton Hall Law School. I was impressed.

Veteran agents also taught us the psychology behind effective interviewing, emphasizing rapport building, preparation, and the simple fact that almost everyone wants to talk if given the chance. No one left that class confused over the fact that although a fine interrogation ploy might elicit an incriminating statement, the statement would likely be worthless without a proper Miranda warning.

Our days were long and opportunities to relax limited. Most evenings, our class congregated in "the boardroom," a bar on the second floor of the academy. It was a sometimes raucous gathering spot for all types: new agent recruits, instructors, veteran agents back for refresher training, agents undergoing SWAT training, policemen from around the world attending the FBI's National Academy, and an occasional VIP. Some nights we would drink too much, but we would always roll out of bed before dawn and run until we left our hangovers somewhere on the back roads of Quantico. We were motivated and we were eager.

Near the end of our sixteen weeks, I was sitting in the boardroom next to an older agent. His class had let out for the day, and I could tell he'd already had a few drinks. I started a conversation, hoping to get a sense of what my future held in store. He turned toward me and fixed his eyes on mine. He looked tired and his words were slurred. "I've spent almost twenty years with the bureau. The worst part was the travel, the moving to different cities. Most of the time I was working far from my hometown, so my kids didn't see my parents much. My father was a terrific guy. I wanted my kids to know him, and I always figured I could get a transfer and be back near him before I retired. Well, I never got back his way. He passed away a few weeks ago. It just didn't work out."

I felt it. I was close to my dad, too. I didn't know what to say, and for the first time my excitement and eagerness were tempered by some harsh reality. I mumbled, "That's too bad."

In a small effort to change the mood, the older agent said, "That's OK. It's not all doom and gloom. This is a good job, and you won't lose it unless you do something really stupid. There's no end to the work out there for the bureau. There will always be plenty of bad guys to keep us busy."

Three

Cold War Warrior

The FBI's New York City office was awash in morale problems. In the early eighties, FBI employees received no cost-of-living adjustment (COLA), so an agent in Los Angeles earned the same salary as one in Des Moines, and a senior FBI street agent in New York made less than a Manhattan police sergeant or a Suffolk County patrol officer.

Under Director William Webster, the bureau made a crude attempt to right the inequity. Many agents spent entire careers in offices where life was relatively inexpensive and manageable, while others worked in one of the so-called top-twelve offices, such big and expensive places as New York City or Los Angeles. Bureau management decided that every agent who had come on board after October 1, 1969, and had not been in a top-twelve office would have to transfer to one. Agents who had spent the better part of twenty years establishing lives in such places as Indianapolis suddenly received transfers to Los Angeles; Chicago; Washington, D.C.; or, worst of all, New York City.

The result was devastating throughout the bureau and compounded further by escalating real estate prices in many of the metropolitan areas around the country. I doubt I could have made ends meet had things continued as they were. Shortly before I arrived in New York, Assistant Director in Charge (ADIC) Thomas Sheer, a square-jawed FBI agent who reminded me of Clark Kent, appeared before a congressional committee that was investigating the effectiveness of the Soviet spy service, primarily the Committee for State Security (KGB). Since two places in particular—New York City, home of the United Nations, and Washington, the seat of the federal government and the site of all nations' embassies—were hotbeds of Soviet activity, the committee wanted to know how an FBI agent matched up against a KGB agent in the counterintelligence business. The ADIC's answer was not encouraging. The average FBI agent had fewer than three years' experience at counterintelligence, but his Soviet adversary did not deploy to the field until he had trained for ten years. Shocked, the committee demanded to know the reason behind this disparity. ADIC Sheer responded that it was simple: many experienced FBI agents could not afford to live in Washington or New York, so they quit. It took months, but Congress did pass a trial COLA for agents in expensive posts, including New York, Washington, Los Angeles, and San Francisco. Soon afterward, the loss of agents fell off to a trickle. Eventually, all FBI offices in high-cost areas got COLAs, and the bloodletting of FBI special agents—people who would have done great service for their country but had to put their families first—ended.

The COLAs improved things for me and for other New York–based agents, but we still could not afford to live in the city. We couldn't even reside within a reasonable commuting distance from work, since train service was also costly. Most of us carpooled, taking turns driving to work and collecting two or three other agents along the way.

Somehow, my carpool got hold of a worn government Impala with over 140,000 hard miles. It should have been retired—in bureau parlance, surveyed—from the bureau inventory but a secretary had neglected to collect the keys, so it was still on the government books. None of us had an extra car, so we used our own money, bought retread tires, and changed the oil ourselves in order to keep the old junker running. Even though our daily carpool in and out of Manhattan meant five hours on the road, beginning and ending near the Pennsylvania border, we were grateful just to have a vehicle.

Another group acquired long-term access to a surveillance van. It was nothing but a stripped-down panel vehicle with only two front seats. The carpoolers took turns driving while the rest sat in the rear in folding lawn chairs. At seventy miles per hour on major highways, an accident would have meant almost certain death for all on board, but they had to get to work and couldn't afford anything else.

In the 1980s, many of the government vehicles, also called G-rides, were typically the tired Plymouth Gran Fury type. These cars practically bellowed: "Feds!" We would try to dress them down with bobblehead dolls or dashboard saints and cover the large government radios with articles of clothing so passersby would not readily spot the equipment. It was makeshift, but most agents were creative and did not wait for Uncle Sam to provide special setups, which rarely arrived.

Our offices were "bull pens"—large, open areas with metal desks grouped in fours. A gray cloud of cigarette smoke hung from the ceiling perpetually, and the din made it virtually impossible to carry on a phone conversation. The carpeting near the heating and air-conditioning wall units was threadbare and covered with mildew. OSHA had shut down the water fountains because of lead contamination. Agents who lived far from the city sometimes stayed the night, sleeping in large office closets. For years, my workday began when I rose at 4:15 a.m. and ended when I returned home somewhere around 7:30 in the evening. These were the conditions of those folks working to counter the massive Cold War spying effort of the Soviets and their allies.

Many agents were embittered and disillusioned. I sat a paper clip toss away from Earl Edwin Pitts and another traitor, Robert Philip Hanssen, later portrayed in the movie *Breach*. If our managers had listened, we agents would have told them that offices like New York's were breeding grounds for treason. We could tell that some of the hard cases were ready to get even for the mess they found themselves in. Mostly qualified, egotistical people, they felt that they were not appreciated and that the U.S. government had let them down. Still, most hung on, because they believed in what we were doing even while FBI Headquarters and Congress treated us with benign neglect.

With some justification, we believed that the managers in headquarters cared more about rubbing elbows with powerful congressmen or their own superiors than about dealing with the complaints of "whining" field agents. The New York office had a reputation as being filled with outspoken employees who were not afraid to give a visiting official, including the director, a piece of their minds, so management found it easier to just avoid New York.

I was on a Soviet counterintelligence (CI) squad, something of a white-collar version of a counterterrorism operation. We shadowed the Russians working out of the United Nations and the Soviet Mission located in midtown Manhattan. It was an era when we relied mainly on hit or miss hand-held radios and curbside public telephones. We tried to spot handoffs, or the covert passing of information from one operative to another, and dead drops, which are secret hiding places for messages. We learned that orange peels often marked dead drops because animals found the scent repugnant and usually left them alone. But how could we put surveillance on every pile of orange peels in the city of New York?

I built a dossier on a Russian diplomat. He either was a Soviet KGB intelligence officer or had been co-opted, that is, forced to work for the organization. No one could be in the Russian diplomatic corps unless he or she cooperated with the KGB. With the exception of certain obvious individuals who usually occupied posts well known to be reserved for the KGB or the Main Intelligence Directorate of the Soviet armed forces (GRU), we could have followed every single Russian diplomat with equal odds of hitting a jackpot.

One of my jobs was monitoring the activities of the Russian deputy secretary to the United Nations. He lived with other Russians in a Soviet housing complex in Riverdale, New York. Every weekend a group of us would be there, waiting for our targets to emerge. Then we would follow them across the five boroughs on the chance that we would spot a clandestine meeting.

The Russians were notorious bargain hunters, often scrounging around in flea markets in the worst parts of town. Because they could easily spot our FBI vehicles, we developed a relationship of sorts. They would wait for our cars to catch up to theirs before they entered the rougher parts of town, happy to know that we were there in case they ran into trouble. On one occasion a bureau surveillance team even stopped to help an appreciative Soviet spy fix a flat tire along the Henry Hudson Parkway. If confused or lost, they would often stop, walk back to an agent's car, and ask for directions.

Although most free people saw the Soviets' communist government and system to be the enemy, I think we agents understood that many of these Russians were simply human beings trying to make a living. Soviet intelligence officers got the best of everything: the nicest stores, the fanciest vehicles, the finest dachas. We knew that many became spies because it guaranteed them and their families a good life, not because they truly believed in the destruction of America and capitalism.

Both sides abided by certain unwritten rules of civility and humanity. The Soviets and their allies would not intentionally kill noncombatants, so we did not have to worry about suicidal Russians flying planes packed with civilians into occupied office buildings. Maybe it was because proclaimed atheists did not believe in a great reward from on high for killing nonbelievers. When something ugly—such as "wet work," or murder—was deemed necessary, however, each group did what was required through proxies. America utilized mercenaries in certain parts of the world but never to the same extent that the Soviets did. The latter used Bulgarians, East Germans, and Cubans, affording themselves some measure of plausible deniability. They were not averse to wet work, and as I would learn some years later, they were anything but circumspect in how they got the job done. Subtlety was not their trademark.

When surveillance was difficult or the target was a high priority, we enlisted special surveillance groups (SSGs), which consist of people specifically trained in clandestine surveillance techniques. They came in all shapes and sizes—older, younger, multiple ethnicities—but were always effective. Unlike us, they knew how not to attract suspicion or raise someone's hackles. We never had enough of them so we had to use them wisely, only on the most important cases.

▪   ▪   ▪

By law, the Central Intelligence Agency (CIA) cannot conduct covert operations within the United States unless it does so in concert with the FBI. We ran one asset, a CI term for an informant, jointly. He was an American who traveled overseas and was in a position to meet with Soviet businessmen and academics. He volunteered to help the U.S. government in any way he could. The CIA had no choice but to bring in the FBI, since the asset was an American citizen who had to be regularly debriefed stateside. I would meet with him and my CIA counterpart in safe houses, unobtrusive locations owned or rented under fictitious names where spy agencies hold secret meetings.

The first get-together was a revelation. After completing the obligatory paperwork, I requisitioned two subway tokens. The bureau operated on a shoestring, and petty cash was virtually nonexistent. I took the train to a better part of town on a sweltering August day and arrived at the brownstone address. Once admitted, I opened an interior door to an opulent apartment packed with people I had never seen before. Most appeared to be support or secretarial staff prepared to take extensive notes. On a linen-covered table were fresh orange juice, bagels, lox, cream cheese, exotic fruit, and a host of additional select foods. The resources at my CIA counterpart's disposal impressed me; it was my first introduction to the widely differing cultures of the bureau and the CIA.

Many times during my career I would meet with valuable FBI informants, men and women who put themselves at personal risk for me, and pay for our meals and drinks out of my own pocket because the bureau, after questioning even the necessity for sharing a meal with the asset or informant, would only subsidize a small portion of the bill. In New York City, bureau regulations would barely cover the cost of a hamburger.

In another case, we received a tip that a code clerk was interested in defecting. A code clerk was an extremely high-value target, and recruiting one from any Eastern Bloc nation was the FBI's top priority. These clerks had access to all the sensitive information flowing through their embassies. They encoded and decoded the secret communications. In the case of a code clerk, even the miserly FBI was willing to pull out the stops and spend whatever was needed.

Someone settled on an ingenious idea. We employed a retired police detective who had specialized in catching pickpockets. He would pass a message to the clerk as he went on his daily afternoon walk with the two security escorts perpetually at his side. The pickpocket "accidentally" bumped into the clerk, slipping a recruitment offer into his jacket pocket. Written in disappearing ink, it was wrapped around a multi-carat diamond. The note read, "If you would like to stay in America, we can arrange it. If you are interested in following through with our offer, this is the signal: Step out of your mission at precisely noon next Monday and light a cigarette." We considered the act skillful tradecraft at the time.

The following Monday, we were positioned across from the Eastern Bloc Mission so we could spot our quarry if he came out to light that cigarette. If he failed to appear, it probably meant no deal or that he was too closely watched. Our entire squad was on edge. If this plan worked, it would be a career win.

There he was, strolling out of the building at noon to light a cigarette!

The plan was in place. Once again, later that week, our pickpocket inserted in the target's pocket another diamond and a note containing specific instructions for his defection. The subject was told that when he left his office to walk home on the following Friday, still accompanied by his guards, he would see a woman wearing a yellow dress. He was to run in her direction. My job, along with another agent, was to tackle his guards so they could not prevent the escape. The woman would be standing by a vehicle, guiding him into it. Then we would take him to a safe location.

We borrowed a clearly marked truck from the U.S. Air Force and three agents in air force uniforms drove it down the street from the mission. There, they were to put a jack under the truck as if they were fixing a flat. It would have been extremely difficult for a foreign security service to acquire an air force vehicle and uniforms. Despite their significant resources, the Soviet bloc just couldn't pull that off in downtown New York City. By using an actual U.S. military vehicle and uniforms, we would prove to the would-be defector that we were not from his own security service just out to test his loyalty, as the communists so often did.

We rented a fabulous penthouse in a midtown hotel, a Hyatt that set the government back eight hundred dollars a night. We intended to deposit our prize there for a day or two, after we had separated him from his controllers. Only the best for a defecting code clerk.

We were in position to watch him enter the mission that Friday morning. But we never saw him leave, not that night or the next day. We had placed a twenty-four-hour visual on the door to that building, but we neither saw him nor heard about him again until three months later, when he appeared in Prague.

It was not the first time a prospective defector lost his nerve. We were certain he had second thoughts after discovering the first note and alerted his superiors immediately. The slightest hesitation could have suggested to them that he had considered taking our offer.

We monitored all the New York airports for weeks after losing him, so we knew he did not fly out of New York. We guessed he had been loaded into the trunk of a car, had crossed into Canada, and was likely secreted out of an airport there.

My counterintelligence responsibility also included monitoring the Communist Workers' Party and Soviet spies posing as UN officials. I followed Vladimir Pozner, a Russian journalist best known in the West for expressing sympathetic views on all issues concerning the Soviet Union during the Cold War. Most people in the intelligence community believed that he was a Russian agent. We would have been remiss not to be suspicious. When he met with a high-ranking Soviet delegation that came to town, a female member of the SSG posed as my girlfriend so we could more easily follow Pozner and the Russians on a cruise ship around Manhattan. We were there to identify members of the delegation and take notice of any unusual familiarity or exchange of items. If anyone turned out to be a known or highly suspected intelligence officer and if that individual spent an inordinate amount of time alone with Pozner, it would be strong circumstantial evidence that Pozner was a spy.

While we were on the boat, I suddenly felt a strange sensation on the back of my neck and managed a casual glance over my shoulder. I sensed we were being watched and realized that I had just walked past men who might have been Cuban (two Hispanic males, fit, with short haircuts, sitting side by side). When I turned, I saw they were carefully watching me and my female partner. As noted earlier, I knew that the Soviets commonly used Cubans to conduct countersurveillance. Cuban agents were tailing me. Had I made a furtive movement, any attempt to approach or interfere with Pozner or any member of the delegation, I would have surely drawn a response from the Cubans. They had identified us, we were now an entry in their database, and they were prepared to use any measure necessary to stop a defection. That Pozner, or someone in his group, warranted countersurveillance was a strong indication that a very important person was present that day.

In this era, paranoia reigned supreme. For those with misguided motivations, with desires to avenge perceived snubs, or who acted out of simple greed, the object justified the means, and that included betraying their country and those who trusted them. It was a convoluted spy-versus-spy game, with double and triple agents and moles. It was a time when senior officials, such as Kim Philby of the British secret intelligence service, the MI6, spied for the Russians and subsequently defected to live out their lives in the Soviet Union. We resided in a house of mirrors where being untrusting made perfect sense.

My counterintelligence work required time on the streets of Manhattan doing surveillance. Dressed as a construction worker, I monitored a meeting of the American Communist Workers' Party in Midtown. We wanted to know who would attend the meeting, particularly any Russians or Eastern Bloc officials. Once, as I took refuge from a cold, late autumn rain in a doorway of a nearby tenement, an unusually large number of strung-out drug addicts passed by, furtively glancing my way. A short time later, I discovered that the door at my back was the entrance to a local heroin shooting gallery. Suddenly, a car with dark-tinted windows pulled up, and someone yelled over the sound of heavy rain, "Hey, cop, you're killing my business standing there. Give me a break!" Then the vehicle pulled away slowly. In parts of Manhattan, the drug dealers had arrangements with some of the cops. That night, when I returned to my car, I found the tires slashed. Heroin was cresting in New York City, and the dealers were brazen.

We had good information that Gus Hall, then head of the American Communist Party, had over a million dollars in cash concealed in his kitchen ceiling, courtesy of the Union of Soviet Socialist Republics. It was illegal to accept money from the Soviet Union or any other communist country without declaring it, but the Soviets had developed an intricate system for moving cash through straw men, using layers of shipping companies and banks to wash funds. They managed to get it to their operatives all over the world without any links to "Red" officials. We were constantly trying to pinpoint the Soviets' cash-filtering system through the media or with academics and nonprofit organizations. We were reasonably confident that the information about Hall was accurate and that the source was reliable. Despite that, the Department of Justice (DOJ) declined to process our application for a search warrant. DOJ lawyers were afraid that if the source was wrong, the American media would have a field day with the FBI and the DOJ lawyers who approved the warrant and again portray the bureau as a dark, evil organization bent upon spying on innocent citizens just because they supported a controversial brand of politics.

No doubt, some of Hoover's methods crossed the line in the light of later sensibilities; however, most of what the early bureau did occurred in the absence of any clear law against a particular action or was in line with early Supreme Court decisions or the attorney general's guidance. The "Red Menace" did exist, and Soviet agents were abundant and well placed among mainstream organizations, particularly labor unions. Nevertheless, the media has always owned the headlines and created the news. Whether before or after Gus Hall, I am sure many agents got away with spying on the United States simply because a risk-averse Department of Justice was afraid of the *New York Times*.

We also investigated Felix Bloch, then the State Department's highest-ranking spy suspect since World War II. State Department officials at times suggested that Bloch may have sold classified information out of pique over not being promoted. A media leak stymied our investigation, so we could never charge him with spying. I spent a number of nights sitting outside his Upper East Side apartment. We were concerned that he would flee the country while we attempted to salvage our case against him. It turned out that he had a friend at the FBI who provided his handlers back in the Soviet Union with advance notice of our intentions. Years later, we discovered the friend was none other than Special Agent Hanssen, the same person who had sat in my bull pen in New York. Hanssen's ongoing acts of treason in ensuing years resulted in the known deaths of nine individuals who had cooperated with us.

Hanssen subsequently moved from New York to become a mid-level executive at FBI HQ, where he helped develop a computer system that afforded access to sensitive information on assets or informants operated by each field division. By this time, John O'Neill was in charge of the National Security Division of the New York office. That division was responsible for developing and managing informants within New York's territory. Mistrustful of Hanssen's system, O'Neill was later popularized in the PBS *Frontline* documentary as "The Man Who Knew" and one of the few who early on recognized al Qaeda's growing influence and the danger it posed. Meanwhile, he did everything he could to keep FBI HQ from connecting to the New York informant data banks. O'Neill knew that New York had one of the two biggest informant or asset pools—the other being Washington—so he was particularly worried about affording wide access to it until he was convinced the system was secure. He stalled until he was convinced it was ready. Sometime later, after Hanssen was finally arrested, it was learned that because of O'Neill's efforts the only office database Hanssen did not penetrate was that of the New York system.

Four

Drug Agent

Counterintelligence agents are lucky if once during their careers they have a hand in catching a spy and getting him thrown out of the country. I thought that capturing drug dealers would be more straightforward and that I might actually see justice meted out as the result of my hard work. After two and a half years, I got the chance to move on to a real criminal squad, the premier counter-narcotics squad in the New York office at that time and, arguably, the best the bureau ever had.

In 1989 I was initially assigned to C-7, one of the New York office's several organized crime (OC) squads. Squad C-7 had just wrapped up the highly publicized "Pizza Connection" case, where seventeen members of a Sicilian family were convicted for selling heroin through pizza parlors used as fronts. However, within just weeks, I was reassigned to C-25, a squad that had lost some personnel to transfers. Geoff, the case agent for the wildly successful "Whitemare" investigation, now headed the squad.

Squad C-25, a task force of New York City detectives and agents, specialized in Golden Triangle heroin, which was king in North America in the 1980s and into the 1990s. Originating in an almost inaccessible area encompassing parts of Thailand, Cambodia, and Laos, it was the highest quality "junk" available in the world. Mexican "brown tar" was a poor substitute, and the Turkish variety that for decades fostered French and Sicilian dominance was drying up because of international cooperation and solid New York Police Department (NYPD) success stories like the Pizza Connection.

Operation Whitemare was a textbook drug case that climaxed in the largest heroin seizure in U.S. counter-narcotics history, netting nearly nine hundred pounds of nearly pure Golden Triangle heroin. It dismantled a far-reaching drug organization, most of the subjects eventually pled guilty, and we had plenty of heroin on our hands. Because of its toxicity, we needed the Environmental Protection Agency's blessing to dispose of the hundreds of pounds of heroin and dozens of small, hard rubber tires that the importers had used to conceal the white powder. It had to burn slowly and at extremely high temperatures to maintain emissions below toxic levels. We destroyed it at a high-tech garbage incineration facility at Fort Dix, New Jersey. Since each tire held about a kilo of heroin, we were heavily armed and constantly looked over our shoulders.

Depending upon market saturation, this amount of pure heroin was huge. Street dealers "cut" heroin multiple times before it reaches the addict, maximizing the dealers' profit margins. Heroin sold on the street is typically only 2–5 percent pure and is mixed with Pabulum or a similarly safe cutting agent. A 5-percent concoction is potent and dangerous. Although the street price fluctuated with supply, a pound and a half, or close to two thirds of a kilo, of quality heroin was selling for seventy thousand dollars to eighty thousand dollars. If the mixture was just a little rich with heroin, particularly if it was good quality, it would be lethal. Dealers gave their clientele only just enough to keep them coming back for more.

Geoff was a young, Chicago-raised Irishman who could be brash and brutally honest. He expected everyone to work as hard as he did. He set the bar high, and during my almost ten years on C-25, only a few came up short. The rest of us melded into a tight-knit group of dedicated agents and cops, taking down case after case. We knew every back alley, one-way street, and short-cut through Manhattan's Chinatown and the Asian communities in Brooklyn and Queens. It was almost uncanny how we could work together during a fast-moving surveillance. Most of our cars carried a "walker," an agent rigged with a concealed radio. The walker could jump out when traffic bogged down and stride alongside the target vehicle, keeping all units advised until another

C-25 vehicle moved ahead on a parallel street and took up position. We often remained on surveillance for two or three days straight, sleeping in our cars or on our desktops. We rarely lost a subject.

Almost every agent on the squad developed a case of his own, but when events in anyone's case called for a surge of manpower, we cops and agents would all unite. It was an amazing display of teamwork from a diverse group of various ethnic backgrounds: Malaysian, Philippine, Thai, Puerto Rican, Chinese, Italian, Irish, and English.

As the new agent on board, I watched and learned, handling many of the loose ends, such as babysitting witnesses in hotel rooms, serving subpoenas, shuttling information back and forth to the U.S. attorney's office, or assisting case agents by analyzing credit card and phone records. I learned the counter-drug business from the inside out in the process. Analysts were virtually unheard of then; indeed, every agent was his own analyst and his instincts almost always provided the missing link between the dots. We did it all and it worked.

Since most counter-drug work takes place after dark, I spent long hours in my car on late-night surveillances, observing giant rats emerge from sewers and scurry through the garbage bags restaurants had heaped out on the curb. The midtown hookers coming off their shifts would stop and chat, knowing we were some kind of cops. They liked that we were out on the street and felt just a little safer. They knew we were after bigger fish.

Sometimes things just fell in our laps. Once, a prosecutor called Geoff about two prisoners who wanted to cut a deal to reduce their sentences. They were drug dealers who owed substantial cash to their Asian heroin supplier. We hatched a plan, furloughed the two convicts, and had them make a call to Korea. Within days, the Asian drug kingpin sent over his courier, a crooked Korean cop, to collect the balance due. We had the two cooperating convicts meet with the Korean cop and pass him the money. We then surveilled him straight to a bank, where he wired it to an Asian account. After we arrested him, he quickly agreed to cooperate. He was our boy then, and we couldn't let him out of our sight.

The two convicts who had tipped us off to the network then told us about some major traffickers operating in Detroit. Our Korean cooperator had supplied them before. A bunch of bad characters, they were number one on the wish list the Drug Enforcement Administration (DEA) had in Michigan. We had our boy reach out to the leader of the Detroit gang and arrange a meeting in a Korean hotel in midtown Manhattan.

The gathering was set for a Saturday night. Our Korean cop was holed up in the hotel, waiting for the Detroit posse. The meeting fell apart after the street-smart Detroit boys made, or identified, our surveillance.

The next morning, my partner and I got to the hotel to take our shift babysitting our Korean cop. The agent going off duty told us to relax. "The dealers were scared off. Those guys are not coming back. They're probably halfway back to Detroit by now."

My partner was an older NYPD detective only days from retirement. The minute he heard the news, he grabbed a newspaper and found an empty room. Before long, I heard him snoring. That was just fine with me. I was tired and didn't feel up to making small talk. Suddenly, the phone rang in our cooperator's room. I told him to answer it. He tried to say something in English, and when he hung up, he was trembling.

"What is it?"

His voice broke, "They are back. They are downstairs."

I knew "they" were our guys from Detroit. We were in a third-floor walk-up, and if these boys got impatient, they would be at the door in seconds, all packing heat. I roused my partner. When he came to, he could not remember where he put his five-shot, .38-caliber Chief's Special, or what we referred to as a back-up gun. I didn't have time to help him look for it. Our Korean was now huddled in the corner of the room, shaking. I had no cell phone (the one or two assigned to our squad were reserved for the bosses), and I knew if I used my handheld radio, the whole building would hear its static. I crept down the stairwell, conscious that my only advantage was surprise. I paused at the bottom, which opened into the small lobby area. Then I heard children's voices.

Damn! I thought. I couldn't make a move with kids there. I pressed my back to the wall and held my pistol in the ready gun position. My training kicked in instinctively. I always point the muzzle of my weapon toward the direction of the threat. (To this day, movies and cop shows drive me crazy when they portray cops entering a dangerous room, pointing their weapons toward the sky or the ground.)

Then I heard the door to the street open, sounds from outside, and children's voices trailing off. Now or never, I thought, and moved into the lobby. I caught one of them, all six feet five inches, sprawled on a small sofa. Before he knew what happened, I had my knee in his chest and my gun in his face. I had only seconds before he would pull his senses together. I shouted at the desk clerk to call 911 and get me uniformed police. Startled and angry with me for disturbing his quiet Sunday morning, he only shouted back louder in Korean.

I told the subject to roll over, and he responded, "Fuck you, you mothafucker." I was starting to lose control of the situation when I noticed two uniformed female cops writing a ticket for a vehicle parked outside the door. I yelled and they heard me. The big women with guns enjoyed taking control of my bad guy, who suddenly became docile. For them it was a helluva lot more interesting than writing parking tickets. I demanded to know who else was with him and where they were, imagining that at any minute his friends would come through the door looking for him.

He said he was alone. When I asked him where he was parked, he just looked at me.

I grabbed his car keys from his pocket. Then I knew I had to look for a Pontiac with Michigan plates, which was not a huge challenge, even in New York City. He'd parked it around the corner, and I found a receipt on the front seat for a motel across the river.

I got on my radio and reached Geoff. "I have a hunch. I don't need you here. Head to the Red Roof Inn in Secaucus. I think you'll find the rest there."

"Roger that." Geoff turned the cavalry north. The group arrived just as the Detroit posse, realizing trouble was afoot, was heading across the motel parking lot toward their car. We got them all and never burned our Korean policeman, who continued to come in handy. I had made my bones with Geoff and the C-25 veterans.

Weeks later, Geoff and I were the only ones in the squad area on a Friday afternoon. The phone rang, and when Geoff took the call, his tone suggested something important was happening. He told me, "Customs just intercepted a crate full of steel pipes containing hockey puck–sized tablets of heroin." When our Korean cop first wired our money back home, we were able to identify the company that had received the transfer. We'd flagged the company in the customs watch list, and it paid off. "Let's get out there."

We arrived at the Korean Air freight terminal to find steel rollers spread out on the floor amid a pile of hockey puck–shaped heroin tablets. Customs had torn the crate open in plain view of every warehouse worker. Two dozen people now knew what had happened, and word would spread quickly outside the warehouse. The protocol was for customs to advise the FBI that a shipment it had marked as suspicious had arrived. Customs agents weren't supposed to open anything until the FBI was on scene. It was our case, our crime scene, our evidence. We'd be the ones doing all the trial work. Customs would claim the stat.

The customs agent was beaming when we walked in, but his demeanor changed when he saw Geoff's face. Geoff said something under his breath and then turned to me, "Ray, you sit on this until I can get some relief out here first thing tomorrow. I want to see who comes to pick it up." I doubted anyone would pick up the shipment now, after customs had broadcast the fact that we had intercepted the goods. However, Geoff was the boss, and I dutifully took up a position for the night while the older customs agent assigned to stand watch with me went out to his car, ready to put his feet up. Looking back over his shoulder, he called out to me, "Remember, kid, this whole airport is mobbed up, and a lot of people know that box contains a fortune in heroin. Stay awake."

Thanks for the help, I thought.

The warehouse was huge, and piles of pallets reached the top of the thirty-foot ceiling. One or two night shift employees dozed in the front office. The air was pungent with a strong smell that resembled ammonia or cleaning fluid. Off in the recesses, I heard strange noises that I wrote off to steel cooling down from the heat of the day. I had been awake for almost twenty-four hours and was feeling it. There were no chairs and the floor was filthy so I sat down on a crate, drifting into sleep. Sometime later, I woke suddenly, sensing that something was just not right. In a scene reminiscent of an old B horror movie, a semicircle of feral cats, as many as eight, sat staring at me. Maybe they'd been sizing me up for dinner. As I sat upright, they scattered into the dim corners of the warehouse. I realized then that the cleaning-fluid smell was cat urine.

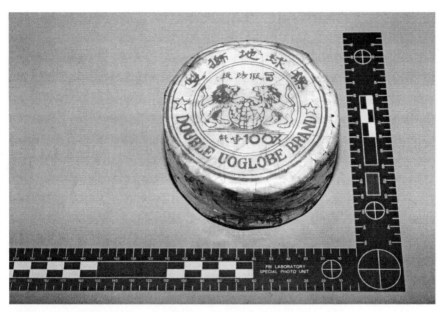

Hockey pucks of Asian death from the Roller Derby investigation.

I stretched and moved around the room, glad that dawn was breaking. By 8 a.m., Geoff and four of my squad mates arrived. I was preparing to hand off the surveillance when someone ran in from the front of the warehouse. "Hey, there's an Asian guy out front. He's here to pick up that pallet!"

We tailed him 24/7 once he picked up the pallet. I did not get home until late Saturday, bone tired but, just like the rest of C-25, enthused. We were off and running on the case, code-named Roller Derby. A series of gut feelings had paid off. Geoff had the finest-honed investigative sense I had seen, and I learned. We followed the crate to a warehouse in Jersey City and set up a round-the-clock watch.

The day of the big takedown came months later. In drug investigations the FBI was nothing but patient, knowing that big, experienced rats take a long time before they go for the cheese. Squad C-25 led teams that fanned out to various locations throughout the city's boroughs. My partner and I were assigned to follow the Asian male who had picked up the container earlier in the year at the Korean Air warehouse. Our orders were to follow (and not lose) him until we received the signal to execute his arrest. He was making delivery rounds in New Jersey that day, and as soon as he pulled onto Interstate 95, he took off like a rocket. I don't know if he suspected a tail or if he just normally drove that way, but I struggled to keep up as he weaved through traffic at breakneck speed. As I pressed the accelerator of my Oldsmobile Cutlass to the floor, my partner buried his fingers into the dashboard and muttered, "We're screwed if we lose him." Nobody wanted to let the team down, and we knew we'd never hear the end of it if we did.

With the needle buried at 110 miles per hour, we blew past cars on the interstate as if they were parked. Then, suddenly, the engine's scream spiraled down to a low hum, and the car slowed to a crawl. I thought I had blown the engine and could hear the ridicule already.

The governor, it turned out, disengaged the engine just before a meltdown. It had done its job, and soon I managed to restart the car and limp down the turnpike but with no subject in sight.

I quickly ran through what we had developed on the guy over the preceding months. His delivery business had him stopping routinely at a number of locations in New Jersey, and I remembered that one of those locations was nearby. I took a chance, exited the turnpike, and headed to the spot, arriving just as our guy left the driveway. The surveillance gods were smiling on us. We were able to follow him back to Queens, where we sat until we received our next order.

There were multiple arrests and multiple heroin seizures. Later that evening all of the arrest teams converged on Twenty-six Federal Plaza. The scene in the basement staging area was bizarre as people were moving in every direction; steel pipes were on the ground, some cut in two; and hockey pucks of heroin were stacked in piles. Power saws sliced through the pipes and bit into the heroin. Clouds of heroin-filled dust floated in the air. The case netted approximately 280 pounds of high-quality heroin and numerous arrests, including that of an affluent South Korean businessman who lived in an estate bordering the presidential residence in Seoul. After Whitemare, it was the second-largest heroin seizure in FBI history, and C-25 had brought them both home.

We had many cases during those years, some large, some small. But to a man, we were constantly kicking over rocks, and the cockroaches were scurrying.

In September 1990, Geoff called me into a meeting with two older Suffolk County detectives, both retired from the NYPD. They had solid intelligence about a wealthy Long Island businessman who was hooked up with the Italian mob and with known Chinese drug dealers. After they left, Geoff told me, "You've got the ball on this one. See if there's anything there." I had just been anointed a case agent. I felt as if I was getting my chance to play with the varsity team, and I was determined not to blow it.

At first, I spent endless hours sifting through dusty, old FBI files. We used an index card system back then. We didn't have computers, just a big warehouse full of hand-typed data that we hoped clerks had filed correctly.

I learned that our guy, Lenny Santangelo, had been chaperoned into the world of mob business by a brutal, old Purple Gang member known as Joe "Pips" Santaniello. Pips was an early mob rogue who had pushed heroin at a time when the Mafia dons pretended to have a moral aversion to selling narcotics. In reality, they ignored drug pushing in Harlem and the black and Hispanic neighborhoods. They were fine with the drug trade as long as they got their taste, and *their* kids weren't hooked.

Files showed that Pips had been a prime suspect in the execution murder of his nephew and his nephew's girlfriend as a payback for ripping off some of Pips's smack in a deal they were supposed to broker. Both of them turned up slouched over the dashboard of a car on Bronx Boulevard, their brains intermingled with the windshield.

I dug deeper and found that Pips had assumed the gambling debts of Chuck Forte, coproducer of ABC's *Monday Night Football*. An inveterate sports bettor and former All-American basketball player from Columbia University, Forte got in over his head with the Jersey mob. He contacted the Genovese family in New York for help, and they sent him Pips. Soon afterward, the cops found one dead New Jersey mobster, and another went permanently missing. Pips then added Forte to the collection of sorry souls he owned.

I found out how the loan sharks worked and how the mob eliminated its competition by preying on the weaknesses and bad luck of legitimate businesses and people. These boys were not good for a free market system.

The dots started to connect. Pips had taken Lenny Santangelo in as a young protégé. Santangelo, married to a woman whose mob father did time for dealing in heroin, gradually built a veneer of respectability by using mob muscle to scare off the competition. He bought a beautiful home on Long Island, enrolled his kids in the best schools, and sent a wad of cash to Pips every week, sometimes as much as forty thousand dollars in hundred-dollar bills. The courier, it came as no surprise, was Pips's son, who was "employed" by Santangelo. We learned through long hours of surveillance that the son's principal responsibility was delivering Daddy's cash.

The harder I dug the more puzzle pieces fit. A Chinese seafood wholesaler, Raymond Luk, employed the brother of one of Santangelo's supervisors. Luk was suspected of being a close associate of and money launderer for Paul Mah, also known as Bucktooth, who was the biggest heroin dealer in town. I knew that good money launderers were always in demand, and I suspected that Pips was using Luk's services as well.

My case, now code-named Pack Horse, was becoming a rainbow coalition. It was an ethnically diverse group of subjects or targets. I was working long days and borrowing agents wherever I could. With every new piece of information, I became more determined to sort things out and get to the ringleaders. As soon as I acquired the probable cause—the facts that justified a wiretap order—I would go to my assistant U.S. attorney (AUSA) and ask him to draft the affidavit requesting the wiretap. He had to send it to an approving office in the FBI, which reviewed it before it went down the street to the Department of Justice. There it had to reach the right person to gain DOJ approval. Invariably, someone in this chain was too busy or on vacation. The process always took time. If the justifying facts were more than two weeks old, we'd have to go back on the street to do surveillance or scrub new phone and credit card records for fresh evidence of criminal activity. I was fortunate that my first AUSA was Pat Fitzgerald. Fresh from Harvard Law School and the son of a Manhattan hotel doorman, he resolutely rewrote our first application for a wiretap on Santangelo's phone twenty-eight times. (As the esteemed Chicago U.S. attorney, Fitzgerald would go on to prosecute the Valerie Plame case. He charged the George W. Bush White House with deliberately outing Plame, a CIA case officer, after her diplomat husband publicly criticized the administration's claims that Iraq had sought materials to make weapons of mass destruction.) I have to laugh whenever I hear uninformed citizens or grandstanding congressmen preach about FBI abuses of civil liberties. If Pat had been an average AUSA, we would never have gotten out of the dugout, let alone to first base on the Pack Horse case. It is extremely hard to get the Department of Justice, let alone a federal judge, to approve any application for a traditional criminal wiretap order.

Eventually I received word that the judge had given us authority to tap Lenny Santangelo's and Joe Pips's phones. Within days, we had our wires up and were listening to cryptic conversations. On its face, my strategy was simple: when we rolled up these two, I felt I had a good chance that they would give up their Asian heroin suppliers for a deal with the prosecutor. While some of the Italian criminals might have felt some small allegiance to another *paisan* (compatriot), they felt nothing toward the Chinese.

Santangelo arranged a Christmas luncheon in town with some "friends." My partner, fresh off a wiretap-monitoring shift, rushed into the squad bay and proclaimed that we needed to put a full-court press on Santangelo when he came to town that afternoon. My senses told me otherwise. I didn't hear enough to warrant the risk. It sounded to me as if it were a legitimate business meeting, but I was overruled when Geoff sided with my partner. Squad C-25 rolled out and caught up with Santangelo on his way into town, following him to a midtown restaurant.

Then things went to hell. Santangelo called his wife, who, it was clear, was just as complicit as her husband was in his mob-supported operation. "Hey, I got people following me," he told her and proceeded to describe every one of our cars and the people in them. The final kick in the head came when, just before hanging up, he told her, "I ain't gonna talk on this phone anymore!"

I sat in the wire room for a few moments in disbelief. I had worked for months to get these wiretaps running, and one impetuous decision had blown it all. I walked into Geoff's office. I always admired his willingness to make hard decisions. In this rare instance, his decision was not correct. "You need to listen to what I just heard." I was calm, but my expression told the story.

We had become soft following the Chinese drug traffickers. For some reason—maybe because they operated in the most congested parts of town—they never seemed to use their rearview mirrors. We could bumper lock them for hours and never once see them glance in the rearview. The Italians, meanwhile, especially the old-timers, were good. They could make surveillance in a heartbeat. I took that much away from the experience, and I would use it to my advantage in the next round.

I thought I could salvage our case. We bugged the office of Pips's son and followed him on his weekly cash run between Santangelo's home and Pips's banks. I clung to hope that someone would slip or get lazy and start talking on the phones again.

Every Tuesday evening, one of Pips's lieutenants, a bruiser named Danny who ran a bookie operation in the Bronx, would drive to Pips's Long Island home. Then the two would drive in together in Pips's car. I had to figure out where Danny was driving him every Tuesday. Since I knew that these boys could make vehicle surveillance, I requested an aerial tail.

A friend named Russ was flying the single-engine bureau plane that night. He asked me to fly backseat and provide another set of eyes. It was a summer night, and I wondered how we were going to track Danny and Pips in Long Island traffic from thousands of feet in the air. I thought it would be a high-tech operation, but it was very low tech. Stationary ground units called out to us when Danny left Pips's home with his passenger. Daylight was fading, but I locked my eyes on Pips's car for the next hour and twenty minutes. We flew big circles while we moved eastward toward Manhattan. Darkness fell, and I locked onto their headlights, hardly blinking and never turning away. Russ called back to me, "Ray, that detergent bottle on the floor is for vomiting and pissing."

"Yeah, thanks," I mumbled as waves of nausea crept over me. Danny and Pips drove into the midtown tunnel. Fortunately, we had anticipated this part, and ground surveillance on the Manhattan side called them out as they emerged from the tunnel. I locked back on. Now I fought the brilliant glare of Manhattan at night from only a few thousand feet up. Suddenly, a huge, black, silhouetted shape roared beneath us, briefly blocking out Manhattan. "Jesus, Russ! What the hell!"

"Hey, we're working through the La Guardia flight patterns, man. They know we're here. I just have to make sure we stay in our lane. It's cool!"

My heart was pounding, and I was struggling to keep from vomiting all over Russ's cute little plane. I lost Danny and Pips just about the time our ground surveillance picked them up and managed to locate them at a known mob social club south of Washington Square Park.

Bingo. Now we knew what the regular Tuesday night dates were about:

Pips was anything but retired. He was making regular visits to pay homage to Vincent "Chin" Gigante, the head of the Genovese family.

The FBI had been trying to tap that social club for years, with limited success. I knew that these two talked about business on the drive in and out, so I applied for a car bug. It was the early 1990s and cellular technology had just arrived. The bureau's black bag experts assured me that they knew how to install innovative cellular car bugs that were a vast improvement on the old line-of-sight transmitters. With a cellular listening device, we could dial it up anytime, just as we would a cell phone, and did not have to be within direct sight of the target vehicle to receive transmissions. I liked the sound of this gadget. I got the financing from FBI Headquarters and devised a plan to install the device in Pips's car. I had to steal his car and keep it long enough for the tech folks to install their equipment. They said they needed about twenty minutes.

Mobsters are convinced that the feds are always trying to bug their cars so they cannot stand to let their vehicles out of their sight. Whenever one of their cars was "stolen" and later recovered, they would torch it rather than risk a fed-planted bug. On Tuesday evenings, Pips and Danny always parked in a mob-controlled garage around the corner from their social club. I knew we could not get his car out of there, so I devised a plan to have NYPD Emergency Services shut down access to his garage minutes before his arrival so he would have to park on the street. Detectives from our squad put on their uniforms and, with the aid of their emergency services pals, forced traffic down a route where we had pre-positioned our own cars along the curb. By radio, I directed my men to pull out just as Pips and Danny arrived, offering them a hard-to-find parking spot on a busy summer night in Manhattan. They bit on the third and last spot, about two blocks from the social club. The minute our lookout radioed that Pips was in the club, our lock expert moved in with a matching key. He was in Pips's Cadillac and on his way within seconds. One of our people, driving a rented look-alike vehicle, took the spot.

"Pips is out of the club pacing the sidewalk," our foot surveillance people told us. "He does not look happy." It had to be killing him. "He's heading back toward the car, and the other guy is with him."

Jesus, I thought, we're only at eighteen minutes, and he's leaving.

"He's turning the corner heading your way."

Just then, radio static, followed by, "Hey, get that look-alike out of there! Here we come!"

Thirty seconds before Pips came in sight of his car, the techies rolled the real Cadillac into the curb where Pips had left it. I worried that the hood of his car would be warm, but he and Danny did not notice. They got in the car and pulled out into traffic. I radioed to activate the bug. Within a minute, we heard voices over the receiver. They were Danny's and Pips's and sounded clear.

We were high-fiving each other when someone broke in, "Hey, reception has gone to shit. We're trying to fix it, but all we hear is a loud rumble."

We crowded around the receiver for the next hour, catching a word or two from time to time in between the noise.

"What's wrong with this thing?" I asked one of the tech installers.

"Don't know. Let's try it out over the next few days and see if it's just some kind of momentary atmospheric anomaly."

"Anomaly! What is that? You didn't tell me about 'anomalies' when I asked you if these things were good."

I learned then that our technical guys had not been entirely honest when they claimed that they had installed the new cellular bugs before. It was their first, and they were learning on the job.

We "stole" Pips's car six more times right from under his nose and attempted to fix the problem. We took it in broad daylight when he was in his favorite barbershop getting his hair cut and a manicure. I recruited a retired NYPD detective who had specialized in catching pickpockets. Dominic was an old paisan and fit right in at the barbershop. We outfitted him with another groundbreaking piece of technology for the time, an eyeglass holder with a built-in short-range transmitter. His job was to let us know when Pips was finishing up so that we could get Pips's car back into the parking spot fast. One time, Pips decided to skip the manicure and finish up early. Dominic was getting a shave, his face wrapped in steaming towels, as a young manicurist flirted with him for a tip. Unbeknownst to Dominic, and part of a developing pattern in my case, the battery in his transmitter went dead. The code word to signal Pips's departure was "Belmont," a reference to the local racetrack. Unaware that his transmitter had failed, Dominic nervously began uttering the code word repeatedly. Of course, he didn't receive the predetermined acknowledgment signal. He panicked, "Belmont, Belmont, Belmont!" Everyone in the barbershop was convinced Dominic had lost his mind. We were lucky that day. Once again, our people returned Pips's car seconds before he came out of the barbershop door. I was watching the entire scene unfold from across the road. I could see Dominic jumping around inside the shop trying to untangle himself from the barber drape. He rushed to the door, thinking all hell was about to unfold when he spied Pips pulling out of his parking spot in his DeVille.

Twenty minutes later, as we gathered at a safe location to test the "repaired" bug, Dominic arrived on the scene and gave me a new lesson in Italian passion. I grew up in a predominantly Italian neighborhood, but Dominic showed me some hand signs I had never seen before. When he finished expressing his displeasure with our technology and assuring me that his imminent heart attack was entirely my fault, he smiled, "Hey, you fuckin' feds got shit for equipment, but you're not bad at swipin' cars."

This attempt to fix the broken surveillance device also failed. I was done waiting on my techies to figure out the problem. I located the inventor of the system on Long Island and paid him a visit. When I described the location where my tech people had placed the bug in Pips's car, he laughed, "The mike should be behind the visor, agent. It's summertime, and he's driving with his windows open. If your people hid that bug over the rear window, it's obvious all you're picking up is the rumble of wind blowing through the car."

This observation made sense to me, but my tech guys figured they knew better than the inventor did. I didn't give up easily so I rented a Cadillac similar to Pips's and bought another cellular system. We installed it with the mike placed over the driver's side visor. I had my guys drive the route Pips usually took into town from Long Island and told them to talk and sing all the way. The recording was clear for most of the ride.

That afternoon I dropped the cassette recording in the tech guys' office. "Listen to it," I said when one of them asked what it was. "It's a recording of how that bug should work. We put the mike where it belongs, and tomorrow we're stealing Pips's car again and fixing it whether you're there or not."

They showed up the next day, sheepish, and reinstalled the mike after we successfully stole Pips's car for an incredible seventh time. Minutes after Pips finished his haircut and got in his car, we had clear audio. He was alone, but we could hear his radio perfectly and even picked up the rustling of his jacket when he shifted in his seat. Touchdown, I yelled inside my head, we have this SOB now!

The following Tuesday we intercepted a landline call from Danny to Pips. The essence of the conversation was that Pips was not feeling well enough for his usual visit to the social club in Manhattan. Pips would never take another drive with Danny again. After seven hard months of trying to fix a bug that had nothing wrong with it and finally getting it right, Pips stopped leaving his home except for running an occasional local errand alone. Touchdown called back.

I could not believe how bad my luck had turned with both Pips and Santangelo. It was as if the god of La Cosa Nostra was protecting them. Then came the final blow, and to this day, I cannot believe it happened. American Express, responding to our subpoena for Santangelo's credit card receipts, boxed them up, attached a copy of the subpoena, and mailed them to Santangelo's home. For the first time I allowed myself to believe this investigation might be over. For a few days, I pushed Pack Horse out of my mind and got absorbed in other cases.

Then one day my partner, who was very smart and had an accountant's background, said to me, "Ray, I think we've got a way to nail that old son of a bitch."

I was only half listening, "Sure." He had been working hard to make up for his insistence on tailing Santangelo and explained to me how Pips's bank records showed a precise pattern of structured deposits over many years, to the tune of millions of dollars.

I looked at him, "So the guy's anal, Keith. So what?"

"Ray, there's a statute, Title 31, that is clear on this. It's illegal to structure transactions to avoid a reporting requirement. If someone consistently, over time, deposits just under ten thousand dollars in cash into their account, there is a presumption that he is trying to avoid triggering CTRs!" He looked at me with that hey-isn't-this-great look on his face, and I looked back blankly. "You should have worn your helmet more when you played ball, dummy! With currency transaction reporting [CTR], banks are required by law to report whenever anyone deposits more than ten thousand dollars in cash, any one time. They're meant to spot people who are trying to avoid paying taxes. They're meant to help the IRS [Internal Revenue Service] track cheats and money launderers! We've got this guy."

A jungle drumbeat started up in the back of my head, "What do we do next, Keith?"

"Get the IRS in here, figure out the details of the arrest and how we can track down all of his cash, and then go arrest him!"

The day we executed the search and arrest warrant on Joe Pips was sweet for me. He was a mean old bastard, and if he had been a few years younger, I'm sure he would have gone for my throat. Within minutes of his arrest, he started clutching his chest, claiming he had a heart condition. This maneuver came straight out of standard Mobster 101 training. The dons always claim a heart condition to avoid pre-bail detention. Geoff looked at him with a half smile, "OK, Joe, get your doctor on the phone, and I'll see if he'll ride in with us or join us at the bail hearing in Manhattan." Of course, the doctor was too busy. As I escorted a handcuffed Pips out his front door, I casually pulled open a drawer in a small table and found it packed with hundred-dollar bills, about twelve thousand dollars' worth.

"Joe, what's this?" I asked him.

"Aw, nothin'. Just my walking-around cash."

We transported him to Manhattan for a preliminary hearing. We seized close to three million dollars in liquid assets from Pips, who had never declared a legitimate job his whole life other than owning a small candy store in East Harlem. These accounts were in his true name. We didn't have the manpower or the time to dig much deeper. I can only guess at what he hid offshore or in a trust with others. In his several safe deposit boxes, we found shoeboxes full of platinum ingots and gold coins worth hundreds of thousands of dollars. Two weeks after we arrested him, Pips died of a heart attack. It was one of the few times a mobster hadn't lied about a heart condition.

One wise guy was down, but another was still on the loose. I hadn't pinned down the Asian heroin connection, but I still believed it would all come back to Santangelo.

In the midst of my case against these two mobsters, another slant developed that would take my unusual little task force down a different road.

Five

Narco Queen

FBI Miami and the DEA were after a group of Hispanic drug and weapons traffickers loosely organized under a Puerto Rican woman named Sonia Berrios-Rodriguez. Berrios-Rodriguez was tougher than most men, and word was that she really liked her women. She was a true entrepreneur, close to the Colombian cartels, and she moved tons of cocaine through Puerto Rico to Florida and New York. She was also connected to the Asians based in New York and had moved heroin into Puerto Rico, which had one of the highest heroin addiction rates in the Western Hemisphere.

After her 1988 indictment on cocaine trafficking charges in the District of Puerto Rico, she became a fugitive, living for a time in New York City. It was there that she further developed her crew and her relationship with major Asian heroin traffickers. In May 1990, the FBI tracked her down at a Key Biscayne, Florida, condominium owned by a Chinese New Yorker named Paul Yang. Sonia likened herself to a narco revolutionary. They found her hiding under a pile of clothes in a closet, along with a half-dozen M16s stolen from a military arsenal. Along with her seized possessions, we found a number of photographs depicting known drug traffickers as well as unknown Asians clearly enjoying a private fishing excursion hosted by Sonia.

Reliable informants confirmed that Sonia had been associating with "Chinese people from New York." They said she and a number of other suspected traffickers had purchased beachfront properties in South Beach, Miami, with cash and that the intermediary for the purchase was a Paul Yang from New York. They also confirmed that Sonia's lieutenant, Ernesto "Ernie" Velasco, along with his brother Frank and most of her crew, continued to run the lucrative business she had developed after she went to prison.

The smoke was turning into fire. I was on to something that could take me right to Paul "Bucktooth" Mah. A middle-aged veteran of the Chinese street gangs that still ruled Chinatown in lower Manhattan, he held the allegiance of more than one gang associated with the powerful tongs, the Chinese version of La Cosa Nostra.

Mah had even been featured in a TV exposé produced by a cub reporter named John Miller, the same Miller who would one day interview Osama bin Laden and become the FBI's head of public relations. Every cop in New York City wanted Paul Mah.

I followed the rules and entered him into the DEA's Drug Enforcement Coordinating System (DECS) in September 1990, surprised that no one had done it before. The system required all counter-drug organizations to file identifying information on any individual or location they were targeting. It was supposed to avoid duplicative efforts by different organizations and, more important, to keep someone's undercover agent or informant from getting shot by an unsuspecting cop during a buy-bust. The system's true purpose was to provide the DEA with an early alert system that tipped it off to new cases or suspects, allowing it to move in on the investigation under any pretext imaginable. I was to learn this lesson the hard way.

The investigation's new Hispanic-Asian angle introduced me to the DEA's case management philosophy, an approach diametrically opposed to the FBI's. On the one hand, the FBI's promotions don't depend on arrest statistics. The FBI encourages patience in getting to the top of a criminal organization. We took the time to work our way up, and if it took a year of sitting on a wiretap to get to the big players, we'd do it. On the other hand, DEA agents got their promotions through strong arrest stats. That meant getting in and closing a case fast.

At about the time FBI Miami was handing its end of the Sonia case off to Squad C-25, two men came to our office—Chuck, a senior investigator with the office of the Pennsylvania attorney general, and his partner, Denny Shook, a good-hearted bear of a man with a huge laugh. They had identified a cocaine ring in Bucks County, Pennsylvania. They believed a Cuban named Velasco, who lived in New York City and kept a common-law wife in a condominium along the Pennsylvania side of the Delaware River, headed the ring. This information matched an informant's report indicating Ernie Velasco and others hung out in New Hope, Pennsylvania, a trendy little town on the Delaware only an hour and a half from New York City. Chuck explained that since his office relied heavily on asset forfeitures to supplement its operating budget, it had authorized him and Denny to work with the FBI in a joint effort.

I applied for approval to deputize state and local officers under the Organized Crime Drug Enforcement Task Force (OCDETF) authority; it provided special funding to pay for overtime and other expenses incurred by nonfederal cops participating in a federally led joint effort against a localized, serious drug problem. Soon I had patched together an unusual group of detectives, cops, and agents all determined to hunt down the reconstituted Berrios-Rodriguez organization. We were a version of Robin Hood's Merry Men, only we were going to take from the rich drug dealers and give at least a portion to the people of Pennsylvania, as well as all those state and local police departments that share in the booty the feds collect.

While our numbers waxed and waned, at any one time our group comprised Pennsylvania State investigators, DEA agents from New York and Philadelphia, and FBI agents from C-25, with assistance from the DEA and FBI Miami, and FBI San Juan. I even deputized most of the New Hope Police Department, particularly since it would have been impossible to conduct surveillance in that town, a place where casual drug use is as normal as drinking beer in any of the steel towns of Pennsylvania. Nervous locals would have identified us quickly, and we didn't need New Hope's finest blowing our case.

After days of running surveillance on the Velasco brothers, we identified their New Hope distributor, a long-haired kid named David, and started by running two attractive female undercover agents against him. David loved to talk about his exploits helping Sonia and others move cocaine through Puerto Rico and to brag about all his local customers. My undercovers were good. Posing as flight attendants who traveled back and forth from Miami, they soon had David eating out of their hands. Eventually I think that David would not have noticed if they had held their transmitters, disguised as pagers, up to his mouth while he droned on about his crimes.

Cell phone records and surveillances in New York, Pennsylvania, and Miami, as well as prison cooperators trying to work off some time, buttressed the case. Every week we identified more members of the crew. When the AUSA for the Southern District of New York (SDNY) dragged his feet on seeking indictments, we took our case to the U.S. attorney's office in Philadelphia, where we found a particularly aggressive AUSA who was happy to show New York how to take down criminals. After the Eastern District of Pennsylvania issued arrest warrants for the Velasco brothers and seven of their associates, the SDNY jumped on board and obtained warrants against Ernesto Velasco and one of his associates, Efraen Santana. It was not the last time that I had to embarrass a prosecutor into doing the right thing.

We needed to take everyone down at the same time or risk people getting tipped off and vanishing. I sent arrest teams to Las Vegas, Miami, and Bucks County, and personally led the team going after Ernie Velasco and Santana, reputedly a former Cuban martial arts champion. Through surveillance, we located Velasco's apartment in a swank, uptown high-rise on Fifth Avenue. We weren't sure that he was in town, and I had made up my mind that only when we had apprehended Ernie Velasco would I give the other teams the green light. I arranged to occupy the apartment across the hall from Velasco's place and had a peephole camera installed so I could monitor his door.

Another agent was supposed to spell me that night, but he had a hard time staying awake. I'd already been up for twenty-plus hours, most of it running back and forth between the U.S. attorney's office and the FBI building. My cell phone rang at 3 a.m. The room was dark, and I bolted to grab the phone. Smashing my shoeless foot into the leg of a chair, I hit the ground in pain and swore through my teeth.

"Hey, buddy," said that familiar booming voice. "We're at Hooters, having a great time. How's it going?'" Denny's laugh was unmistakable, and I imagined everyone in our building could hear him.

"Hey, I didn't send you to Las Vegas to party. You've got to take down your guy in just hours. What the hell are you doing?"

"Don't sweat, buddy. Got to get loose. Can't get too stressed or you can't perform!" He hung up, and the pain of a broken toe consumed me.

I wasn't in a great mood at 9 a.m. when I heard someone knocking on Velasco's door. I limped to the peephole as a vaguely familiar figure with long, greasy hair entered the apartment. I heard a muffled conversation between two males. That was good enough for me. I rolled my lethargic partner out of bed and told him to call all the teams and tell them to get in position. I called Mark, who was my AUSA, and informed him I was reasonably confident Velasco was home. Mark was not a courageous AUSA. "I think you need more probable cause. It'll be on you if he's not there."

"Mark, I can't hold back the guys much longer, and this thing is going to get tripped up if we wait any longer. I'm going in. Talk to you."

I turned to my now relatively awake partner. "Tell the guys downstairs to start moving up here now. We go in ten minutes."

I moved to Velasco's door, careful to stand outside the doorframe when I knocked. A female voice asked, "Who is it?"

"Special delivery for Ernie Velasco." I gambled that she was either hung over or coked up. She opened the door slightly. "FBI, miss. I've got a warrant. Just don't interfere." My training told me to scan the room for danger, my head moving in unison with my weapon.

"Who is that?" asked a male Hispanic voice from one of the bedrooms.

"FBI! Step out here now! Show us your hands first!" Moments passed until we heard the hobble of footsteps, and then Ernie stumbled into the room, eyes bleary and red, stomach hanging over his boxer shorts. "Who's in the other bedroom?"

"A friend with his gal," replied Ernie. As I dragged Velasco to the floor, I motioned for one of my men to cuff him and then quickly moved to the other door with a detective named Benny.

"FBI! Come out now! Show your hands first!" I had to bellow the command twice before the doorknob began to turn and two male hands protruded, followed by a naked, stoned Efraen Santana. One of my men spread-eagled Efraen on the floor and handcuffed him, and Benny and I moved into the room to clear it. I entered first, trying to adjust my eyes to the darkness. I could tell someone was on the bed. Then I heard a female voice pleading in broken English for her clothes. When Benny found the light switch, we saw a stunningly attractive naked woman kneeling on all fours, blinded by the light, and groping to find some item of clothing.

"Benny, clear the closet, then the hallway! Benny! Clear the goddamn closet!"

Benny was a lady's man, and he could not stop staring.

"Damn it! Give her some clothes."

I proceeded to clear the rest of the suite, but I admit that the beautiful Brazilian model challenged my focus considerably. When I returned to the bedroom, Benny, grinning and transfixed, was holding out thong underpants between his thumb and index finger, dangling them as if he was tempting his cat with its favorite toy.

We took inventory and found extensive drug records, small quantities of cocaine, a pistol, and another one of Velasco's sidekicks hiding in a third room. He identified himself as Tony, but he looked suspiciously similar to someone photographed on one of our many surveillances of Velasco's crew. We already had information that local police in New Hope had previously picked up a Tony for discharging a weapon within city limits. I remembered an intercepted conversation between Velasco and a male Hispanic referred to as El Loco. I called my AUSA back and told him, "I have to hold this guy until the other teams report in."

"You can't do that without probable cause. You know that," he was adamant. "Let him go."

I thought, To hell I will, and walked over to the guy, "So, pal, what is your name and what are you doing here?"

"My name is Tony, and I just met these guys. They asked me to make a grocery run for them this morning."

"You have any other names, Tony?"

"Yeah, I'm Tony Ruiz from Brooklyn. Now I need to leave if you're not going to arrest me."

He got up and started to walk toward the door. He would be on the first phone he could find once he stepped out of the building.

"Hey, El Loco!" I called out.

"What?" he replied, clearly responding to the nickname we had heard repeatedly on our wiretap.

"Thanks. You're under arrest." That was enough probable cause for me.

We bagged four other Velasco associates that day, along with plenty of incriminating records, some drugs, and a couple of expensive cars. My plan was coalescing. At least one of these guys would talk, and our next stop would be Ernie Lee, also known as Cuba Boy, the same guy who had invested in the

Miami properties with Sonia and was a close associate of Bucktooth Mah. This bust was going to be a classic roll-up, and we were zeroing in on the biggest heroin dealer on the East Coast.

About a week and a half later, on a Saturday afternoon in May 1994, I received a phone call from the DEA office in midtown Manhattan. "Agent Holcomb, I'm patching through a call from Agent Marchese." I knew this news could not be good.

"Hey, Ray, this is Pete. Wanted to let you know we picked up—well, it's a little more complicated than that—but Cuba Boy is cooperating with us and we had him buy two keys from Bucktooth Mah this morning. I thought you might want to know."

"What are you talking about? Why would Cuba Boy cooperate with you, and why would you turn him around on Mah when you know I have the case on Mah?"

"Well, we couldn't wait to get a hold of you."

"That's bullshit."

"Talk to my boss on Monday." He hung up.

I was stunned. How had this happened? Everything had been going according to plan. Squad C-25 had done a lot of hard work—a year plus—and we had flushed Cuba Boy right into the hands of the U.S. attorney's office in Brooklyn, where the assistant on duty that weekend just happened to be the brother of the DEA agent who had called me.

That Monday a little bit of hell broke loose between the FBI and the DEA. The matter went to the top of both organizations. The DEA had plainly ignored its own guidelines, but a bad guy was in custody and cooperating against the biggest bad guy in New York, Bucktooth Mah.

Cuba Boy's cooperation gave the DEA what it needed to get a wiretap on Mah. Their agents allowed me to sit in during the monitoring. Every day I would travel to their office and review the wiretap transcript. I hated being there, and it took every ounce of control I had to keep from busting the DEA agent who snaked me along with the others, right in the nose. In any event, the intercepted conversations were good, some of the best I had ever heard. There were phone calls between Mah and people in Canada, then calls to Thailand and other points in Southeast Asia. I knew this investigation was going to develop into a very big case, regardless of who got the credit. It was going straight to the top of the Golden Triangle.

I watched as the DEA had Cuba Boy buy five more keys from Mah. Then, only days later, they announced that they were taking down the case. "You're crazy!" I snapped. "This thing is just beginning. Why would you want to take it down now? Mah is old school. He won't cooperate. He won't give you the top dogs. He won't give you anything!"

"Just our policy. We generally don't run a wire much more than sixty days. Too many scumbags to get off the street."

"Jesus! With some patience, you could take down a huge organization. You could take down this organization from New York City through Canada to Southeast Asia. That's not more important than those shit heads pushing dime bags in the Bronx?"

It was a done deal and one of the more shortsighted decisions I have seen during my law enforcement career. Mah got nine years and never talked. I am sure he served far less. A DEA agent got his promotion, but heroin kept flowing into New York.

I was durable, but this disappointment was a major hit. Just as when we blew the surveillance on Santangelo after a year of hard work, it took some time for me to clear my head and accept what had happened. Some in Berrios-Rodriguez's crew were still out there dealing, though, and I was determined to get every one of them. Geoff understood and gave me as much rope as I needed. We arrested people at sunrise in the mountains of Puerto Rico, tracked some of them down in the back alleys of Miami, and finally put a case together against Berrios-Rodriguez.

Tony Ruiz, aka El Loco, skipped bail days after his release. I tasked one of my informants to track him down, suspecting that he was in Miami. Several weeks later, my source found Ruiz at a run-down hotel in South Beach, registered under a false name. FBI Miami seized him an hour later, and this time I was determined we wouldn't lose him again. I had learned a great deal about prosecutors. As in every other profession, there are those who care and those who collect a paycheck. As it turned out, we did not win the lottery with this one. I flew down and arrived on the day of Ruiz's bail hearing. When I met the AUSA handling the case, with his long, bleached-blond hair and wearing boat shoes without socks, I knew we were in trouble. He twirled a pencil and stared at the ceiling as I tried to impart to him the importance of holding Ruiz without bail. "My informant is sure Ruiz will head for Cuba the minute he is released," I said.

"Sure, sure, got it covered." He was not convincing.

By the time our matter was called, the female magistrate had made apparent her penchant for setting all but the worst ax murderers free pending trial. When the surfer boy–prosecutor addressed the court, his presentation was lackluster, and he failed to convey any of the pertinent information I had given him. I could not stand it. I got up from my seat and sat down next to him, grabbed his elbow in a vice grip, and hissed through my clenched teeth, "You'd better goddamn ask Ruiz the following questions, or he's walking and I will never forget that!"

"OK, OK, relax man. What is it?"

I spelled out for the third time all the facts that he needed to convince the magistrate that Ruiz was a flight risk. He recited them to the judge. She stated that in view of the new information, Tony Ruiz was clearly a risk. She remanded him until trial. Maybe Surfer Boy learned something but probably not. At least Ruiz was in jail for the time being.

In early 1995, when Sonia was finishing her nine-year sentence for massive cocaine trafficking, we hit her with a new indictment, charging her with being the principal administrator of a continuing criminal enterprise, conspiracy to traffic in heroin, and illegal weapons trafficking. My prosecutor from Manhattan accompanied me to San Juan to discuss the matter with the U.S. attorney for the District of Puerto Rico. He greeted us cordially, at first, and then became visibly upset. He was pissed that we had gone after Sonia. He felt that seven to nine years was more than enough punishment for selling a ton of cocaine and heroin. I could not believe his arrogance as he asserted that Sonia had "paid her dues." As I walked out of his office that day, I was compelled to turn back, "Now I understand why Puerto Rico has the second biggest addict population in the Western Hemisphere." He glared in disbelief that I would dare to speak to him in that manner.

The day Sonia Berrios-Rodriguez was sentenced to twenty-three years in the Southern District of New York, all of her women friends appeared in court in their finest stiletto heels and sausage dresses. They were sending her a message that they would be waiting for her. Although she tried to appear tough, the reality of what lay ahead had begun to penetrate. She left the stand handcuffed and escorted by marshals, doing her best to wink and smile at her adoring friends as if she were a movie star at the Oscars. As she started to pass me, I momentarily blocked her path and bent forward so no one but she could hear: "Sonia, you've been screwed by a man." She froze and glared at me before her marshal escort dragged her away.

I was not done with the Berrios-Rodriguez operation. I knew from my early days of working narcotics that visiting jail time on these parasites is only half the game. We did not put the ball in the end zone until we had tracked down and taken the proceeds of the criminal enterprise. With enough money stashed away, the criminals can continue to operate effectively from behind bars. Take away their resources and they become just more nameless members of the prison community.

Pack Horse was a seven-year Ferris wheel ride of some great ups and a number of rough downs. I developed enough information over the course of the operation to build a solid case against money launderer Paul Chang. Chang had taken over $2 million in cash from Berrios-Rodriguez, Luk, Cuba Boy, and others and purchased two valuable properties on Ocean Avenue in South Beach. One of the properties was just two doors down from the Versace mansion. I arrested Chang and searched his offices, discovering overwhelming evidence: coded handwritten diaries with notations clearly referring to Berrios-Rodriguez, Cuba Boy, and Luk, along with cash amounts, and references to meetings with these individuals in Miami.

At trial, both Cuba Boy and Luk testified that they had delivered boxes full of cash to Chang in Miami. In spite of my AUSA's inexperience and fumbling throughout our trial, I felt confident that we had presented a slam-dunk case. Chang admitted that he had purchased the properties largely with cash provided by Berrios-Rodriguez, Cuba Boy, and Luk, but he claimed that he believed them to be honest business people and that "in the Chinese community we always deal in cash."

The jury adjourned and remained deadlocked for five days. I was worried. It finally returned with a verdict of not guilty after the judge had issued an incomprehensible instruction. I was astounded when the judge directed the jurors to disregard witness testimony that almost everyone in Chinatown knew Cuba Boy and Paul Mah to be drug dealers. In effect, he directed them to accept the defendant's claim that he did not realize he was dealing with bad people. I glared at Mark, the assistant prosecutor, in disbelief while he sat frozen and said nothing. The case was over. The next day I had to turn over a check for $1.2 million from the U.S. Marshals Service to Chang's lead attorney. It represented the proceeds from the sale of one of the Miami properties. We had seized the two properties and sold one of them subject to an agreement to hold the funds in escrow pending the outcome of our trial.

Chang's attorney practically laughed in my face as he snatched the check from my hand. I wanted to knock the hell out of him, but as usual I managed to control my rage.

I knew Chang was guilty. Some of the jurors confessed to me as they filed out of the jury room that they believed he was, too, but that the judge's instruction had left them no alternative.

About a week later, I received a phone call from one of the assistant U.S. attorneys who had helped with my case. "Ray, you won't believe what just happened. One of Chang's lawyers called me. He said he felt uncomfortable about something and needed to come forward. He said the jury foreman called him several days after our trial and asked him if he would hire his daughter who had just graduated from law school!"

"That son of a bitch!" I yelled into the receiver. "How do we find out who held out in that jury room?"

"Well, I told Mark, and he said that he wouldn't take it back to the judge. He said it's over, Ray."

The judge had been less than friendly to Mark throughout the trial. To some degree, he deserved it. Mark had not exactly been stellar in presenting our case, dropping his notes, forgetting his line of questioning in mid sentence, and repeatedly failing to object when even I saw the necessity. His first serious trial broke him. He had no backbone left to go up against the judge, and I knew the SDNY would not turn on one of its own.

The words of my Georgia partner, Ed, came back to me: "Justice is only a word. We have to drag it screaming and kicking through the system. No one else will." I had dragged this case as far as I could, but the system had beaten me one more time. I was not ready to quit just yet, though.

As we continued to build cases on the few associates of Berrios-Rodriguez who were still on the loose, sources provided information that Sonia's parents had moved from Puerto Rico to the Florida Panhandle. They had paid cash for a home next door to her prison. They were visiting her every day and acting as couriers, carrying instructions and cash money orders.

My southern district AUSA had all but disappeared. Within weeks, he left the U.S. attorney's office for a job in a private firm handling civil matters. I found an assistant who specialized in forfeitures, and he helped us put our case together.

Several days later, we headed to the Panhandle, where we obtained and executed a search warrant from the local U.S. attorney's office. Mom and Dad Berrios-Rodriguez were not home when we arrived. We managed to let ourselves in, doing little damage, and found all the records we needed, including dozens of money order receipts totaling tens of thousands of dollars. We left our notice and inventory at the house. I am sure it was not a pleasant moment for them when they returned and realized we had been there. We interrupted Sonia's cash flow. The ball had crossed the goal line.

The U.S. government seized over a quarter of a million dollars in cash from Sonia's parents. She was no longer the Drug Queen of Puerto Rico. Sure, someone or a group of someones eventually replaced her, but that was a problem for the next DEA or FBI agent.

Pack Horse culminated in the arrest and prosecution of twenty-one individuals, including two of the most notorious heroin traffickers in New York history. Also meted out were total accumulated jail sentences of 145 years, and we arranged for the seizure and forfeiture of $4.4 million.

A couple associates got away, but we bagged most of them. My philosophy had always been that we would win in never giving up, and I was certain that for at least a time, narcotics dealers in eastern Pennsylvania, Miami, New York, and Puerto Rico were looking over their shoulders. After arresting Ernie Velasco and his brother, we pulled the tapes of their phone calls from the prison. During one conversation, a buddy of Velasco's in Miami, who was also feeling our heat, complained, "They're down here poking into everything! Who are these guys?"

Six

SWAT Training

"In accordance with U.S. counterterrorism policy, the FBI considers terrorists to be criminals. FBI efforts in countering terrorist threats are multifaceted. Information obtained through FBI investigations is analyzed and used to prevent terrorist activity and, whenever possible, to effect the arrest and prosecution of potential perpetrators. The FBI further describes terrorism as either domestic or international, depending on the origin, base, and objectives of the terrorists. Domestic terrorism is defined as the unlawful use, or threatened use, of force or violence by a group or individual based and operating entirely within the United States or its territories without foreign direction committed against persons or property to intimidate or coerce a government, the civilian population, or any segment thereof, in furtherance of political or social objectives."
—FBI Counterterrorism Division report, *Terrorism 2002–2005*

Beginning in the mid-1960s, with the Cold War raging, America found itself confronting a new kind of threat. Violent elements of the radical left and the anti–Vietnam War movement, resurgent anarchists, pro-Palestinian groups, communist ideologues, and Soviet-manipulated dupes all threatened the fabric of American life. They did so in a way unknown since the darkest, most turbulent days of the Great Depression. The Weather Underground, an

American radical leftist organization whose leaders and members had split from the Students for a Democratic Society (SDS), engaged in a series of bombings, riots, and a jailbreak as part of a "Declaration of a State of War" against the U.S. government. The majority of the bombings were directed against government buildings; in most instances, the group sent out advance communiqués providing evacuation warnings. Between 1971 and 1975, it struck the U.S. Capitol, the Pentagon, and the State Department.

The Black Liberation Army (BLA), an underground nationalist-Marxist militant organization, undertook a program of "armed struggle" with the stated goal of "taking up arms for the liberation and self-determination of black people in the United States." It was most active in the United States from the mid-1960s and through the 1970s. The BLA carried out a spate of bombings, robberies (what participants termed "expropriations"), and prison breaks. Authorities suspected that the BLA was to blame for over sixty incidents of violence between 1970 and 1976. The Fraternal Order of Police blamed the BLA for the murders of thirteen police officers, including that of a San Francisco officer killed while working at his desk and the ambush and murder of two officers with the NYPD. They also bombed a San Francisco church full of mourners attending the funeral of a police officer killed while responding to a bank robbery.

At the 1972 Summer Olympics in Munich, Germany, members of the Israeli Olympic team were taken hostage and eventually murdered by Black September, a militant group with ties to Yasser Arafat's Fatah organization. As the athletes slept, eight tracksuit-clad terrorists, carrying duffel bags loaded with AK-47 assault rifles, Tokarev pistols, and grenades, scaled a two-meter chain-link fence with the unwitting assistance of American athletes who were sneaking back into the Olympic Village. Once inside, the terrorists used stolen keys to enter the Israeli team's two apartments. By the end of the ordeal, the terrorist group had killed eleven Israeli athletes and coaches and one German police officer.

From the 1960s through the 1970s, over 150 commercial aircraft were hijacked in the United States. At the direction of the hijackers, the majority of them were flown to Cuba. It was an epidemic.

Just like the police, the FBI found itself ill prepared to face this new kind of enemy. Heavily armed and vicious, these criminals, crazies, and ideologues had no remorse about executing "pigs" (their term for law enforcement officers) and blowing up the symbols of capitalism or government.

Clearly our well-trained agents, armed just with revolvers, were outgunned. The FBI needed specialized tactical teams at a field office or local level that had superior training and better firepower than the bad guys had. Even the most self-centered FBI careerist didn't want to explain to dead agents' families that their loved ones had died because they hadn't been given the training or the tools to defend themselves.

By 1972, the Los Angeles Police Department (LAPD) had begun to attract considerable media attention with its special weapons and tactics team, made up mostly of military veterans and outfitted with the latest weaponry and body armor. Unlike big federal bureaucracies, the LAPD answered only to the mayor and the city council. As a result, and unlike the federal government, the LAPD could adapt with lightning speed.

In the New York office of the FBI, the biggest of over fifty bureau field divisions, a group of older agents began to map out a course toward creating an FBI SWAT team. In the process, they remained sensitive to the perception of large segments of the populace that the FBI was only a step away from becoming an Orwellian Big Brother bent on trampling the U.S. Constitution into the ground.

The New York office ordered the creation of a shooting club–rifle team with the best rifle shooters in the division. In the spring of 1971, after tryouts at the bureau's range in Peekskill, New York, twenty club members were selected out of a substantial pool of talent. Each member was issued his own Remington 760 pump-action, .308-caliber, scoped rifle, equipped with a quick-disconnect mount that held the scope. The problem was that the mount was faulty. It would often choose on its own to discard the scope after only several rounds were fired.

It wasn't long before the rifle team was doing more than just competitive target practice. In January 1972, Trans World Airlines (TWA) Flight 2 was hijacked as it traveled from Los Angeles to New York. Once on the ground at John F. Kennedy International Airport, Garrett Trapnell, a bank robber and con man, demanded over $300,000, freedom for militant Angela Davis, and a face-to-face meeting with President Richard Nixon. He threatened to ram the Boeing 707 into the TWA terminal if his demands were not met. One of the new rifle team members arrived on the scene and took up a position behind the blast fence on the tarmac. He waited until Trapnell stepped into view, then shot him twice, hitting him in the arm and hand, and ending the standoff. No one else was injured.

In the New York division, management handpicked agents it considered the go-to guys in time of crisis and assigned them to the bank robbery and fugitive squads, often referred to as the reactive or violent crime squads. Among these mature men were war veterans, former street cops, and former professional athletes. Many were the best shooters in the office. Proven, self-assured, even cocky egos were not lacking in the reactive squads. These men were the kind we wanted to send into buildings after hardened criminals. They formed the cadre of the next tactical team evolution in the New York office.

In 1973 the tragic terrorist attack in Munich was still a fresh memory. So was the violent seventy-one-day standoff at Wounded Knee, South Dakota, between members of the American Indian Movement and a hastily assembled group of U.S. marshals and FBI agents. That year, the FBI's New York office formally ordered the creation of four apprehension teams. These five-man squads received some limited, specialized training with scoped rifles, M14 and M16 automatic rifles, tear gas delivery systems, and 12-gauge shotguns. Just as the rifle team had, they soon found themselves dealing with kidnappings, barricaded violent subjects, hijackings, and the arrests of violent gang members.

During this time, the domestic threat continued to spiral upward. A few weeks didn't pass without some extremist group trying to collect headlines for its cause by hijacking or killing. Police officers were gunned down and bombs continued to explode. In 1974, a violent Puerto Rican Marxist-Leninist group known as the Armed Forces of National Liberation (FALN) initiated a bombing spree, seriously wounding police officer Angel Poggi in East Harlem, New York. Over the next nine years, the FALN was responsible for over a hundred bombings in the United States, including the January 24, 1975, attack on Fraunces Tavern, a lower Manhattan landmark and popular gathering place, that killed four and wounded fifty.

Within a year of establishing the apprehension teams in New York, FBI HQ approved the creation of SWAT teams within each field division. A July 1974 memorandum directed a two-week in-service at Quantico for selected agents. They were instructed to bring "well worn hunting boots, . . . old blue denim jeans, a baseball cap, and your grays."

During the early years of field-based SWAT, the fledging teams received only limited support and training from FBI HQ and the training unit at Quantico. In large measure, they relied on their own ingenuity. Soon, each division had its own unique selection process and training program. As could be expected, the quality of these teams varied widely, depending largely on the personality of the leadership and the support of its local management.

The New York office had a pool of almost nine hundred agents to draw from, and the core of its new SWAT team revolved around the same people who had made up the original rifle and then apprehension teams. Some of these veterans, such as Danny Coulson, who would later form the elite Hostage Rescue Team (HRT) based in Quantico, eventually transferred out of New York. However, a unit of veterans—men from the New York area—remained with the team for years. These agents were respected throughout the office and included such men as Mike Henehan, Tom Lagatol, and Dave Carmen, who provided long-term continuity that was unique to the New York SWAT program.

In short order, the New York team took the lead among field SWAT teams in nearly every respect. Blessed with some of the bureau's top marksmen, the team took advantage of the close ties some of its members held with the military. With the support of his team leader and office management, Bob Aldridge, former Special Forces soldier and a Vietnam veteran, developed a mutually beneficial relationship with the U.S. Marine Corps. The corps wanted to learn more about operating in an urban environment, and its commandant specifically asked for veteran cops and agents to teach his men how to handle themselves on the streets of a big city.

The late 1970s were heady times for the New York SWAT program. In the words of one former team member, "We were rockin' and rollin'." Hindered only by a short supply of time and money, the team developed and honed new tactics for law enforcement. Tom Lagatol, one of the best shooters in the New York office, became an advocate of the "quick kill" shooting method that the U.S. Army had developed in the early 1960s. It is also called instinctive shooting, and the key is to make the weapon an extension of one's eye. This technique recognizes that while snipers use sights, people engaged in close-range gunfights generally do not, and even if they attempt to find their sights in the heat of a firefight, they will never take the time to find a perfect sight picture. When adrenaline is screaming through the system, all that works is muscle memory. The shooter is barely aware as the gun comes up to a certain spot and he or she embraces and pulls the trigger. Agents and police who have been in close-proximity gunfights will tell you that they never thought about their sights.

To be effective, you must repeat the basic steps. You must practice the same drawing motion, the same grip, the same placement of the trigger finger, and the same final position of the weapon. If the threat is near and there is no time, the gun discharges at belt level. As the threat distance extends, the level of the weapon will generally be more elevated until it is almost at eye level. If the threat is somewhat less imminent yet real, then the officer or agent has the luxury of raising his or her weapon to eye level but must watch the target for any furtive or deadly movement; therefore, the officer or agent still isn't looking at his or her sights.

Lagatol's skill at teaching quick kill soon came to the attention of the Marine Corps. In short order, he and several handpicked teammates were instructing Marines, who, in turn, took the skill back to the corps.

Bob Aldridge, again with the approval of team management, also developed a fast-rope capability for New York SWAT. Developed by the military in Vietnam, this helicopter insertion technique uses heavy ropes extended from gantries, or arms, attached to the sides of Huey helicopters. It had clear applicability to some civilian law enforcement scenarios. When people need to be put into a difficult location quickly, and the terrain does not allow helicopters to set down—such as on rooftops covered with antennae, vent pipes, and chimneys—it is the next best way to get operators where they need to be.

Functioning almost as autonomous units, FBI field SWAT teams had to address local threats as they saw fit. City teams, such as New York's, developed door rams, other entry capabilities, and surveillance techniques that worked for them. Teams in more rural jurisdictions cultivated tracking and woodland patrolling skills.

Teams were also on their own when developing a rapport with local police departments. They did so on the strength of personalities. As FBI and police leadership changed, so did the groups' relationships.

Despite generally decent associations between SWAT teams and local police departments, there were some rocky times between the NYPD and FBI SWAT in New York during the 1960s and well into the 1980s. In most cases, the detectives, investigators, and street agents tried to work through the problems for the good of the common mission. It was trickier on a management level. There has always been a tense relationship at the upper echelons between the two New York groups. It had begun around 1932, when Charles Lindbergh's infant son was kidnapped. The FBI, under a young Hoover, tracked the suspect to a spot in the Bronx and didn't inform the police. Ostensibly, the bureau didn't want the police to know because the agents thought officers in local police departments might be fast and loose with the information. It actually had more to do with rivalry and jealousy and about grabbing newspaper headlines and the glory and fame of making the big case.

The bad taste from the Lindbergh kidnapping lingered and, through the years, merged with perceived and actual slights. The friction escalated, fueled by the fact that federal and state laws overlap in most criminal matters. In an effort to alleviate the destructive ill feeling, the FBI and the NYPD created a joint bank robbery task force in the late 1980s and the Joint Terrorism Task Force (JTTF) shortly afterward.

I began my career with the New York FBI SWAT team when I was still working counterintelligence. Participation on a field office SWAT team is ancillary to every member's full-time job. Tom Bara, a veteran agent and long-time SWAT team member, invited me to try out for the team. Things were much less formal in those days. My college roommate was Bara's best friend and had vouched for me. I was considered a stand-up guy; that assessment, combined with my athletic background, was enough to get me a look. The team members had to feel they could trust me. Their philosophy was that while many FBI agents had the requisite skills to learn how to shoot well, to enter barricaded apartments, and to subdue violent criminals, the team couldn't teach character or teamwork. It's either part of an agent's makeup or it isn't. In an organization filled with confident people, it is not easy to find those who can keep their egos subservient to the good of the squad. More important, no one wanted to go on a risky mission with someone he or she could not trust.

We were at team tryouts at Camp Smith, the old National Guard base high above the Hudson near Peekskill and only a few miles south of West Point. For decades, Camp Smith had served as the site of the New York office's principal firearms range, with a full-time staff, classrooms, and barracks for overnight training. The winding roads that lead up to the site can suggest a serene autumn portrait, but my visit was on a harsh, late fall day with hard ice on the ground. Following a cursory interview, we went out to the firearms range. The wind howled as we new recruits strode up to the firing line along with the regular team of mostly grizzled veterans. Even with gloves on, my hands nearly froze as I shot two pistol qualification courses, each one a total of fifty rounds from various firing positions. I did miserably, more worried about losing my footing and shooting someone than hitting the target. My fellow recruits did not fare much better.

Clint Guenther, the team leader, then told us to call it a day, so we eagerly slid our way back inside to the gun-cleaning room where the pungent smell of oil and Hoppes cleaning fluid filled the warm air. No one took this part of the day lightly. A dirty weapon has a high potential for malfunctioning, and the semiautomatics we were transitioning to were less tolerant of dirt than the old six-shooters. If you drop a six-shooter in a mud puddle and pick it up, it will generally still work. If you fire a semiautomatic frequently, carbon builds up inside its mechanism at critical points, and eventually it will malfunction. The slide will lock back, and if you are well trained, you will instantly go into the "tap, rack, bang" clear drill, which may not solve the problem. If you fire hundreds of rounds at a range and don't clean that gun, there's a strong possibility that it won't work correctly when you have to draw it in the line of duty.

After our freezing audition, we headed to the local gin mill. The owner treated the SWAT guys well, so it had become a popular hangout. Out came the steaming hot chili and hamburgers. Then we toasted agents, the FBI, law enforcement in general, wives, girlfriends, pets, and the New York Yankees. Starting light on beer and graduating to Goldschläger, a heavy and syrupy schnapps-like drink speckled with gold, we drank for three hours. We blended our fest with a post-operational "hot wash," comparing notes and exchanging information. Before the party dispersed, Tom Lagatol, a legend to me, came over and wrote his phone number on a slip of paper. I was in a haze, but I heard him say, "Give me a call at the office tomorrow morning."

The drinking had been part of the interview process. They wanted to see how we handled ourselves with a few drinks under our belts. When I called the number the next morning, I got the good news that I was a probationary SWAT team member.

During the early years of FBI SWAT, agents still carried revolvers or, as Hollywood cops referred to them, "cookie cutters," since that's what the cylinder resembles. Many team members carried standard bureau-issue .357 Magnums, a powerful revolver. Although all agent recruits trained on the M16 and the 870 shotgun at Quantico, there was little specialized equipment to go around, most of it being reserved for the violent crimes squads. Only a few tactical-type weapons had found their way to the field SWAT teams. Generally, we had to serve for years before an M16 rifle or Heckler & Koch (H&K) MP5 submachine gun found its way into our hands. Each weapon had a pedigree, and every team member could recite the names of the previous two or three owners. The SWAT arsenal could only be described as a real hodgepodge— an eclectic assortment of shotguns, M16s, MP5s, various revolvers, and 9mm automatics (Browning and Smith & Wesson)—as well as personally owned but bureau-approved handguns in all sizes and calibers. There was even a silenced .22-caliber pistol for taking out streetlights when we needed the mask of darkness. Uniformity, or interoperability, was not the rule of the day. If I ran out of ammunition in a gunfight, I had to hope someone nearby was carrying the same weapon; otherwise, I'd have to crawl off elsewhere to find a reload.

By the mid 1990s, the bureau had transitioned to semiautomatic pistols as the standard agent-issued sidearm. First, it used the Swiss-made SIG Sauer 9mm, followed by a disastrous 10mm Smith & Wesson, and finally the Austrian-made Glock in several calibers. A violent FBI firefight had made the bureau take a long, hard look at its firepower. In the spring of 1986, two men committed a series of brutal bank robberies in southern Miami. Afterward, an elite FBI unit staked out a section of the South Dixie Highway on the morning of April 11, having learned that the robbers would be heading there. Within minutes of their arrival, Agents Ben Grogan and Jerry Dove saw a vehicle carrying two males that fit the description of the suspects' car. They pursued it while other agents converged on the scene. Following the decision to carry out a felony car stop, there were a series of violent collisions with three bureau cars ramming the target vehicle, forcing it up onto the curb and into a tree. Immediately after coming to a crashing halt, the suspects, Michael Platt and William Matix, opened fire on the agents with high-powered, semiautomatic weapons. Only one of the agents was carrying a 9mm semiautomatic. Ben Grogan, SWAT trained and possibly the best shot of all, lost his eyeglasses during the collision and could not see well enough to find his weapon on the floor of his vehicle.

The FBI agents fought back with a fury, firing with amazing accuracy and hitting the robbers repeatedly in critical areas—the groin, chest, and head—but to virtually no effect. Despite many gunshot wounds, Platt casually strolled through the carnage and murdered Grogan and Dove execution style. Agents Gordon McNeill, Ed Mireles, and John Hanlon were seriously injured. Agents Dick Manauzzi and Gil Orrantia suffered less devastating injuries. Only one agent, Ron Risner, was uninjured.

This tragedy made the FBI reappraise its standard-issue handgun and run through a series of exercises to find the right weapon, one that would stop an adversary cold in his or her tracks. The agent selected to spearhead the project was a lawyer who taught constitutional law at the academy.

After running extensive ballistic tests on gelatinous forms that resembled human torsos, the decision makers concluded that a 10mm bullet was the solution. It was a massive round backed by plenty of powder. It seems, however, that no one seriously considered what type of handgun could manage so colossal and powerful a bullet. Only Smith &Wesson returned a competitive bid, but since a Brazilian company had bought the manufacturer, it was not the Smith & Wesson of yesteryear. It was not long before the new stainless steel gun earned the moniker "boat anchor" from skeptical agents. It was so cumbersome that most agents shied away from it soon after trying it, reverting to using their personally owned weapons. Not only was the new gun virtually impossible to conceal, but smaller hands had difficulty controlling it. Soon, fissures appeared in the frames of a number of the guns, and the FBI could not deny that it had made a big mistake. It had been a tremendous waste of money, but certainly it would not be the last time the FBI would charge forward on an expensive project without considering the opinions of those who would actually use the product. Ironically, a gun and bullet already existed—and had for decades—that more than fit the man-stopper bill. It was the time-tested

.45-caliber Colt M1911A1. By the late 1990s, all FBI tactical teams, as well as any agent willing to buy his or her own, had an updated version of a seventy-year-old gun the U.S. Army originally designed to stop the Moro rebels during the Philippine-American War. The Moros, high on drugs and promises of heaven, had fearlessly stormed U.S. troops who carried .38-caliber revolvers at the time. When the FBI scratched its head and tried to prevent a recurrence of the 1986 firefight debacle, instead of reviewing what the U.S. military did in 1911 under similar circumstances, the agency consulted a lawyer and backed into the problem.

By the late 1990s, after discarding the boat anchor, the bureau settled on the Austrian-made Glock as the standard issue for all FBI agents. Agents now can opt for a 9mm, .40-caliber, or .45-caliber version of this quality, time-tested handgun. There is now some version to fit every hand and almost every condition.

Firearms people will continue to argue the merits of the 9mm, .40-caliber, and .45-caliber bullet. On the one hand, the 9mm is a smaller and lighter round, ideal for military combat missions. Troops can carry a lot of this ammunition, and it is easier to train them to use it, regardless of their hand size or strength. Police, on the other hand, rarely engage in gunfights that last more than seconds. They usually take place in close range, where the .40-caliber and the .45-caliber rounds are most effective.

▪   ▪   ▪

When I first joined the team, headquarters spooned out a paltry fifty dollars per agent for equipment. We wore watch caps instead of ballistic helmets, and our dark blue fatigues and boots were hand-me-downs. It is one thing to get someone else's gun but an entirely different matter when you are talking about boots. I am not squeamish, but I made a serious effort to disinfect the boots I finally received, after two months of waiting. The former owner was not renowned for his personal hygiene, and they smelled bad. My method was not scientific. I threw a couple of ounces of Desenex antifungal foot powder into each boot, shook the boots as if they were martini shakers, and let them sit for days.

We had to work hard to stay on the team, and many agents thought it bordered on nuts to want to be a SWAT team member in the first place. We put in extra hours, normally earned no extra money, and got no slack on our regular jobs since SWAT was a second job for agents still working their criminal cases. Moreover, the nature of the SWAT job called for middle-of-the-night calls, often with little or no warning.

My first serious SWAT training occurred in Fahnestock State Park in rural New York State, where the team stayed in unheated park cabins for a week in the late fall. We took a course in orienteering, finding our way through miles of deep forest using a topographical map and a compass. We learned how to rappel—that is, to make a controlled descent on a special rope, a technique we would later use from a hovering helicopter—and how to ascend the rope using cams, devices commonly known as jumars.

One afternoon, I hiked up a mountain with Tom Lagatol. Tom and Bob Aldridge had been running the block of rappel training that week. We had to tie together two 200-foot ropes to make the distance. We anchored them at the top of a cliff overlooking a stone quarry. Tom tossed the ropes off the side of the precipice, which was about a 300-foot drop to the bottom of the pit. The crag extended well out over the face of the rock wall so that we could not see below. I knew that Tom was testing me when he said, "OK, Holcomb. You go first." I hooked up my rappel system, my figure eight, and carabiner and launched myself over the edge of the crag. After descending 10 feet, I saw right below me all my rope tangled in a little tree protruding from the mountain-side. The rope heap looked like a massive bird's nest.

Tom couldn't see me from his position above. I could hear him shouting, "Holcomb, why the hell aren't you descending?

"I can't. It's all stuck in a branch."

I was hanging about 290 feet off the ground with the wind tossing me about like a Frisbee. Tom shouted back, "Well, tie off and fix it!"

With only a day and a half of training, I did it. It was tricky, but I was able to recoil over 300 feet of rope in my arm, fling it beyond and clearing the tree, and hurl it down to the ground. Then I smoothly released my tie off—essentially a brake—and rappelled down to the ground.

Tom Bara came down after me and reached a jagged outcropping. When he kicked off from it, the wind caught his body and spun him 180 degrees. He swung back into the rock, unable to absorb the impact with his feet, and broke his right arm when he hit the rock. A serrated ledge cut through his arm like a carving knife. He was bleeding badly and still about 200 feet up in the air. The belay man, the person on the ground who can control a climber's descent by pulling the rope taut, realized Tom was in trouble. Tom's camouflage fatigues were blood soaked by the time he reached the ground. He tried to laugh it off while our medic, always present and the most important man on the team, went into action. Tom was not the last casualty that week.

I never had a problem with heights. I guess that in another life I could have been a steel worker constructing high-rise buildings. Team leader Guenther, a bureau-certified rappel master, recognized this advantage and offered me as the Manhattan office's candidate for rappel master school held at Quantico. As part of the school, we spent two days in the mountains of West Virginia, climbing and descending the same cliffs that the U.S. Army Rangers had scaled when they prepared to assault the beaches of Normandy on D-Day. For the next twelve years, I was the team's primary rappel instructor, arranging and overseeing rappel instruction for every new recruit. We rappelled often, whenever we could gain access to a helicopter or a rappel tower, and I never lost an agent. No one even incurred a serious rope burn.

During our training at Fahnestock, an air horn blew every day, summoning us out of bed before dawn to train in the cold. After calisthenics and a run, we moved through a series of other drills, including boxing, weapons retention, and a military-style confidence course. You have seen them in movies, where trainees run through pipes and climb up walls. We made our way through the course in virtual pitch darkness, leaping from one belly-buster telephone pole, mounted horizontally four feet or so off the ground and just as far apart, to the next. We couldn't see where the next one was, but we sure weren't going to show any fear. One of our teammates landed so hard on a pole that he broke his rib. Impressively, he was able to finish the course.

Team members had to re-qualify every year to stay on SWAT. The whole team watched, and close was not good enough. We had to do a minimum of three pull-ups, lifting our chins over the bar, while wearing all our SWAT gear; run a timed obstacle course, which included a simulated body drag; and shoot a score of ninety in full SWAT uniform, including the heavy ballistic vest and helmet, or we were off the team. Many of us lost sleep while thinking about the consequences of failure. Most agents have a healthy dose of competitive instinct. SWAT team members have even more. No one needed to apply pressure on us; we did a fine job on ourselves.

We always looked for opportunities to train with elite units of the armed forces, such as the U.S. Navy Sea, Air, and Land (SEAL) teams; Marine Force Reconnaissance teams; and U.S. Air Force Pararescue. When I had been on the team for a year, we had the chance to use a state-of-the-art training facility at Fort Bragg, North Carolina. Typically, somebody on a SWAT team knew someone in a military unit and worked out some joint training. Civilian-military training is highly encouraged since each side normally takes something positive away from it.

Military special ops people from Fort Bragg observed us during our drills. Of course, we wanted to impress them and prove that we were more than just a bunch of ragtag cops. We gathered at the entrance of the army's shooting house. Clint divided us into pairs, and my partner Russ and I were designated to be first. It was a "live fire" drill; that is, we used real bullets and real flash bangs. A flash bang is a hand grenade without the shrapnel and is designed to momentarily stun or disorient the senses of those nearby with a blinding flash, smoke, and concussive sound and to allow the assaulters to gain the upper hand. There is no room for error during live fire. Only well-trained and well-disciplined teams can even consider practicing this way.

Hard-bitten instructors watched us to observe our tactics. They were looking to see whether we sought cover and concealment and whether one of us was always in a position to fire on the threat while the other reloaded. Most important, though, they were looking to see if we could shoot.

On Clint's signal we entered the first door simulating a dynamic, or violent, breach. Another teammate had rolled a flash bang into the hallway before our entry. Within a split second of the detonation, I moved into the hallway and confronted a hostile target that was about thirty-five feet away, engaging it immediately. All of Tom Lagatol's quick kill training kicked in as I fired three rounds, two to the chest and one to the head. Like a precision machine, the rest of the team continued to move down the hallway and clear the adjoining rooms. No one stopped to admire the handiwork. We instinctively moved on with our partners to the next threat. All the while, team members barked out observations while flash bangs exploded and weapons fired. Then suddenly, from the very far end of the shooting house hallway, we heard, "All clear! All clear! All clear! Safeties on, weapons holstered!" followed by momentary silence.

When the drill ended, the special ops guys inspected our targets. I was an average shooter on the team, certainly not one of the best, but I had been trained by some of the best. I noticed Clint and two of the army instructors lingering over my target at the entrance. As he walked past me Clint muttered, without looking my way, "Good job, Ray." I could tell he was pleased. Without using my sights, I had managed to pull off an excellent three-round burst, placing one in the forehead and two directly in the heart from thirty-five feet.

We usually spent the bulk of our training time on what the military calls close quarter battle (CQB) drills. Simply put, it is a dynamic, fast-moving way to rout bad guys in dense urban settings. It is physically and mentally demanding, and whether employed by the military or police, it can only be done effectively by groups or teams that have worked so closely together that they can anticipate each other's every move. The assaulters must be adept at quick kill shooting.

One of the key tools in CQB is the flash bang. After forcing a door open, a team rolls this small bomb into the room. If it detonates in a hand or near a person, it can hurt, maim, or kill. Once the designated assaulter, or "banger," removes the pin, being careful to slip the pin's pull ring over one of his fingers, he must maintain a grip on the spoon of the flash bang; otherwise, it will discharge just like a military hand grenade. If the banger removes the pin and finds that circumstances have suddenly changed—for example, innocent people are unexpectedly in the danger zone—he will have to find a way, while being jostled by his teammates, to move forward with the group while holding the small bomb in one hand until he can safely reinsert the pin or safely discharge the flash bang. On at least two missions I witnessed teammates calmly control a prepped flash bang until the opportunity arose to reinsert the pin. It takes a very cool head.

SWAT team tactics are in constant evolution, and conditions will often dictate the type of entry or assault. The military has largely adopted the dynamic approach to clearing dangerous areas. On the civilian side, where collateral damage is a primary concern and surprise is rarely available, police and FBI SWAT teams still rely heavily on what is known as a deliberate police clear. It is a slow and methodical process, employing heavy ballistic shields, lights, and handheld mirrors to detect an adversary who might be lurking at the end of a winding hallway, in the corner of a basement or bedroom, or up in an attic. Movement is measured, and constant communication, whether by radio or hand signals, is critical. No corner is left unchecked, no matter how long it takes. When a large building is cleared this way, it takes multiple teams of assaulters to relieve each other as the weight of gear and the grind and stress of the slow process take their toll on even the fittest policeman or agent.

Clint and his senior team members constantly searched out new opportunities to learn skills and test our character. Military special ops teams use a technique known as spy rigging to airlift, or extract, personnel out of heavy brush or other difficult terrain where helicopters cannot land. A long, heavy rope extends from the helicopter's belly, and soldiers, using carabiners, clip themselves into D-rings sewn into their harnesses and the spy rope. Up to eight people can hang thousands of feet up in the air, bound to one long rope, and fly for miles until out of danger and in a safe landing zone (LZ). We practiced this training over the mountains of Hershey, Pennsylvania. I dangled with my harness biting into my groin, the wind buffeting me violently, and someone's feet flapping just above my head while mine did the same to the guy below me. It had no real application to our work but conveyed to the uncommitted that SWAT was not a game.

Since the first days when Bob Aldridge brought fast roping to New York SWAT, air operations had always been a strong suit of the New York team. Whenever we could access a helicopter, we would practice extractions and insertions using rappel ropes, fast ropes, and spy rigs. During a biannual regional SWAT training near Hershey, Air National Guard helicopters flew a squad of team members to a planned LZ miles out into the mountains while another squad, using orienteering and patrolling techniques, worked its way on foot to the same coordinates. After ensuring that the area was clear and secure, they then dropped smoke for the incoming helicopter. With the aid of specially trained SWAT team members who had served in the army or air force as forward ground controllers, they guided the helicopter to a safe landing using military hand signals.

In this era, domestic terrorists, particularly survivalist and Aryan Nations types, were on everyone's mind. Intelligence disclosed that after the Ruby Ridge incident in 1992, a number of cults had stockpiled weapons, often at locations deep in America's hinterlands, for what they deemed the inevitable showdown with the federal government. If there was another standoff or a

New York SWAT brings fast roping to field tactical teams.

Spy rigging—nothing but a gut check.

kidnapping deep in the mountains, SWAT might have had to respond on foot. We would have been on their turf, and the mountain men and the survivalists know their forests and valleys. We didn't, so we needed to prepare just as a military unit trains for patrols in hostile territory.

▪ ▪ ▪

Since we were part of an FBI division on the East Coast in a city surrounded by water, our ability to operate on or in water was crucial. During annual training, the U.S. Coast Guard dropped us off a long way from a beach, and while wearing safety vests capable of inflation in an emergency, we'd swim through the grinding surf to shore. Just like hanging from under the belly of a helicopter at three thousand feet, it was another way of testing us. We practiced body casting, or rolling off the side of fast-moving rigid-hull inflatable craft, into the Atlantic. Navy and Marine special teams use this technique to insert units onto hostile beaches. Again, it had little practical use for FBI SWAT team operators. For us, though, it was another gut check, a confirmation that every operator understood and accepted that the job implied an element of danger.

There was a more practical side to our water training. We learned how to operate boats; to board larger, moving vessels without falling into the ocean while encumbered by forty pounds of gear; and then to search the strange bulkhead compartments and engine room nooks that landlubbers have no idea about. We would pull alongside the starboard and port sides of an inter-coastal cruise ship as the vessel headed toward the Atlantic Ocean. Simulating a boat hijacking with hostages on board, we threw flash bangs as distractions, and with 150 tourists watching, we scrambled on board, fanned out to every corner of the ship, and conducted clearing operations. After the first successful demonstration, the boat owner regularly called the U.S. Coast Guard for the date of the next FBI exercise, since he had customers who lined up for tickets.

We also trained with Navy SEALs, warriors who were always looking for urban training settings where they could practice their skills and techniques. We watched them move up and down the inside of elevator shafts with special ascending devices that will grab even slick steel cables. We studied their CQB techniques, which gave the term "dynamic" new meaning. Just as the Marine Force Recon teams at Camp Lejeune, North Carolina, and army folks down at

Fort Bragg, these remarkable teams fight wars. They are not consumed with avoiding collateral damage at all cost, and the term "liability" is not a legal reference to them. The concept of being second-guessed by a grand jury or internal affairs investigators, processes that constantly look over the collective shoulders of police and FBI agents, are unknown to them and rightly so. Still, although their world was dramatically different than ours, we always took something away from their training that helped us be more effective.

▪   ▪   ▪

Although the HRT based at Quantico jealously controlled special explosive breaching techniques used for taking back hijacked aircraft, we routinely practiced dealing with hijack situations, particularly since two of the country's largest airports, Kennedy International and LaGuardia, were within miles of our office. Both the special ops people at Fort Bragg and the Federal Air Marshals at Pomona, New Jersey, allowed us to use their training facilities. Both locations offered mock wide-bodied commercial aircraft with realistically configured seats and ballistic capability, meaning we could fire live ammunition at simulated adversaries. Taking back a hijacked aircraft requires far more practice and fine-tuning of skills than any other challenge facing tactical teams. Every member must understand his or her specific assignment. A single individual's mistake can put everyone in jeopardy.

A perfect example of how badly things can go during an attempt to take back an aircraft occurred after the 1985 hijacking of EgyptAir Flight 648 as it was en route from Athens to Cairo. The terrorists, heavily armed with guns and grenades, hijacked the plane shortly after takeoff. When the terrorist leader was checking passports, an Egyptian Security Service agent aboard the aircraft opened fire. He killed one terrorist before being shot dozens of times. The exchange of gunfire punctured the fuselage, forcing the aircraft to descend. Although the terrorists wanted to get to Libya, the crippled aircraft had to land in Malta. The Maltese authorities permitted an Egyptian combat unit known as Thunderbolt to attempt to take back the aircraft. Early the next morning Egyptian commandos attacked the plane with explosives. The Maltese claimed the commandos' stun grenades caused fires and widespread suffocation. Other reports indicated the commandos inadvertently killed many passengers during their struggle to escape, and other witnesses claimed the hijackers tossed their own grenades into the passengers' midst. In any event, storming the aircraft killed fifty-six of the remaining eighty-eight passengers, two crewmembers, and one terrorist. Until the events of 9/11, it was the deadliest hijacking in history.

In the live-fire aircraft fuselage at Fort Bragg, army special ops personnel demonstrated their dynamic assault technique. When the aircraft door was breached, one operator stepped inside and instantly shot any target he determined, in the wink of an eye, to represent a bad guy. In the meantime, two-man teams flowed in behind him and ran down the aisles, engaging bad guys without stopping until they reached the aircraft's tail and nose ends. It took only seconds for the operators to differentiate the bad guys from the good guys and to eliminate them with surgically precise shooting. The technique required perfect choreography. If the aisle runners veered inches left or right, they would have stepped right into the cover man's field of fire.

Clint gathered us in a huddle. "OK. You all saw how they do it. Does anybody think he can't?" Nobody was about to admit it. Clint designated the breachers, the cover men, and the aisle runners. "Let's dry run this once, then it's live. You are being watched and graded here, men, so let's get an A."

Tom Bara, always looking to break the tension, piped up, "So, Clint, a B is only one dead SWAT guy, and I guess a B-minus would be one dead and one wounded, right?"

The run-through went smoothly. Now it was time for the real thing. Despite experiencing many live-fire drills, it crossed my mind how close to my head those bullets would soon be passing.

I was designated an aisle runner. On the signal, the door was breached, and our cover man hooked inside. He started to fire on the bad-guy targets that were randomly placed throughout the dozens of seats. Entering mid fuselage, my partner and I, hip to hip, spun right, while another pair moved left toward the tail. I engaged all seats to the right and my partner took on the middle. I could hear the crack of the cover man's MP5 as we flowed up the aisle, hesitating only slightly to double "tap" an occasional bad target tucked low in a seat, and finally gaining and clearing the forward galley and head. "Clear! Clear!" came the shout from each of the aisle-running teams. In unison, we holstered and moved out of the fuselage to the deck. We had nailed every unfriendly target without hitting any friendly ones. Most took two or three rounds in the head or neck. The army people said little, but we could tell from the way they treated us that evening, over beers in their special bar, that we had earned their respect.

Among all of these special groups, military or civilian, none was more important to our team than the 106th Air Force Rescue Wing based on Long Island. Pararescue is the U.S. Air Force's version of the Navy SEALs. While an elite combat unit, it has a primary search-and-rescue role. Based on both coasts, the units save downed pilots, respond to ships lost at sea, and have primary rescue accountability for every shuttle launch out of Cape Canaveral, Florida. These same personnel helped recover the remains of the space shuttle *Challenger* after it exploded shortly after launch in 1986. For many years, they served as backup medics to our team when we executed arrests, and they regularly provided us with air transport for missions, any type of air operations training we asked for, and first-class camaraderie. They taught us about survival under harsh conditions. Together, we hiked portions of the Appalachian Trail and climbed New Hampshire's Mount Washington in sub-freezing temperatures and a winter storm whiteout. They were as much a part of our team in those days as any of our FBI personnel.

▪   ▪   ▪

All of these training missions were physically and mentally challenging, but for me, none compared to the fear-laced challenge of firearms instructor school. Assigned to the range at Fort Dix, New Jersey, Glenn was the number two firearms instructor for the New York office. The New York division maintained three firearms ranges in the mid-1990s: Fort Dix, Camp Smith in Peekskill, and a range on Long Island. These ranges had to accommodate more than a thousand agents, all of whom had to qualify with their weapons every three months. It was a mammoth undertaking with serious risk concerns. Glenn had the ideal shooter personality; he was similar to Obi-Wan Kenobi of *Star Wars*, becoming one with his gun and blocking out the world when he stood in front of a target.

My SWAT team leader wanted as many of us as possible to become qualified as firearms instructors. For one, it allowed us to fit in mandatory FBI weapons qualification courses during our regular monthly SWAT training. Further, it would mean not having to show up for an additional day of training with the general agent population and not having to contend with supervisors who already resented the time we were devoting to SWAT training.

I hesitated to try out for the upcoming regional firearms instructor school. Although a better-than-average shooter, I was never great. When I finally decided to make a run at it, Glenn offered me his cherished target pistol. I didn't want to embarrass my team or Glenn. The FBI community, just like everyone else, loves to gossip. Not only do many firearms instructors have big egos, but there is an undercurrent of jealousy in every office when it comes to the SWAT team. I knew if I failed, it would be almost impossible for me to show my face in the New York office again. The pressure began to build.

Glenn showed me how to shoot his beautiful stainless .38 with special grip and sights. He recommended that I try to qualify single-handed since the qualifying score for single-handed shooting was 250 points instead of 270 out of 300 points. That idea made sense to me so I practiced in the old style, like one of Hoover's early G-Men, blading my body and turning my head to look straight down my extended arm at what should have been a perfect sight picture. I should have realized after the first two or three practice shoots that this single-handed style did not work that well for me. From my first week at Quantico, I knew the two-handed technique, which is supportive and allows for a more steady hold on the target. Somehow, even though my practice runs were just shy of the minimum score, I felt I could pull it out when the adrenaline kicked in on game day. Big mistake.

It was a grueling course. We started out from the twenty-five-yard line, where remotely controlled mechanical targets turned to face us for only several seconds. That was the signal to draw and fire. A team of Quantico instructors ran the regional qualification course at Fort Dix and had brought in close to sixty agents from all over the mid-Atlantic and the Northeast, all vying to become firearms instructors.

I went down to Dix the night before the three-day course was to begin with my friend Paul Sutherland, who was also on the SWAT team. The first day was for warming up and getting comfortable. That night I had trouble sleeping, worried about my shooting and listening to a storm beginning to brew outside. Shooting is a big deal for any law enforcement officer, a major tool of the trade. Everyone on the team, the squad, and the force knows who can and cannot shoot. Understandably, no one wants to go on a high-risk arrest or a dangerous mission with a partner who can't handle a gun.

On the morning of the qualification, the weather was gale-like, with winds blowing horizontally at about forty-five miles per hour and pouring rain. I knocked on Paul's door, and he answered with his toothbrush still in his mouth. "Paul, this one-handed thing is not going to work. Can you show me how to hold this pistol with two hands?" Paul nodded and tried to say OK through the toothpaste. He walked into my room and gave me five minutes of instruction about where to place each finger on both hands.

Then he looked at me and asked, "You're switching on the day of the test?"

The instructors ran the qualification three times. Once an agent made it, the agent could step out of line, get dry and warm up, and watch the poor souls who remained, trying to avoid humiliation. The wind was gusting and tearing targets off the racks when we stepped from the range classroom to take up our assigned lanes. More than a dozen times the instructors had to stop the course to repair targets. Although I was breathing properly, squeezing the trigger correctly, and, I thought, acquiring a good sight picture, my performance was not good enough. I shot a 222 on the first round. Embarrassing as it was, I was not going to quit. I noticed other agents high-fiving each other as they walked off to have lunch. The pressure mounted.

We went for the second round. This time I improved but barely. I shot 242. Seventy percent had passed, and my friends were telling me to hang in there. Turning my fear of humiliation around, I became angry with myself and my attitude. I said out loud, "Hey, screw this." Looking up at the ominous sky, I said, "OK, big guy, pick up the wind and the rain. Throw it all at me because if I'm going down, I'm going down fighting against everything you can throw at me." What happened next caused me to think that maybe he took a moment from his busy schedule to listen.

I'd heard that nobody makes it through on the third try, that a third try was just staving off the inevitable. Most shooters by the third try are so demoralized that they don't have the confidence left to pull it out. I took my position on the line and tried to relax, then I heard a low voice behind me, "Hey, so what are you doing, guy?" It was my Obi-Wan Kenobi, Glenn. Even though he didn't need to be out there, he offered to step in for a Quantico instructor who'd had enough of the rain. "Listen, Ray, like I've told you before, the only thing you want to see is that front sight line up with the rear sight. That target should be nothing but a white blur. Now, just focus on that sight post, and do it."

The public-address system from the range house blasted, "Shooters, take your positions! On the signal, draw and fire two rounds in three seconds!"

On the honk of the air horn, the targets snapped around. I drew my pistol, acquired the best sight picture I could, and fired. After drawing and firing two rounds six times, we moved to the fifteen-yard line. I would not look at my target, partly out of fear and partly because I didn't want to lose my ability to concentrate.

I tried to relax my shoulders. Glenn was still behind me. He whispered, "Man, you are so dead on."

With that reassurance, everything came back. When the air horn blared, I shot, this time with more confidence. Again and again, the targets turned and I shot, never looking down range. When we finished our last of thirty rounds from the fifteen-yard line, the instructor spoke, "Shooters, retrieve your targets and report your scores. This portion of the course is concluded. Those of you who have not obtained the minimum score are free to leave. Thanks for your time."

I walked around the berm to retrieve my target, refusing to look until I was within arms reach. "Holy shit!" I said to myself, aloud. The entire center of the bull's-eye was missing, completely blown away. I wanted to jump in the air and scream. A short time later, the head instructor announced that I had shot 287 out of 300. It was, he said, probably the highest score of the day and, admittedly, pretty damn good under the weather conditions. I wanted to find Glenn and give him a big kiss, but SWAT guys don't do that.

Seven

Early SWAT Missions—
and a New Kind of Enemy

For most of us, SWAT was a frequent and welcome break from the routine of our primary jobs as investigators. This is not to say that developing a criminal case and tracking down offenders weren't interesting. However, that done, we were sentenced to the blandness of trial preparation, conducting interview after interview, followed by preparing subpoenas for more information. Then, we would sit in a room and analyze it all for what often felt like eternity.

Our regular jobs usually required a large amount of desk work and meetings with prosecutors. So we didn't mind that the training meant working fifty- or sixty-hour weeks. We handled the two jobs, moving almost effortlessly from our SWAT utilities to our pressed trial suits and white shirts.

It wasn't that we thought SWAT was a game. We understood the danger. Not a week went by that some cop wasn't shot during an arrest. Still, we needed the rush of going after dangerous people and executing arrest plans.

In the early summer of 1989, we got information about a Puerto Rican separatist planning to set off a bomb at a New York City monument on the Fourth of July. The source of the information was working for another government organization and pinpointed the subject's apartment in lower Manhattan.

That same organization had specialized technical expertise, so it sent a team to the identified residence armed with a sniffing device that could detect explosive chemicals in the air. Under the guise of utility men, they took a

Author on the right during SWAT training, where the bullets aren't paint or rubber.

sample from under the door. It showed positive for explosives, and we got the green light to raid the apartment on the East Side, which was in a neighborhood we used to call Alphabet City. This mission was my first as a SWAT team member. After attending a briefing earlier that morning, Clint met us at a staging area a few blocks from the raid site. He said, "Ray, you'll be the breacher."

The breacher generally stands near the front of the assault team. Once he has successfully forced open the door, he steps aside momentarily, allowing the first two or three operators to quickly enter the location. Depending on the entry team's size, the breacher may be the third or fourth man into the room. It seems counterintuitive, but the first person busting through is usually less likely to be shot than those following him. Most folks need a few seconds to organize their thoughts when their front door suddenly explodes. By the time the average criminal is clearheaded enough to pull a gun and start shooting, the first one or two agents are already in the room, and the third guy is most likely to catch a bullet. That being said, the first person in is not necessarily home free; booby traps and fierce dogs respond instantaneously.

Actually, anytime you are outside a door with a bad guy inside, you are at risk. Law enforcement officers have been injured or killed because they stood too long in what tacticians call the funnel of death. It doesn't take a marksman to hit someone coming through an entryway. You just pump bullets into the middle of the opening when you hear someone approaching. One SWAT guy was hit between the eyes, above his bulletproof vest and below his helmet, because he hesitated in that funnel. He had lowered his ballistic shield, trying to see into a dark bedroom, and made a perfect target as he stood at the door, backlit by the hallway light.

We were after a former army demolitions expert, trained in booby traps. Clint warned, "Don't turn on any light switches when you enter. One of the booby trap techniques they commonly use is drilling a tiny hole in a light bulb and filling it with gasoline. Watch out for trip wires, usually a few inches above the floor. Good luck."

Good luck? That was it? If the bureau had conducted that same raid today, with that same intelligence in hand, there would be an army of bureaucrats, attorneys, explosives experts, and medical personnel in a huddle weighing the possible ramifications of our mission. What if we set off booby traps and a tenement building collapsed or caught on fire? In the end, the lawyers would probably prevail, and they'd scrub the mission.

It was a hot Saturday, and at 7 a.m., we were already cooking inside our ballistic vests, tactical rigs, helmets, and dark blue utilities. The temperature would top out at over a hundred degrees that day. As we pulled up to the site, Tom Bara tapped me on the helmet and in his signature deadpan way said, "Remember one thing, kid." I locked onto his next words, anticipating some advice that might save my life. He paused for effect, then said simply, "Souvenirs."

Barreling out of the truck in typical SWAT fashion, we entered the building and moved through the hallway as quietly as possible. I carried a heavy battering ram and waited for the signal to swing the ram back, then forward, nailing the apartment doorknob dead-on. I chucked it clear of our path so nobody tripped over it. Guns drawn, two of the men stepped through the doorway with me on their tail. The room was dark, and as we struggled to acquire our night vision, an intolerable stench hammered us. It felt like 105 degrees inside, but we kept moving, peeling off, one to the right and one to the left, just as in a well-drilled football play. It reminded me of the Green Bay Packers' power sweep during the Vince Lombardi era.

The stink was unbearable, and we were slipping and sliding on something. Somebody yelled, "We've got a body in here!" We drew back a curtain, exposing a pile of filthy blankets mixed with what appeared to be a human being. Although he grunted and his body twitched, he was in a drug stupor and did not respond to our orders. The toilet must have been overflowing for days, and we stood in an inch of excrement and urine. The sniffing device had detected ammonia, a natural byproduct of human waste. It was a pointed reminder that we couldn't solely rely on informants or on science. Finding criminals, including terrorists, is a very imperfect business.

By the time we left the building, the NYPD had sealed off the neighborhood, and marked cars were parked up and down the block. In hushed tones, the residents were confiding in the cops, "You got the wrong place. You really want apartment 26A." And, "There's something bad going on in 12C." This Manhattan neighborhood was awash in heroin, and good people would try anything they could to clean it up.

On these early operations, I realized that I had the right mental makeup for SWAT missions. I liked the quick tempo—the faster the better—and I was good at taking it all in. Some people under stress develop tunnel vision, but I could see more. When the pressure built and the danger level became intense, my mind would slip into an almost Zen-like state of peace and clarity.

On another early SWAT mission, we trailed the murderer of undercover DEA agent Everett Hatcher. Hatcher had been on his way to meet a dangerous drug dealer when he lost his backup in heavy Brooklyn traffic. He went ahead anyway and met up with steroid-abusing Costabile "Gus" Farace, who shot Hatcher execution style and stole his narcotics in a drug rip-off. We launched an intensive search for the killer, hitting locations every night, but were always just a step or two behind him. We had information that Farace's friend, another heavy steroid user, was letting him hide out in his Staten Island townhome. Sources told us the friend carried a gun and had a pit bull as a pet.

We timed the raid for sunup and staged and finalized our plan nearby. It would be a modified "deliberate police clear" operation, meaning that owing to the small size of the townhouse and the subject's inclination toward violence, we would move quickly but with our ballistic shields. We would hit the patio's sliding door and the front door simultaneously to prevent an escape. Basic tactics call for positioning men at every exit and containing a target. We didn't want a foot chase or a gunfight that could jeopardize bystanders. The principal breacher was Kirby Scott, already a team veteran when I joined and a terrific athlete. This former pro football running back, as with others on our team, always got the job done without fanfare. We approached the house silently with streaks of sunrise just appearing in the east and received the entry signal over our radios. Kirby struck the sliding door with a sledgehammer as if he were hitting a grand slam home run. The hammer slipped through the glass so effortlessly that he lost control, and the hammer careened across the room. The fugitive's friend had just stumbled into the kitchen, narrowly avoiding the flying sledgehammer. He turned and tried to run back into the bedroom. Then an avalanche of helmeted SWAT operators smashed through the front door and buried him before he could grab a gun from his dresser.

We immediately scanned the room, looking for the dog. Someone yelled, "Look at this!" The pit bull had been asleep near the glass door when Kirby slammed it, and a trail of excrement led from the door to under the bed. We had a hard time dragging out that shuddering animal. We turned the dog over to Animal Services and then handed Farace's friend to the case squad for processing. He had been aiding and abetting a killer, and he was going to find out that the weight room in a federal prison is a little different from his local gym.

Unfortunately, Farace wasn't there. However, after a couple raids, the message got out to the mob that the FBI was not going to stop till it found him. Farace was seeing the daughter of a Mafia capo and had violated an unwritten but critical code of organized crime by bringing on the heat from the feds and police. Just as some veterans in the office predicted, the mob got to Gus before we did. His uncle, Greg Scarpa, a Colombo family member, executed him on a Manhattan sidewalk nine months after he had killed Agent Hatcher. There was some poetic justice. It spared taxpayers an expensive, drawn-out trial, and Farace died just as he had killed the DEA agent. I hope that for at least a moment before his uncle shot him, Costabile "Gus" Farace realized what was about to happen.

■   ■   ■

Occasionally, because of their special training in entry techniques, individual SWAT team members would be detailed to help other criminal squads with arrests. On one detail, I was assigned to help an organized crime squad arrest a mob hit man at his Bronx home. The case agent knocked heavily on the front door, announcing that the FBI had an arrest warrant. I was standing close by, aware that I should not stand immediately in front of the door, when the mobster's wife opened the door slightly. She glared at the case agent for a moment and then tried to slam the door in his face. I jammed my sturdy SWAT-issued boot between the door and its frame, only to have it pinned within seconds by an entire extended family. It turned out that Gino had more than a few grown kids living with him. There was screaming, cursing, hysteria. My foot stood between the FBI and our subject and at least six people who were leaning against that door.

I noticed that most of my team began to scatter for cover, probably expecting a couple of rounds to come through the door any minute. That thought was definitely occurring to me when Joe, another SWAT team member who had also played football in his former life, stepped up and gave me a nod. In unison we both slammed into the door, and our combined force toppled the crowd on the other side. In an instant I found myself lying in a mass of screaming Bronx Italians.

The sight was *Three Stooges* hysterical, until I looked squarely in the face of a snarling pit bull. It is very strange, the thoughts that come at such moments. I recall thinking that a 9mm round from my SIG Sauer might not penetrate the animal's thick skull. Fortunately, the dog's handler must have read my thoughts and didn't want to test my theory. Or maybe it was the crowd of agents clambering over my back, using it as a drawbridge that changed his mind. He pulled hard on the leash and restrained the angry animal. Soon things were under control, but it might have turned out differently if we hadn't managed to get inside before the family really got it together.

FBI divisional SWAT teams were more than just a local resource. Headquarters regularly called on field divisions for agents and SWAT personnel in times of major crisis.

In the early 1990s a number of teams, including New York's, were sent to Fort Lauderdale, Florida, to provide security for the Racketeer Influenced and Corrupt Organizations (RICO) Act prosecution of the leaders of a Miami cult. A notorious sect of Black Hebrew Israelites terrorized people in the 1980s. At its height, it controlled an $8 million empire of properties. Its doomsday leader was Oklahoma native Hulon Mitchell Jr., aka Yahweh Ben Yahweh, which is Hebrew for "God, Son of God." Mitchell controlled his congregation with threats and murder. He would have defectors from his church killed so that others would stay in line, and he ordered the random murders of whites as part of an initiation to a secret temple "brotherhood." Those ordered to kill had to prove they had done the deed by bringing him victims' heads or ears.

After the presiding trial judge's secretary was shot and killed in her driveway, it was evident that the local FBI office had insufficient manpower for an extended trial. SWAT teams from across the country arrived to provide courtroom and witness security and to send a message that the government was in control. Witnesses would not be intimidated or harmed.

When the case agents needed to run down investigative leads, they called on us. On one particular occasion we were sent to find a potential witness in a part of Miami that the case agent described as dangerous. When we pulled up in front of our first location, we glanced at each other and started to laugh. Mowed lawns, palm trees, and whitewashed, one-story Florida-style houses were nicer than some of the tough parts of the New York boroughs where we spent most of our working time. It was all just relative.

Taking first in the "weird assignment" category, one SWAT group from Chicago had to spend a night deep in the Florida Everglades. The body of one cult murder victim had been found there, and the prosecutor wanted someone to testify about the night air temperatures. Since maggot size relates directly to air temperatures and humidity, the prosecutor would use the data these fellas collected to argue that the victim had been dead for a specific period, refuting a defendant's alibi. So well-trained, tough SWAT guys stayed up all night reading thermometers in the Everglades.

▪ ▪ ▪

In September 1995 Hurricane Marilyn roared into the Virgin Islands, punishing St. Thomas. During the storm, violent criminals escaped from the island's prison. Afterward, some of the locals, taking advantage of the lack of authority, went on a looting rampage. As days passed the looting spread, and even some of the local police and National Guardsmen joined in the scramble for booty. After a U.S. Coast Guard patrol reported a complete breakdown of authority, six cutters headed for the island to evacuate panicked vacationers. With the arrival of twelve hundred U.S. military police, federal marshals, and FBI agents, including elements of the New York team, order was restored.

One SWAT raid took us to Brooklyn, where a Jamaican posse—a highly structured and usually dangerous version of a street gang—had taken over an entire square block. We had to clear a multistory apartment complex that housed a drug operation and other criminal enterprises. We moved in late at night with every man we had, cordoned off the surrounding area, and put agents at every conceivable exit. We focused on what we believed was the main entrance and primary drug distribution point. One of my teammates, Russ, was trying to slice through a door reinforced with diamond plate, which are thick sheets of steel. Russ was using a new metal-cutting power saw that had been issued to the team only a few weeks earlier.

Sparks splattering everywhere, Russ was so focused on using the metal saw that he didn't notice his pant leg had ignited. We had a problem. How could we let him know he was on fire without startling him? We were a little worried about getting ourselves sliced in half if, while we tried to get his attention, he started suddenly and turned around. We didn't have to worry long because he figured it out when the flames reached his groin area. Someone grabbed the sputtering saw from his hand as others helped him smother the flames.

The main door came down, and a team of SWAT operators flowed into the vestibule, breaking off in different directions to execute their piece of the overall mission. We located the apartment of one of the principal posse members and tried to enter using a high-tech breaching tool. We wedged one end against the door and the other against the wall. A canister released pressurized air, driving the lever forward. The door gave a little at first; then the ram snapped in two, the pieces ricocheting off shins and walls.

Frustrated after pounding and beating on his door with every tool in our arsenal, we were nearly ready to punch a hole through the cinder block wall with sledgehammers when a male on the other side, with a heavy island accent, pleaded, "Enough, enough, enough! I'll let you in, mahn!" The door to his apartment, similar to those in many a bad city neighborhood, was protected with a steel plate and fox lock, a device in the center of the door that, when engaged, projects bolts into the door frame in three directions—the top and both sides. Two thick boards wedged into holes chiseled in the concrete floor further protected the steel-clad door, forming a fortress-like defense that only explosives could penetrate.

We couldn't have gotten inside until he opened the door, highlighting the value of reconnaissance. We wouldn't have been futilely flailing like Keystone Kops if we had had good inside information. An informant who has infiltrated the criminal enterprise is often how we got a warrant in the first instance. Best case, a source could describe who was usually at home, where everyone slept, where weapons were stored, and the kind of lock on the door that we'd encounter. If we couldn't develop a source inside the organization, we always tried to make a "friend" with the building maintenance crew, utility servicemen, or anyone who knew the interior layout; otherwise, we were walking in blind just as we had done that night in the Bronx. Preparation was everything.

It was always our team's policy to check out a location ourselves before hitting it. Many agents and cops are involved in bringing a case to the point where people are about to be arrested. The more people involved, the more likely there will be miscommunication. Before all arrests, representatives from every FBI element would attend a briefing to coordinate everyone and minimize confusion. However, with so many different players in the mix, somebody along the way invariably missed something. That's why whenever the team was tasked with the entry, we always made sure to verify the target address with our own eyes. The thing about criminal investigative work and arresting people is that the case agent is always up to his eyeballs in high-pressure work and a thousand last-minute details. Whether you are the case agent or the SWAT team leader, you have to remind yourself that every detail counts, no matter how jammed up you are.

Later in my SWAT career, after I became the team leader, I sent a young team member to a pre-arrest briefing. He returned with the details, including the target location we were going to hit. I asked him, "Jin, did you drive out and check the spot? What did the front door look like?" He responded that the case agent had given him a copy of the tax records for our location that included a photo. I took a look at the copy and noticed that the address didn't match what we had been originally told. The target location was now listed as a street instead of an avenue. "Jin, get in the car with me. We're taking a ride." It was late in the day and the office was almost empty, but verifying this information was important, really important. We fought heavy traffic out to the address in Brooklyn while most everybody else in the office was fighting traffic to get home. When we found it, we discovered the location Jin had been given was fifteen blocks away from the right address and the entrance was unlike what we would have to contend with at the correct location the next morning. If we had hit the wrong location at five in the morning, we would have seriously ruined some family's sleep and never have made it to the right location on time. Jin got it. I didn't have to say another word.

Every SWAT mission was a learning experience for those who were open to learning. We had our hands full one night while arresting a member of a violent gang at his family's house near the Throgs Neck Bridge. He was one of a group of young mob wannabes who'd held up armored cars and banks. He had recently figured out that the bureau had developed a female informant in his group, and he had tried to kill her with a knife.

The case squad called in SWAT to handle the arrest. We approached the subject's building in a typically crowded New York neighborhood where, after dark, it was hard to tell one row house from the next. We didn't have what is known as a "no-knock" warrant, so we were required by law to announce ourselves and to allow a reasonable amount of time for the occupants to comply (aka load their guns). The legal rationale is that average frightened citizens, particularly after dark, not knowing who is breaking down their door, might respond violently out of fear and in self-defense. Normally that response would make sense. However, if we needed an arrest warrant for someone with a violent history or someone known to possess weapons, judges would, on occasion, issue a no-knock warrant to give the police a split-second advantage. Some judges, that is.

In this case, we pounded on the door, and a middle-aged man peered out its small glass window. We announced, "FBI! Open up!" When he didn't, Kirby gave the order, and our designated breacher jammed the Halligan tool, a firefighters' crowbar, between the frame and door. With the tug of two SWAT operators, the door locks exploded, and we faced an onrushing lunatic, a big woman in her late forties wearing a housedress and all but foaming at the mouth. She screamed expletives I'd never heard before. Paul Sutherland tried his normal firm but polite demeanor on the banshee. When she got right in his face, swinging violently at his head, he gently put her down on the floor. She got right back up, swinging and cursing. We couldn't let her slow us down. We had to get to the subject before he had time to collect himself, so this time Paul wasn't gentle. With his huge forearm, he caught her across the face, and her feet left the floor. I admit that I enjoyed the sounds of her body slamming to the ground and the air exploding from her lungs.

Then the basement door flew open. A teenage male emerged with a pit bull straining at his leash, primed to rip out somebody's throat. One of our men pointed his gun at the animal, "If you let that dog off the leash, I will shoot it." His voice was calm and controlled, and the kid restrained the dog.

Then the dad came at us, but he wasn't half the man his wife had been. After we handcuffed him, our immense target showed up at the top of the stairs, clothed solely in boxer shorts. He defiantly loomed over us, a big, fat, slobbering nightmare.

"Come and get me you, motherfuckers!" he bellowed, spraying spit everywhere.

Tom Lagatol led the way up the stairs, and I was right behind him.

The kid wasn't done waxing poetic. "I'm gonna rip your fuckin' heads off, and then I'm gonna shit down your cop throats!"

I was a little concerned about how this arrest was going to play out. My mind's eye pictured him leaping off the landing and crashing on top of us, followed by a mass of humanity tumbling down the stairs, and a melee of flesh wrestling for guns.

Tom fixed his hard, black eyes on the subject. Then he pointed his M16 carbine at him and quietly but clearly told him, "There's no one but my friends on this stairway. You can't win a fight with so many of us here. When I advance toward you and you grab my weapon, it will probably go off. You'll probably get gut shot, and that's real painful." I could see that Tom was maneuvering for some space on the top of the small stair landing.

The subject hesitated for just a moment, backing away from the muzzle of Tom's gun, and then his mouth started back up. He was in the middle of another "motherfucker" diatribe when the palm of Tom's hand exploded into the subject's face just below the nose, sending the giant reeling back against the wall. Again, with lightning speed, Tom swung his carbine to his back and landed a short but powerful kick to the inside of the subject's knee. He buckled enough for Tom to put him in a choke hold. If the carotid artery is squeezed off for five to seven seconds, most people will black out. For a brief moment, Tom resembled a cowboy roping an angry steer. They careened off the wall once, maybe twice, and then down they went, a combined total of almost five hundred pounds. The building shook. Our tough guy flopped like a beached whale while Tom handcuffed him. He had to borrow my cuffs and link them to his in order to reach from one of the subject's wrists to the other.

I learned more that night about defusing a dangerous situation than I had during my entire sixteen weeks at the academy. Screaming epithets back at an enraged subject only escalates a bad situation. Good cops and good agents control the situation with their presence and tone of voice; then at a precise moment, after quickly sizing up the alternatives, they move swiftly. Screaming only tells the bad guy that you're just as scared as he is. You want him to think you are more than human.

You can't get that type of education behind a desk staring at a computer. You have to be on the street.

■ ■ ■

In 1991, when Sammy Gravano turned on former Mafia don John Gotti, he went into an abbreviated FBI version of the U.S. Marshals Service Federal Witness Security (WITSEC) program. The FBI's Hostage Rescue Team handled his security initially. The problem was that Gravano didn't like his HRT babysitters. Most were military-like in demeanor and took their prison guard work seriously. To them, Gravano was nothing but a criminal from some strange place called Brooklyn, and their approach to the job was simple hard ass. While they were bent on keeping him alive, they weren't concerned about his morale, even though he was critical to taking apart the biggest crime syndicate in New York. Like a spoiled kid, Gravano, a native New Yorker, proclaimed he would stop cooperating until the bureau surrounded him with people who understood him, meaning people from New York. Focused completely on putting Gotti away, the case agents and the AUSA from the Eastern District of New York demanded that New York SWAT team members, people they knew and could deal with, come down to Quantico and take over. We did and virtually lived with Gravano for months, hiding him in different locations and never letting him out of our sight.

Gravano was nicknamed the Bull for his thick neck and aggressiveness. He also had a penchant for boxing. Only Sammy Gravano would have the grit to go toe to toe in a courtroom, or anywhere else for that matter, with John Gotti, who had taken his "family" to the top of the ladder of New York organized crime. Gravano already admitted to having murdered eighteen people on Gotti's orders. He offered that information up to the U.S. attorney after learning that Gotti, through his mob mouthpiece Bruce Cutler, had started negotiating a deal to distance himself from those homicides and claiming he had never ordered any of the killings. Gravano was angry and wanted to get Gotti before his former don got him.

When the trial date was close, we moved Gravano into a wing of the vacant married officers' quarters at Fort Monmouth in New Jersey. We always had at least four people with him, so he knew he wasn't going anywhere, and we didn't cut him any slack. We never forgot what he had done or what he represented, but since we were stuck with him and wanted to see Gotti put away for life, we made the best of the situation.

Gravano would get antsy, stuck with his jailors in a small townhouse, 24-7. I decided that we all needed to burn off some steam, so I offered to box with him. He used to brag about his sparring bouts with professional contenders at Gleason's, the legendary Brooklyn gym in which he reportedly had an interest. I figured I could hold my own with him since I had received decent instruction from both my father, a middleweight naval fleet champ, and Tom Lagatol, who'd fought in the Golden Gloves in New York. We cleared out the furniture in the living room, and it became our ring. After a jog, push-ups, and sit-ups, we'd box five-minute rounds with a minute break in between them. There was only one rule: no deliberate headshots. Inevitably, we'd catch each other with a glancing blow or inadvertently land a hard one to the head when one of us ducked or weaved at the wrong time. It was thirty-five minutes of practically nonstop pounding. He was in good shape—definitely one of the few senior mafiosos I had met who was fit—and his shots to my body were powerful, sending shock waves from my head down to my toes. But I wouldn't let him know that he rocked me. A few times, I saw the psychotic flash of a killer's eyes when I hit him in the jaw, and I was reminded that he was an admitted murderer.

We took him out for occasional jogs or for rounds of racquetball at the base gym. I'd pick his brain about the mob when we would cook dinner together. I once asked him why he killed so many people for Gotti, and he told me that he grew up in a world where the mob was his family and his country. He told me that as a kid he had learned that no one else took care of or rewarded him except the mob, so he would do anything to protect that family.

Another time I asked him whether it was easy to spot FBI surveillance.

"Sure, you guys think you're blendin' in, but you walk around in runnin' shoes and wear those cheap plastic exercise watches. Plus none of you are fat! Who the hell do you think we think you are?"

On the trial's first day, Gotti's people took over the front two rows of the courtroom, glaring at the jurors in a blatant intimidation attempt. The following day, my entire SWAT team showed up in the courtroom. Supplemented by other agents from the office, we controlled the first rows for the balance of the trial. I sat directly behind Gotti the first day that Gravano testified against him. It was a day that I won't forget. From the moment Gravano took the stand until he was excused an hour and a half later, he and Gotti locked eyes in a visual death grip. I did not see Gravano blink once while he answered questions about his relationship with Gotti and the murders he had committed. The Bull testified over a period of weeks, and in the end he took Gotti down. Gotti went to prison, where he died of cancer. The family never recovered. The don's son tried to run things, but he was incompetent and soon found himself following his father to prison.

Gravano couldn't change. He flunked out of the WITSEC program when he tried to start his own drug syndicate in the Southwest and went to prison where he was, again, caught dealing in drugs.

▪   ▪   ▪

In 1993 an explosion rocked the foundation of Tower One of New York's World Trade Center (WTC), marking the first time that America was successfully attacked by people who found their inspiration in the preaching of Islamic extremists. Although their spiritual leader, Omar Abdel-Rahman, aka the Blind Sheikh, had taken refuge in the United States, he hated the very place that offered him peace, security, and a pulpit. Abdel-Rahman and his plotters, operating out of a mosque in Brooklyn, had hoped to bring down the towers and kill tens of thousands of people in the process.

The first WTC bombing should have been a wake-up call. Right in our very midst, a group of Middle Eastern men who gathered across the river in Brooklyn had plotted and seriously damaged a major American landmark. An operational mastermind of that attack, a Pakistani named Ramzi Yousef, subsequently went to the Philippines and with the help of his uncle, Khalid Sheikh Mohammed (KSM), went to work developing the so-called Bojinka Plot. Yousef and KSM intended to bomb twelve U.S. commercial jumbo jets over the Pacific in the course of two days. When a bomb detonator accidentally exploded in Yousef's apartment, the Philippine police responded and, realizing what they had stumbled upon, turned the evidence over to American authorities. By this time, a small cadre of New York FBI agents was beginning to see the bigger picture. This strange, relatively unknown international group really hated America and, for starters, wanted to drive everything Western from the Arabian Peninsula.

Abdel-Rahman's Egypt-based group, al-Gama'a al-Islamiyya, had links to another little-known extremist group that some referred to as al Qaeda, or "the Base." Its members seemed to be following a Saudi-Yemeni known as Osama bin Laden. Meanwhile, it took some time, but the FBI put a strong case together against Yousef, who was tracked down in Pakistan in 1995. Yousef was prosecuted in the Southern District of New York and sentenced to life without parole.

While the WTC bombers were formulating their plan, a member of their group, an Egyptian informant named Emad Salem, was providing his FBI handler with worrisome information. Salem had worked his way into the inner circle surrounding the Blind Sheikh. In a pattern to be repeated eight years later, FBI management just didn't get it. More concerned over possible impropriety between the handler and her informant and the informant's unwillingness to testify in open court than with the nature of the threat, New York management all but shut Salem down just before the attack.

The bureau's failure to heed his warnings is well documented, and I won't revisit that debate. However, after the first attack, an embarrassed FBI resurrected the Egyptian informant with the help of a lot of cash. Very soon, Salem put investigators on the trail of another, more serious impending threat from the same location. Once again he identified the plotters who intended to strike a number of Manhattan landmarks.

The FBI installed closed-circuit television monitoring inside the Queens warehouse where the plotters collected and began to prepare massive bombs that were meant to destroy the Lincoln and Holland tunnels, the federal building that I worked in, the United Nations Building, and the George Washington Bridge. The investigative squad monitored the conspirators' every movement, right up until they began mixing their deadly stew in fifty-five-gallon drums. We moved in on the "Day of Terror" cell late at night on June 24, 1993. Sitting in the back of our SWAT truck that strangely cold evening, we waited for the signal to enter the desolate warehouse and arrest the terrorists. At 1:30 a.m., members of our team raised the rolling, steel warehouse door. As they did, one team member's helmet smacked against it, and the sound reverberated throughout the warehouse.

"Who is there?" one of the terrorists called out calmly, without lifting his head, his eyes affixed to the ammonium nitrate mix.

"Pizza delivery," responded the SWAT team member.

The five terrorists didn't know their personal jihad was over until they felt the barrels of our weapons in their backs. They were making the bombs, using wooden spoons to mix fertilizer and diesel fuel into an explosive paste. We arrested them at the last minute, patiently biding our time because the U.S. attorney wanted the case to be airtight.

In Washington, President Bill Clinton said the American people should feel "an enormous sense of pride" that the terrorist plot had failed. The media billed it the Landmarks Plot, and in describing the takedown the *New York Daily News* headline read, "FBI Foils Plot to BLOW UP NEW YORK." Further, it credited the SWAT team with the line, "Raiders swift as lightning."

Not surprising, the media quickly learned our informant's identity. He was clearly a target for murder, so the office decided to help him relocate. The SWAT team was assigned to help Salem move from his uptown apartment and provided security every step of the way. Of course, it wasn't a traditional SWAT operation, and we dressed to blend in. As was often the case, when management needed a group of motivated, well-trained, and well-equipped agents who could rally quickly and get the job done, they usually turned to the SWAT team. It was an omen of even bigger and broader missions to come.

Subsequent to the arrest of the Landmarks plotters, the ringleader of the second plot, Ali Siddig, decided to cooperate. The SWAT team was given the mission of secreting him until he could testify. We trusted him even less than we did Gravano. He was something that none of us had a handle on. We could understand the drug dealers, the mob arm breakers, and bank robbers, but we were not really capable of fully understanding the motivations of a religious fanatic like Siddig. We kept him in the stockade at Fort Monmouth and staffed it around the clock, while the case agents constructed the case against the other plotters.

There were a few embarrassing moments for the FBI during the trial, such as the disclosure of tape recordings Salem had been secretly making whenever he met with his FBI handlers; however, in the end the case was tight enough to convict all the conspirators. In 1995 the Blind Sheikh was convicted and sentenced to life in prison. Nine other conspirators received a range of sentences based upon their cooperation, all with the help of "Brother" Siddig.

With the exception of a few terrorism agents in the New York office such as Dan Coleman, most of us put the WTC bombing and the Landmarks Plot in the back of our collective mind. We had dealt with terrorism before but not Muslim fanatics. We were used to activity involving white supremacists, the Weather Underground, the BLA, the Irish Republican Army, the FALN, the Cubans, the Unabomber, and so on. We weren't accustomed, however, to religious fanatics coming at us from outside the United States and didn't yet know how determined and widespread their movement would be. It is easier to ignore things that are nearly incomprehensible, particularly when we wanted to believe that the problem has been handled.

Much easier for our Western investigative minds to comprehend, the Unabomber had terrorized the country over nearly seventeen years. The terror he spread stemmed more from his irrational, Manson-like ramblings and incredible arrogance than from the death and destruction he caused. Theodore Kaczynski had excelled in academics at a young age and had an IQ of 167. He received an undergraduate degree from Harvard, earned a PhD in mathematics from the University of Michigan, and became an assistant professor at the University of California–Berkeley by age twenty-five. He resigned two years later. In 1971, he moved to a remote cabin in Lincoln, Montana. From 1978 to 1995, he sent sixteen bombs to various targets, including universities and airlines. His campaign killed three people and injured twenty-three.

Standard FBI practice is to assign a code name to investigations. Before Kaczynski's identity was known, the FBI referred to his case as UNABOM, for the *university* and *airline bomb*er. Kaczynski sent a letter to the *New York Times* on April 24, 1995, and promised to end his bombings if the *Times* or the *Washington Post* published a manifesto he'd written that addressed his fear of the erosion of human freedom.

When an FBI behavioral psychologist hypothesized that good might come of it, the *Washington Post* published his ramblings. The psychologist thought that the writing style and content were so unique that someone might recognize the author. As it turned out, Kaczynski's own brother recognized the style and beliefs and tipped off the FBI.

After his capture in April 1996, the New York SWAT team and other squads from throughout the country went to the deep Montana woods to protect Kaczynski's cabin and property. We knew the place would be swarming with souvenir hunters and the media, so we secured the perimeter around the cabin to prevent valuable evidence from being tainted, lost, or stolen.

In 1996 we were part of the security detail at the Summer Olympics in Atlanta when a blast tore through the crowd of revelers in Centennial Olympic Park. Two people died and 111 were injured. If not for two young men who tried to steal the unattended backpack the bomber had planted in the park, many more would have died. The backpack was too heavy for them to carry, and when they tried to run with it, it fell on its back. A steel plate inside would have propelled the explosion into the crowd if the bag had remained upright. I arrived at the bomb site a short time after the explosion. It was apparent that we had been lucky.

Two more bombings struck an abortion clinic and a gay nightclub in the Atlanta area. Similarities in the bombs' design—sticks of dynamite wrapped in nails—suggested the same individual was responsible for all the attacks. The bombing of an abortion clinic in Birmingham, Alabama, provided the FBI with crucial clues, including a partial license plate. That information and other evidence led the FBI to identify Eric Robert Rudolph, a former explosives expert for the U.S. Army, as a suspect. He eluded capture and became a

Author (center, back to camera) assists with security survey of underground sewers, Atlanta Summer Olympics.

fugitive, hiding in the Appalachian Mountains. The New York team went to the heart of the rural South and, with FBI SWAT teams from other parts of the nation, searched the mountains, gullies, and ravines daily over a period of months with the aid of local trackers.

I had been promoted to section leader, responsible for half of the team. Although my men were more accustomed to climbing stairwells in inner-city housing projects, they handled themselves well during long days moving through the rugged and dense Smoky Mountains, a subrange of the Appalachians. In a first for the FBI, I called for a helicopter medevac after a team member fell ill while on patrol far from any access road. Our medic initially diagnosed the problem as a possible stroke, so I made a decision to call for our helicopter, which was based in the small town nearby. Never in the bureau's history had it been done, but our pilot was a Vietnam War–trained vet, and our medic performed like a star. We built a signal fire, and with machetes we carved enough of an opening in the forest canopy so the penetrator could be lowered from about forty feet while the helicopter held in a hover at treetop level. It was a dangerous maneuver, particularly once the weight of two men swayed in the prop wash from the belly of the chopper, but our pilot was a master. That helicopter didn't move until our men were on board.

Rudolph eluded the FBI for years. He was captured by a twenty-one-year-old local police officer in May 2003 when he was discovered behind a store in Murphy, North Carolina. After his arrest he pleaded guilty to all four bombings, including the Centennial Olympic Park attack. He received five consecutive life sentences and now lives in solitary confinement in the supermax Administrative Maximum (ADX) federal prison in Florence, Colorado. Omar Abdel-Rahman lives just down the hall.

Back home in New York, one of our violent street crime squads was on to a group of uptown Dominicans posing as police officers in Morris Heights, a congested part of the city not far from Bronx Community College. Flashing phony credentials, they'd convince residents to crack the door and then push their way inside. They weren't much more than stickup guys interested in cash and jewelry, but they were armed and dangerous and liked to prey on the weak. In police parlance, they were known as push-in robbers.

We got an informant to infiltrate the group. One morning, he lured them with the promise of a good place to hit and arranged to meet the cop impersonators late that same night. It was a particularly cold winter day, when the temperature topped out at eighteen degrees. Kirby had recently taken over the SWAT team, and he sent me to reconnoiter the meeting site. After walking the area, I decided that we needed to position men along the wall near the Harlem River and next to the Major Deegan Expressway. I saw a single escape route, a ramp that descended from the elevated highway and curled around to a couple of acres of an open public works' parking area. My senses screamed disaster. It was obvious that if we tried to arrest the Dominicans underneath the highway, they might try to drive out of it. The last thing we wanted was a wild police chase through crowded neighborhoods.

Early that evening, I hid a couple of SWAT vehicles, positioning them as close as possible to the top of the exit ramp. The Dominicans were driving a Chevy Caprice decked out to resemble an unmarked police car. We spotted them two hours into our surveillance, when they turned down the exit ramp heading for their appointment with our informant. When our concealed arrest team moved in, the Dominicans panicked and charged back up the exit ramp. We radioed our blocking vehicles to obstruct the ramp, and our truck arrived just as the Caprice came roaring to the top. The panic level was spiking. My men exited their vehicles and wielded their M4 semiautomatic weapons (a newer version of the military's M16) and Remington 870 shotguns, both relatively effective at penetrating a vehicle. When they directed spotlights into the Caprice to blind the occupants, the driver threw the vehicle into reverse and tried to back down the ramp, just as we had anticipated. We blocked the ramp from both directions. They had nowhere to go.

Then one of them bolted from the car and took off toward the river. I had thought of that possibility too, and my men were pre-positioned in the field below the ramp. What I hadn't counted on was that anyone would jump. Without breaking stride, he leaped over the seawall into the Harlem River. We stopped one of my men, who was beginning to tear off his body armor, from following him. The river was dark, ice cold, churning, and ferocious. There was no way anyone could survive it.

Our NYPD backup had a police helicopter hover over the river, its searchlights darting in all directions, but the Dominican was gone. Here was an instance where I thought I had predicted every possible response, and I still missed one. Although fortunate that none of my men were hurt, I was still hard on myself. I should have known better by this stage of my career. I vowed not to let it happen again.

Eight

Al Qaeda in Africa: SWAT Overseas

"International terrorism involves violent acts or acts dangerous to human life that are a violation of the criminal laws of the United States or any state, or that would be a criminal violation if committed within the jurisdiction of the United States or any state. These acts appear to be intended to intimidate or coerce a civilian population, influence the policy of a government by intimidation or coercion, or affect the conduct of a government by assassination or kidnapping. International terrorist acts occur outside the United States or transcend national boundaries in terms of the means by which they are accomplished, the persons they appear intended to coerce or intimidate, or the locale in which the perpetrators operate or seek asylum."

—FBI Counterterrorism Division report, *Terrorism 2002–2005*

When the U.S. embassies in Tanzania and Kenya were bombed simultaneously in late August 1998, the FBI's Washington Field Office (WFO) landed the investigative ticket and sent an evidence response team (ERT), investigators, and SWAT personnel to provide security, or what the military calls force protection. Only blocks from FBI Headquarters, members of the Washington division claimed the investigation as theirs because their extraterritorial (ET) squads had been working criminal matters in that part of the world for years. They wanted the case. They were always in competition with New York to be the bigger and more successful office, and this investigation was a high-profile matter. FBI HQ was just a short walk from their office, and they had high-level friends pulling for them. New York, however, had been investigating Osama bin Laden and al Qaeda for years and was just weeks away from obtaining an indictment. Unless the U.S. attorney for the Southern District of New York agreed to relocate the case, New York had jurisdiction. Within days of the attack, largely as a result of the lobbying of John O'Neill, then the special agent in charge of national security for the New York office, the investigation was reassigned to our division. John had also done a recent tour with the Counterterrorism Division in headquarters, and he knew the Washington people, too.

Before the African embassy bombings, FBI SWAT teams had little experience providing force protection for overseas or international investigations. Although FBI ERTs and investigative teams in the past had been granted access to overseas crime scenes that involved attacks against U.S. property or interests, not until the East African strikes was a host nation willing to give the bureau virtually free reign within its borders. Kenya and Tanzania were ill equipped to address the carnage and the investigative effort that would be required, particularly since the case would undoubtedly reach across many borders. As a result, the State Department requested and received authorization for the FBI to bring over the equivalent of what would later be known as a rapid deployment team (RDT), which in essence was a complete office staffed with managers, investigators, technicians, SWAT personnel for security, and all the basic gear necessary to function independently. We were breaking new ground.

My Squad C-25 supervisor, Geoff, was now also the SWAT team coordinator. This double duty was commonplace. Although running a fifty-man SWAT team would, by most anyone's standards, qualify as a full-time job, the New York office still hadn't seen fit to make the coordinator position full time. Geoff would be serving as second in command of the Tanzanian investigation, and Ken Maxwell, a counterterrorism boss, would head it. Geoff reached me on the road and told me I was going to Africa. He directed me to gather seven SWAT team members and get ready. At this point, I was also working for John O'Neill in New York's National Security Division. We enlisted seven SWAT team operators and a communications specialist. We were to meet in

Africa with six investigators from the New York office's international terrorism squad who had already departed the States.

We would be flying on a C-5 Galaxy, an air force airlifter jet and one of a fleet of older aircraft that date back to 1970. The FBI did not have the airlift capacity to transport substantial personnel and equipment around the world. As a result, the bureau had to request assistance from the Department of Defense in times of crisis. Not until after the attacks on the embassies and the realization that more attacks might follow did the FBI, as part of the official RDT program, enter into a full contract with the air force to guarantee transport capability for worldwide events.

The air force load master at McGuire Air Force Base in central New Jersey, home of the 305th Air Mobility Wing, told us where to place our containers of ammunition, weapons, duffel bags, communications gear, "meals ready to eat" (MREs, the same fare issued to the military), and cases of bottled water. I tried to make sure I had thought of everything we would need—not want—in Africa. We were used to taking care of ourselves and relying on no one else for our own safety, so we tried to cover all the bases. Compared to the military, the State Department, and the CIA, the FBI was an underequipped, rank amateur at matters such as these. What we did have, however, were talented, creative people who knew how to get the job done.

I thought about the horror stories already filtering back from Africa. It was difficult to distinguish the African equivalent of urban legends from the truth. I'd been warned not to hang my laundry outdoors to dry because flies would settle in my boxers and lay eggs in them, and when they hatched, the maggots would burrow into my skin. There were stories of thieving monkeys that would take anything not nailed down and of aggressive ones that were diseased and would bite if confronted. One story I could validate involved an FBI supervisor who, in an ill-advised move, was jogging on the beach in the predawn hours when some locals attacked him. He returned from his run battered, bruised, and barefoot. His Nikes, the only item on him of any value, were gone.

We took off from McGuire at midnight. We had been in the air for hours when the crew chief came back to where we were sitting. He shined a flashlight out of the small portholes that functioned as windows. This maneuver did not augur well. A minute later, the pilot announced on the intercom system that we had developed a fuel leak and had to turn back.

The C-5 went into a steep bank, turning 180 degrees, and we were back at McGuire at 3 a.m. We took off again early that afternoon. I wanted to be part of this FBI milestone, even though it wasn't the first time the FBI had deployed overseas after a terrorist attack. In 1995, the FBI was in the Balkans, under the protection of U.S. and UN troops, where it helped uncover evidence of genocide during the Bosnian War. The FBI had also gone to Saudi Arabia after a massive truck bomb exploded outside the Khobar Towers in 1996. That explosion, near an apartment complex housing American military personnel, killed 19 Americans and wounded over 300. It was the worst terrorist attack on Americans in the Middle East since the bombing of the Marine Corps barracks in Beirut, Lebanon, in 1983. In that attack, 241 Americans had been killed.

The bureau couldn't sneeze in Saudi Arabia without authorization, and the atmosphere in Lebanon and the Balkans was difficult and intolerant. This African operation would be different. Finally, the bureau was going somewhere where it could conduct a full investigation with little restraint, free to do what it does best.

Air force regulations required we overnight at Naval Air Station Sigonella, Sicily, en route, so that the flight crew could rest and refuel our plane. We bivouacked at the base of Mount Etna, where the views and lush foliage were astounding.

From Sigonella we flew nonstop to Nairobi, Kenya, where we were briefed on the information developed to date, and we shifted some personnel, taking on two additional investigators. During that two-day layover, I had my first opportunity to see what a powerful vehicle-borne improvised explosive device (VBIED) can do. Much of the embassy's structure remained; however, the devastation to surrounding buildings was horrific because of less demanding construction requirements. Hundreds of civilians had died. In a fit of ecstasy, Osama bin Laden proclaimed al Qaeda's role in the carnage. Once just a shadowy figure known only to a few terrorism investigators and intelligence officers, he was now fully out in the open, and he professed to be acting as "the hand of God."

New York SWAT (author on far left) in Dar es Salaam.

We left Kenya for Dar es Salaam (Arabic for "House of Peace"), Tanzania's capital. When we touched down in a semi-deserted military airport on the city's outskirts, the WFO SWAT team was there.

As the C-5 ramp lowered to the runway, sunlight blasting the interior, our senses were overwhelmed with the scent of the Third World—auto exhaust fumes, tropical flowers, rotting vegetation, food cooking, and garbage burning—all aloft on heavy, humid air. We stepped down to the tarmac stiff legged and unloaded our gear from the pallets. A few yards away, strewn haphazardly among the grass and weeds, were rusting helicopters and more arcane Soviet military equipment, remnants of communist influence during the Cold War.

Four sport utility vehicles headed toward us through shimmering waves of heat. From another direction, the WFO agents we were replacing, packs slung over their shoulders, tramped toward us in a single column. I assumed that we would exchange a quick greeting before they boarded the C-5 and returned to the States, but they were so angry that New York was taking over the investigation, they wouldn't even look at us. We didn't even hear a grunt.

We loaded our gear into the vehicles. A group of Tanzanian soldiers was outside a dilapidated barracks near the airport entrance. From the loud voices and exaggerated gestures, it was clear they were high on something. Half of them were out of uniform, and if someone was in charge, it was impossible to tell who that was. They didn't even look up as our motorcade pulled out, and these guys were supposed to be guarding the air base.

Our native contract drivers took off down the highway toward the city as if in a race for their lives. We entered the downtown area after the sun had set and just as a big soccer match ended and the stadium crowd hit the streets. There were no working traffic lights, most of the street lamps didn't function, and the minimal light was from the commercial buildings in the area. Our drivers were not inclined to slow down, and in the narrow beams of our headlights, we saw masses of people leaping out of our way as we careened through the streets. I was amazed that we hit no one, but soon realized that this style of driving was the standard in Tanzania. We traversed an old road that ran parallel to a cliff along the ocean, dust rolling by the car windows. Our vehicles lurched violently from side to side as our drivers dodged goats and cows in the street.

We pulled up in front of a masonry wall that reminded me of a Spanish hacienda, and walking through it we were stunned to see a five-star hotel built in an African style. It had a thatched roof and stood only three stories high, seamlessly blending into the landscape. Although quite different from a typical modern Western structure, it was no less pleasing. My understanding was that it was one of the best hotels in Tanzania and was owned by a South African company. There was a Hyatt downtown, but we wanted nothing to do with a location in the heart of any city. At this hotel, the Sea Cliff, we had our back covered by a steep precipice that ran straight down to the sea and a single approach to the hotel entrance that we could, to a degree, control. No one knew how many more truck bombs were out there, and we were a logical target. As a precaution, we situated our people in rooms as far as possible from the street side of the hotel.

We stood in the middle of a luxurious lobby in our SWAT casuals—khaki cargo pants and black golf shirts. The employees wore crisp white jackets, and it was obvious that well-to-do Americans, Europeans, South Africans, and Indians patronized the hotel. Tanzania was popular for its minerals, game preserves, Mount Kilimanjaro, and the Serengeti National Park. Many well-dressed tourists and businesspeople were milling about in the hotel's cocktail bars and restaurants, and I remarked that we weren't going to pass ourselves off as big game hunters. I obtained access to a service elevator so we could secure our weapons, ammunition, and communications equipment in a room designated to be our temporary operations center.

The hotel overlooked the crystal green-blue water of the Indian Ocean, where the occasional fishermen cast nets into the sea from their traditional dhows rigged with distinctive triangular sails. The inland view reminded us that this place was not a resort. Naked children walked past herding goats, and colored plastic garbage bags blew in the wind as some form of African tumbleweed, occasionally attaching themselves to tall cacti. Dust swirls, or devils, and piles of garbage dotted the landscape. At the same time, the sun was a brilliant fireball in a clear, blue sky, another of the many dichotomies that prevail in that part of the world.

The hotel suite that the Washington team had occupied was empty. We thought we would find records of what the agents had accomplished to date, but they had left nothing—no instructions, no advice, and no records. They had been so furious about our replacing them that they had sanitized the room, leaving nothing of any value, not even a pencil. They had taken out their frustration on us. It was not a stunt worthy of FBI agents.

We configured our command post in another suite, our technicians installing satellite dishes, encryption equipment, and fax machines so we could communicate with headquarters and the New York office. It was cramped, it was not secure enough, and reception was poor. Geoff saw that it wasn't working, so, in his typical fashion, he recognized an opportunity and sought out the hotel manager. "We would like to take over the unfinished third floor and create a command post. What will it take to finish the third floor of the hotel?"

"About twenty-five thousand dollars."

"OK, it's done. Let's finish it."

They finished construction in about ten days, which was probably a record for that part of Africa. The hotel's management included some no-nonsense Indians who personally oversaw the work, running several shifts a day without weekend breaks. We ended up with one of the most magnificent command posts the bureau ever had, complete with a view of the sun as it rose each morning over the Indian Ocean. It was the only time in my FBI career that I witnessed agents returning to a command post after their shift was over just so they could hang out.

Since this investigation was the first time FBI SWAT teams had deployed to a major overseas incident, Geoff had no blueprint to follow. Nevertheless, when he knew we were going, the first thing he did was to requisition a large amount of cash. This move was smart, since the U.S. dollar speaks volumes anywhere in the world. Because we were a cash cow, hotel management seemed to overlook the obvious: that we were terrorist targets and putting everyone in our vicinity at some risk. Even in Tanzania, our cash found most everything that we needed, from copy machines to local cell phones.

The day after our arrival, we gathered as a group at the main police station in Dar es Salaam to meet with the interior minister, who was in charge of the Tanzanian National Police Force. Ken Maxwell, the FBI on-scene commander, and Geoff wore suits and ties; the rest of us were less formal but still presentable. The British-built, nine-story building had once been impressive; however, it had suffered from neglect over the years and was now a commentary on the current state of the former British Empire. Our destination was the top floor, and the broken elevators had not worked for a long time. As we headed toward the stairwell, I noticed a puddle of something dark on the floor and motioned for the others to step around. I realized that it was blood. No one working in the building seemed to notice or care.

Seventeen of us—our entire FBI team of investigators, technicians, and the SWAT team members—climbed the nine flights in extremely oppressive heat and humidity. I was behind Ken, who wore a light tan tropical suit. As we trudged step by step, I focused on the sweat stain spreading on Ken's back like a Rorschach test, and I thought how lucky I was that I wasn't part of management. The minister, a large and somewhat intimidating-looking man, sat at a long table in a conference room flanked by a half dozen of his men. Despite not having a good command of the English language, he was determined to talk to us in our native tongue. He spoke slowly, with lengthy pauses between each word, "I . . . am . . . very . . . happy . . . to . . . assist . . . the . . . FBI."

The wall behind the minister was all glass windows. Four enormous ravens landed outside on top of the broken air-conditioning unit and simultaneously began an ungodly screeching. For those of us sitting directly in front of the minister, it almost appeared as if the birds were dancing and screeching on top of his head. The minister was oblivious and droned on although we couldn't hear a word over the cacophony. It was as if the ravens were mocking him or furious at us. Somehow we managed, as a group, to maintain a serious demeanor, although I shot an occasional don't-even-think-of-it glare at one or two of my men who were prone to be cutups.

When we finally left, Ken was sweating like a fire hose and his face was bright red. He alluded to the bizarre scene, "Do you believe that? Was that the most unbelievable thing you've ever sat through?"

That afternoon, I walked down Embassy Row, a once stately area of tree-lined streets on the edge of Dar es Salaam. Built in a time when terrorist attacks on embassies were outside the limits of a civilized imagination, there was virtually no setback from the street to the buildings. I could fathom the power of the terrorists' explosion when I saw the cab of a truck embedded in the second story of the U.S. Embassy. The driver of the VBIED had parked alongside a large tanker truck filled with thousands of gallons of water. The ensuing explosion had been absorbed in good part by the truck, possibly saving lives. Twenty-five yards away, right across the street, an ancient tree with a circumference as wide as a small house and standing sixty-five feet tall was shredded and embedded with thousands of pieces of jagged metal and glass. It looked as if a giant had blasted it with a shotgun.

The U.S. Embassy in Dar es Salaam before the attack.
Photo courtesy of Leo West.

The U.S. Embassy after the blast. Photo courtesy of Leo West.

It was very quiet until I heard a strange clucking. I know birds and their sounds. My father was a woodsman and used to practice birdcalls with a small device, asking me to match the call to the bird. This call was unfamiliar. Then I noticed two beautiful peacocks walking along the top edge of the embassy's roof, fanning out their wings and tail feathers. I marveled at the irony of these impressive birds atop the devastation, silhouetted against the setting African sun.

This trip made me realize the extent of the threat we now faced from terrorism. I saw that these determined people could accomplish their goals despite relatively crude tools. That they were able to coordinate nearly simultaneous attacks in Tanzania and Kenya was not lost on me. It required substantial patience, planning, and knowledge of bomb making. Their operational security had been amazing. They knew how to keep a secret.

The ambassador had relocated the U.S. Embassy to a residence outside of town. Just like every nice house in Africa, it too was a walled compound. A

The critical evidence, the bomb truck's vehicle identification number.
Photo courtesy of Leo West.

Tanzanian military contingent, sporting the same worn Soviet uniforms and equipment we'd seen on our arrival, was guarding it. The men sat clustered under a lean-to, sitting in old stuffed chairs, some with their boots resting on a rickety old table that supported a dangerous-looking heavy machine gun. One round from that weapon, assuming it worked, and I was sure the table would collapse.

The embassy personnel were demoralized and still shaken by the attack. One of the ambassador's assistants confided in me, "We were so relieved when we saw your men arrive. Here we are, on the edge of Africa, and the embassy blows up. We were afraid of what would happen to us next." She pointed, "As you can see, our Marine security guard is very small, and we have no faith in the Tanzanians."

We didn't get that kind of welcome in many places.

Take the regional security officers (RSOs), for example. Almost all of the RSOs I have dealt with were happier when we left than when we arrived. Largely former military or police officers, RSOs are responsible for the security of the U.S. ambassadors in foreign nations. They are also in charge of protecting other Americans employed at the embassy and of ensuring that visiting Americans stay out of trouble. They usually oversee a number of locals, or Foreign Service nationals (FSNs), who serve as security guards for the embassy. They have a lot on their plate.

Ambassadors tend to have big egos. They are impatient and generally don't have the time to fully understand the difficulties RSOs face in trying to keep the embassy community safe. So, many places have a short-tempered, frustrated RSO serving an ambassador who is, at best, disdainful of him. Visitors, as we were, were a perfect target for venting their frustrations. We were more than an annoyance to the RSO; we were a big gaggle of armed career stoppers.

I can understand the RSO's viewpoint. I wouldn't want these FBI agents rolling into my territory either. Western visitors to a place such as Dar es Salaam are just potential crime victims who will invariably make the RSO's day a great deal harder.

When we showed up in Tanzania, the RSO dressed us down as if we were children and let us know that he was the only sheriff in town. His demeaning tone was enough to make us want to take off his head. Some of the guys on my team looked as if they were close to doing just that. After our lecture, I pulled my group aside and said, "Look, guys, you have no idea what kind of hell he has just been through. He is responsible for the embassy's security, and his embassy was just blown up. How would you like to be in his place? So, we will swallow his crap with a smile, and we will be professional. Got it?"

The second night, in a morale-building gesture, we were invited to the temporary embassy for an African cookout. Native dancers performed around a bonfire to the sound of traditional instruments: flutes, drums, and rattles. They spiraled about, thrusting their spears into the sky, wearing next to nothing, and looking as if they'd just stepped out of *National Geographic*. It was the first time the embassy staff and their Marine guards let their hair down since the bombing. I took in the spectacle: the roasting food; light chatter punctuated by occasional laughter; a blazing fire and dancers; the black, clear night sky; immense stars; and throbbing native drums. I was here to help find terrorists, but this night I was enjoying Africa.

Nine

Tracking the Bombers

Some of the bureau's most experienced forensic examiners who dealt with explosives dug through the rubble and debris at both embassy bombing sites within hours of arriving in Africa. Men who had already proven themselves just two years earlier at the Khobar Towers bombing in Saudi Arabia and at sites elsewhere reviewed the embassies' destruction. They were from the FBI's Laboratory Division based in the academy at Quantico. The explosives unit was part of the scientific analysis section, which consisted of one unit chief and eight supervisory special agents (SSAs). They were volunteers, men who loved this kind of work and who devoted much of their spare time to learning more. Only someone with such a passion could have sustained this kind of tempo. They dug through the rubble and debris for long days, day after day in the hot sun, retaining their concentration and enthusiasm.

In Dar es Salaam, the FBI's evidence response team comprised several forensic examiners out of the explosives unit and specially trained agents from the Washington Field Office. On Friday, August 14, only one week after the bomb went off, Greg, one of the FBI investigators, pulled a twisted piece of steel from a mass of three or four almost unrecognizable vehicles resting close to twenty-five yards from the blast crater. Just as forensic investigators had done in the basement of New York's World Trade Center and at other bombing locations, they were methodically scouring the blast site for clues. Dozens had examined the area surrounding the point of detonation in a coordinated progression and fanned out from ground zero at a tortoise's pace. To the unpracticed eye, they may have appeared to be searching without a particular goal, but they knew exactly what they wanted to find.

With muted excitement, the investigators carried their find over to their lead examiner, Leo West, who was in charge of collecting and processing all the evidence at the scene. It was part of a chassis, and, like an engine block, it usually holds the key to determining the type of vehicle used. Standing in the heat and glare of the African day, they struggled to find the vehicle identification number (VIN). Unique to every vehicle manufactured, the VIN unlocks the vehicle's entire history. Then with a fresh set of eyes, Iggy, an FBI physical science technician, walked over and asked, "Hey, what are you guys doing?" Iggy realized that his teammates were on to something. He took one look at the object and immediately pointed to a series of letters and numbers. The damaged metal was a vehicle frame section bearing VIN MH40-060500. The Japanese manufacturer would identify it as part of a 1987 Nissan Atlas two-ton truck. Once the VIN was determined to belong to a Nissan vehicle, taskings (leads) were sent to the FBI legal attaché, or legat, in Tokyo for all records pertaining to the truck's history. In November 1994 the truck had been shipped to Tanzania, where a Mr. Zahoro had bought it for $9,290.00. The investigation was off and running.

In another classic case of great forensic work, within weeks FBI investigators, with the help of the Tanzanian police, began to identify subjects. They also pieced together how the attack was planned and executed.

During the investigation, one of our native drivers took us to meet an informant who claimed he could tell us about the conspirators who bombed the embassy. The promise of reward money ensured a constant flow of tips and leads. We waited for the informant while parked in front of a local police station, running the car's engine so we could have some air conditioning. Then I detected an unusual sound above the din. I asked the driver to turn off the car engine and heard the high-pitched screams of a woman coming from within the station house. Her shrieks were nearly in cadence with a loud cracking sound. My Tanzanian driver, unaffected, told me that the police were either whipping or caning a woman who had broken some law. "What crime would call for caning?" I asked.

He shrugged his shoulders, "Anything. She might have told lies about her neighbors."

▪   ▪   ▪

A young Tanzanian named Rashid had rented his house, a walled compound, to the bombers. When questioned, he acknowledged only knowing one of them on a limited social basis. We knew he was lying and that his connection was greater. They had all lived together, and he knew them well. After his arrest, he admitted to supplying his renters with cell phones and other resources but refused to concede that he knew what they were plotting.

Subjects such as Rashid were assigned investigative teams made up of FBI and Tanzanian investigators. In Rashid's case, the Tanzanian government provided us with police translators, a necessity as none of our team spoke the local dialect. These translators were some of the hardest-working people I had ever met, struggling mightily to translate rapid-fire questions and answers for hours at a time. We learned to watch for signs of fatigue and call for routine breaks to give them a chance to regain their strength. As a backup interrogator on the team, I was still working to overcome a seven-hour time change and trying to get some sleep despite nightmares, which were likely induced by antimalarial drugs.

During one session, I could see the translator was cotton mouthed and tired. I was not thinking clearly, and being used to working in downtown Manhattan, I suggested we stop and get a cup of coffee at the local coffee shop. Everyone looked at me strangely. They had no idea what a coffee shop was, and even if they did they would never admit that they had no money for coffee. We learned to bring bottled water and share our MREs with our hosts. They were careful with the MREs, usually eating only one or two of the items contained in the pouch and saving the rest for their families that evening.

I soon realized that almost to a man, the Tanzanians suffered from malaria. The symptoms—profuse shaking, sweating, and acute fatigue—were impossible to ignore. When someone had a recurrence, we would lose him for days. It reinforced our need to continue with our antimalarial medication despite its side effects.

The interrogations took place in the Tanzanian version of what I referred to as 1 Police Plaza, which was the address of the NYPD's headquarters. It was a four-story complex with a relatively modern facade and a badly neglected interior.

One long afternoon, I needed to use a bathroom. I went down the hall to the steno pool, where women sat at manual typewriters, some that actually worked. They were the classic high ones with handles and ribbons, and the secretaries typed on them at beat-up wooden desks. One of the women directed me toward a small louvered door. Inside was a large, square concrete box not quite two feet off the floor that had a hole in the middle. Effluent overflowed from the box and trickled in a small stream toward the steno pool. I stood there thinking, I don't even know how to use this thing. Do you stand up as close to the box as you can and try to reach the hole or do you get up on the box and pee down into it? I did the best I could, but the whole time I was thinking, There's no lock on the door and I'm probably doing this wrong and any second there will probably be twenty Tanzanian women standing out there looking at me and wondering how come I can't pee right.

After a couple of weeks, we started making some progress, with Rashid finally admitting to prior knowledge of the terrorists' plan. I called FBI HQ with the good news but instead of offering a "hip hip hooray," the legal counsel told me to back off. We could not ask any more questions unless we read the subject a Miranda warning and provided him with a defense lawyer.

"Do you remember where we are?" I said in as hushed a tone as possible.

"If we are to build a prosecutable case, you will need to follow the rules, agent."

When I explained the problem to the senior Tanzanian officer, he responded, "We do have a university and there is a law school. We will call and see if anyone is available."

The Tanzanian interrogators still looked befuddled. I told them, "Anything we obtain from the subject that is an admission of guilt can't be used to prosecute him unless we first advise him that he has rights and the danger he faces if he admits guilt."

"How do you convict anyone?"

"Well, it is very hard." I also told them about discovery: "We also have to give the defense lawyer all the information we have that we will use against his client in the trial."

One of them pondered this news and offered, "Sometimes the day of the trial we give them some things. I still do not understand how you can convict anyone with all these restrictions."

In the interim, the Tanzanians had sent a car to the local university and borrowed the senior professor of law. He arrived, still wearing his legal robe and carrying his wig. He was terrified, wondering why we wanted him. The Tanzanians, just as citizens of many underdeveloped countries, were afraid and suspicious of the police. Once I explained to the professor that we needed his help and that he was not in trouble, he relaxed a little. Unexpectedly, providing our subject with counsel was the best thing we could have done. Not only was the professor a competent translator, but, after sizing up his client's dilemma, he also advised him that he would be much better off standing trial in America. He told him, "The Americans will feed you while you are in their jail." Tanzanian prisoners do not receive sustenance from the authorities, relying entirely on family and friends to bring them food.

Then we received word that we needed to go to Zanzibar, an island off the coast of Tanzania. There was new information regarding suspects who were from the island, and we were to interview witnesses. We had two Tanzanian detectives and a Tanzania Intelligence Service (TIS) officer with us when we flew into Zanzibar. We went on a South African jet that the bureau had contracted for, along with a South African medical team to support us in the event of emergency. This arrangement wasn't unusual. Stateside, we always had medical personnel in tow when we went out on a dangerous raid. We really needed the medical team in Tanzania. The closest acceptable hospital was in Nairobi; after that, we'd have to go to Johannesburg or Tel Aviv.

The first night, Paul Sutherland and I conducted an interview in the Zanzibar police station, finishing up late. The police had turned off the lights, so we had to feel our way down the stairwell to reach the parking lot. We didn't know how we'd get back to the hotel since we had no idea where we were. Only one car was in the compound's lot, a TIS vehicle. It belonged to the old Tanzanian intelligence agent who had joined us on our trip from the mainland. The old agent was well spoken. He had spent time in embassies around the world and had worked for the government when Tanzania had fallen under the sway of communist powers. He found us groping about in the dark parking lot and asked if we'd like a ride back to our hotel. He was our only option so we got in the car with his driver.

As soon as we pulled out in the street, two police officers, federal police paramilitary types with AK-47s, approached. I figured this encounter was not going to be a problem. They were police officers and we were with a member of the TIS. The FBI was a combination of both of these elements—the counterintelligence and the federal law enforcement sides—so I assumed that the cops and the TIS agent should be pals. The body language of the old agent and his driver told a different story. They avoided all eye contact with the gendarmes. One of them circled the car and the other shouted inches from the driver's face while our host just stared ahead nervously. Both cops held their weapons in a ready gun position, with their fingers on the triggers. I eased my SIG Sauer semiautomatic out of my hip pack and held it tight to the side of my leg.

Sensing the danger, I went into that Zen place again. I envisioned a bullet in the back of my head, my body devoured by creatures in a Zanzibar swamp and my loved ones back home never really knowing what happened to me. Then the snarling cop glanced into the backseat of our SUV and noticed us. He was obviously startled by our presence. His temperament changed to mild disgust, and he motioned us on. Paul and I were relieved.

A quarter mile down the street, two more gendarmes spoiling for a fight stopped us. The street lighting was better here. They spotted us in the backseat right away and let us proceed.

Communist-trained security apparatuses around the world had a reputation for being cruel and in some cases outright murderous. Under the old Soviet-leaning regime, the TIS would carry out reprisals against the families of anyone who stepped out of line. Now that democracy had come to Tanzania, I guessed grudges remained. It wasn't wise to be hanging out with TIS guys. You could almost equate it to Nazi Germany's Gestapo agents going back to work after losing the war.

Before dropping us off, the TIS agent told me, "There is a man being held here in solitary that you need to look into." He told me his name. "But you can't let the police know I gave you this information."

"Why do you think I need to talk to him?"

"You'll see."

Our hotel was located in the center of Zanzibar City in the ancient section called Stone Town. It reminded me of a scene from the *Arabian Nights*. The rooms were sanitary, with no window screens but at least mosquito nets draped the beds. My only complaint was that the plumbing was so strange I couldn't figure out how to use most of it. Plumbing in Africa continually humbled us.

When our group—Paul, Gary, some investigators, and I—had dinner on the veranda that evening, the ocean lapped up against the other side of the seawall, and the dhows were so close we could see the faces of their crews as they sailed past. As darkness fell, the sky once again sprouted stars that seemed close enough to touch. Small native men catered to us, as we ate food we couldn't begin to identify. Then, someone suggested going down the street to check out the local bars.

Zanzibar has a different feel from the mainland. It has a stronger Muslim influence, having been under intermittent Arab control until 1963. First settled by Persian traders, Zanzibar became an important center of the slave trade on the East African coast. When we walked down to the old harbor, we saw a plaque and a monument near the wharf denoting the very spot that had once served as an auction platform for Africans being sold to slave traders. We stood there for a moment, trying to comprehend what that place symbolized.

We walked on in silence until Paul noticed a bar that looked as if it was out of the 1800s, a place that sailors and crusty sea dogs might have frequented. Inside, it looked more like a pirates' den. As unbelievable as it sounds, there was even one character wearing an eye patch at the bar. Smoky, crowded with locals, the bar had a number of working women trying to ply their trade. Some even had teeth. While a few of the gals were focused on a drunken Brit at the bar, the rest quickly turned their attention to us. Even though the beer was ice cold, it wasn't enough to make me want to stay. Gary and Paul were particularly big and we were all armed and relatively fit, but that didn't intimidate our new friends. The crowd started moving in on us and I could see the plan. The women were the bait or the shills, teaming with the weaselly looking men who were positioning themselves to try to pick our pockets or possibly worse.

I'd made up my mind to leave when two women began to sandwich me, repeatedly asking if I knew their cousin in Brooklyn. I covered my gun with one hand and my wallet with the other and nodded to the others to back out of the place. We left together, the last man walking backward to cover us. The Brit at the bar stumbled over to us, red faced, and mumbled, "Mates, mind if I leave with you?" Even in his stupor, he realized that if we left him there alone he was in trouble. Part of the crowd followed us down the dark, narrow cobblestone streets all the way to our hotel.

As most nights in Africa, that night I slept with my pistol close by.

The next morning, I returned to the Zanzibar police station with a young FBI investigator. To protect my TIS source, I made up a story that we were looking for an Iraqi individual last seen in Tanzania who went by several names. The chief was in a gracious mood. "Yes, agent, I will look into this. Please wait outside." A little while after we had left the room, the chief of police called me back, "I think we can help you with this. Stand by, and we will have this individual brought over."

They called us into a room with a long conference table and ushered in a short, swarthy man in his forties who was neither African nor necessarily Semitic. The police chief said, "We detained this man when he arrived in Zanzibar the day after the American embassy was attacked. He was carrying two sets of identification. Here are copies." I glanced at the documents; one set was Iraqi, the second set issued by the Red Cross in Geneva, Switzerland, and in a different name. This was classic spy tradecraft.

My partner reminded me that our aircraft was departing for the mainland in an hour, so I had to cut quickly to the heart of the matter. The Iraqi only spoke Arabic. The Zanzibaris provided two translators, one to translate English to Swahili and the other Swahili to Arabic. The prisoner looked desperate. I was convinced that he was an Iraqi spy or operative of some kind and wondered whether he could have any connection to the bombing. Or did he just fear the inevitable dragnet for foreigners? He had tried to leave Tanzania right after the attack and was so anxious that he got sloppy.

"Massoud, why were you in Tanzania?" His answer did not make much sense. He claimed he had come to Tanzania for a business opportunity; however, his friend never met him and did not return any calls.

Wrong answer, I thought. "Massoud, are you in the service of the Iraqi government?"

He replied that he had been a major in the Iraqi army and that he had deserted after the Gulf War. Then he claimed he had been hiding in western Iraq and in Iran since 1991.

Time was running out. "Massoud, are you now, or have you ever served, in the Iraqi Intelligence Service?" I listened to the chain of translation around the table finally reach him. His gaze went to the floor. "No," he said quietly.

I stood up and turned once as I walked away. He looked as if he was about to cry. Damn it, I thought, I had worked counterintelligence for a while, and this man had to be a spy. My every instinct told me there was a reason he was in Dar es Salaam when our embassy was decimated.

I would have loved to have stayed and gotten to the bottom of Massoud's story, but my team was waiting at the airport, the weather was turning bad, and it was outside my lane to work a spy case. However, I was determined to impress upon my bosses that this man deserved attention. My sense was that he would have done almost anything to get out of the black hole the Zanzibaris were keeping him in, and the Tanzanians would have given him to us for a grin. On my return to the hotel, I filed my report and hoped that someone ultimately followed through on this big opportunity.

I worked long, hard days while I was in country, but in my limited spare time, I found Tanzania to be a place of interesting customs and people. One people stood out from the rest, the fierce-looking Masai warriors who earned their manhood only after killing a lion using nothing but a spear. Ebony black, extremely tall, and thin, they donned lion and leopard skins and danced with their mouths wide open. They would come to town on broken-down buses from the Serengeti, hundreds of miles away, to work as guards for the wealthy townsfolk. For a few dollars a day, they stood watch over their homes, holding their spears and clubs, wearing their full, colorful garb. I suspected no one was willing to take on a man who had faced down a lion with a spear.

Three months after first setting foot in Tanzania and after tracking endless leads and conducting dozens of interviews with both Tanzanians and Kenyans, the FBI found the bomb factory in Dar es Salaam. New York SWAT team members secured the perimeter until evidence technicians could arrive and scour the location. It was a monsoon night, and the downpour was so bad that agents were standing with rainwater up to their shins. The water flushed huge spiders out of their holes, and they desperately sought high ground by climbing up the agents' pant legs. At one point, someone flashed a red laser beam across some of the men and created alarm since laser-sighting systems had become a common feature for many tactical weapons. It turned out to be only local kids fooling around, but the incident made the night that much more miserable.

The team kept the perimeter all night in the rain. Once the forensic guys arrived, they were able to collect a windfall of DNA samples, fingerprints, explosive or chemical traces, and the other clues that helped to identify and eventually track down most of the people involved in the bombings. FBI agents were part of the capture and interrogation of five of the embassy bombers. They were extradited to the States for trial in the Southern District of New York. Since they were all dangerous people, the SWAT team routinely provided their transport and security. I handled the logistics once the subjects were on American soil, keeping their arrival from becoming a media event by moving them late at night into lower Manhattan. If the weather permitted, we brought them into town by bureau helicopter.

On one occasion, a terrorist was flown into Stewart Air Force Base in New York State. From there a bureau helicopter transported him to New York City. On his own accord, the pilot took a detour and flew past the West 30th Street Heliport, heading south until the Huey was eye level with the illuminated face of the Statue of Liberty. He hovered close for a while so that the prisoner could see little else but her huge staring eyes.

The five captured embassy bombers would all eventually receive life sentences. In the interim, however, some weeks after returning to New York, we received a call that there had been a serious problem at the Metropolitan Correctional Center facility involving two of the embassy bombers who were housed there pending trial. These seemingly passive individuals, men who never missed their daily prayers and who had pretended to befriend the guard assigned to their floor, had tried to take hostages so they could demand the release of Omar Abdel-Rahman, the Blind Sheikh.

In order to ensure that the prisoners were provided full protection under U.S. law and upon the insistence of their defense attorneys, the Federal Bureau of Prisons had changed its policy and had stopped inspecting their cells for contraband. The men therefore had had the time and the privacy they needed to fashion a shiv from a long-handled comb, stripping off its teeth and sharpening the handle to a point. They had also managed to concoct a pepper spray from ingredients they stole from the prison's kitchen.

That day, the regular floor guard carried the only set of keys to the cell. A second set was kept several floors below. When the guard entered the cell, the prisoners jumped him. They punched and kicked him and then jammed the shiv through his eye and into his brain. It all took place in minutes while open-mouthed defense lawyers watched from behind the glass doors of an adjoining conference room. Other guards stationed below grabbed the second set of keys and quickly took control of the situation. The guard who'd been attacked by the prisoners he had befriended walked out of the building in shock with the shiv protruding from his eye.

This attack clearly highlighted the nature of the people we were dealing with.

Ten

The Secret Years

During his prime, a period covering almost fifteen years, one valuable, well-placed individual helped the United States penetrate and gather information on some of our most serious enemies. Just prior to my deployment with the SWAT team to Tanzania, I made a decision to leave Squad C-25 and take on an assignment related to this man. At the time, I did not appreciate that I would be leaving behind much of what I loved about my work. Nor was I fully aware that I would be entering a shadowy realm where distrust and secrecy were job requirements.

I will refer to my charge as Ivan. In bureau-speak of the time, Ivan was an asset, or an individual who provided counterintelligence information that helped us stop other nations from spying on us. Assets are often motivated by politics. Some do it because of their aversion to communism or to the brutal regimes that had crushed democracies throughout Eastern Europe and large parts of the world. For others, it was a way to help those they cared about escape an oppressive regime.

Unlike informants, many of whom are criminals or have close access to criminal activity, an asset is not usually from a criminal culture. In fact, the person often becomes a trusted partner and, as in my case, a friend. The corollary is that, as in any relationship, you must be honest enough to tell your friend when that person is really screwing up. As capable and perceptive as an asset can be, Ivan was up there with the best of them, but he had his share of foibles. In the normal course of events, the consequences of a friend's mistake are not life changing. An asset's error, however, can compromise or disassemble valuable spying operations and place lives at risk. There can be public relations damage, as in the case of Jonathan Pollard, a U.S. Navy intelligence analyst charged with selling classified material to Israel. Arrested by the FBI in 1985 and sentenced to life imprisonment for espionage, his case set back U.S.-Israeli relations for many years.

I was not Ivan's first handler. For many years and until the late 1990s, Ivan had had good relationships with other seasoned handlers. Then management in the New York office decided that he and his handlers had become too comfortable with one another. When word filtered down that changes were imminent in the Ivan operation, I let it be known that I was interested. I thought that if I took on this new assignment, I could stop doing surveillance every other night and working with prosecutors preparing cases for trial until late the other evenings. I thought I would have more time with family and friends and live a more "normal" life. I was wrong. I didn't fully understand the demands of the job and the impact it would have on my personal life.

On the one hand, criminal work, no matter how complex an investigation or how devious the suspects, is relatively simple. Once you're fairly sure a crime has been committed, you go to work using every tool available and with a singular goal—to bring the bad guys to justice. Your job is to stop crime and put criminals in jail. As an FBI criminal investigator, once you are on the team, you are part of everything it does and knows. "Law enforcement sensitive" is the only caveat circumscribing information you uncover, and even then you can still share information with cops and prosecutors who have a good reason to know about it. It was the same team attitude that I enjoyed about sports. I liked that sense of working together for a good cause.

On the other hand, in the world of the spy and the counterspy, you're never sure who your friends are, and there is rarely a finale. Your prime concern is protecting intelligence from everyone, including your own people. Every report must be scrutinized to ensure an important bit of information isn't accidentally turned over to the enemy or to the wrong "friend." Those who uncover valuable information hold it closely and jealously withhold it from others.

Now I would be working for people who didn't always mean what they said and who didn't trust me enough to use their real names. I would be vetted routinely to ensure my honesty. I couldn't take it personally; they trusted me no less than they trusted anyone within their own organization. I would not be able to divulge what I did to anyone at home. My day at work would not be for discussion at the dinner table. There would be periods without telephone contact and many unexplained absences. Counter-espionage is a line of work that tests the most trusting relationships, often to the breaking point.

My new partner and I went to our first meeting with the sister agency, the organization that paid the bills for our operation and was the direct benefi-ciary of Ivan's efforts. Having virtually no prior contact with this group, I was taken aback almost immediately by the feigned cordiality. My years of work-ing with street people told me that what I saw was not what I was going to get with this crowd. We learned that Ivan didn't take well to losing his former handlers. His relationship with them was almost brotherly, and Ivan's world toppled when they were taken away. Our job, we were told, was to make him productive again.

"Whatever it takes, Ray, get this guy back on track. We need to know what those folks are planning, and this guy is our best source."

I am restricted from discussing Ivan's specialty or the nature of our tar-gets; however, I can say Ivan was extremely good at his calling and unusually successful. Characteristically, my partner and I took our instructions to heart, and after much patient hand-holding, we got Ivan back in stride.

As experienced street agents, we brought an element of common sense to the operation. Our sister agency provided most of the technical expertise; their personnel were the geeks and we were the knuckle draggers. They some-times insisted that one of their operatives pose as Ivan's assistant so he could accompany him on assignment. Before we launched Ivan and his temporary assistant on a new mission, I would order the assistant to turn all his pockets inside out. Usually indignant, the assistant would comply once he saw that I was serious and would not budge. Invariably, I would find a second form of identification, either a driver's license or library card that would identify the assistant as someone other than what his cover identity showed. This slip was not merely an excusable mistake that would be awkward if discovered by the wrong people. The error would have destroyed the operation. More than once, Ivan had had a gun stuck in his chest when a suspicious guard noticed furtive action. Ivan had been able to talk his way out of the situation, but he knew there was no guarantee of success the next time it happened. I had controlled criminal informants before and knew the risk of wiring up a guy and sending him into a meeting with dangerous, suspicious people. One small slip could end it.

Of course, as in any large entity, the FBI also had people who couldn't survive on their own, let alone be responsible for the well-being of others. For example, at one point I called Bob, my FBI counterpart in another territory, to tell him that we had an opportunity for Ivan with a special target. I asked if he could provide some cleared contractors for manual work that we couldn't do ourselves. This request wasn't unusual, and Bob assured me that he had trusted men who could do the job. We arranged to meet Bob and the contractors at a hotel to discuss the plan. On the day of the meeting, I was running late, and in my rush to get to the hotel room, I locked my keys in my unmarked G-car. I'll deal with that later, I thought—first things first.

Bob opened the hotel room door, and I saw that Ivan was already there with my partner. Bob proudly introduced me to his two contractors. "Ray, I want you to meet Shlomo and Efran, who've done work for me in the past.

The men were in their early thirties, very fit, with high and tight military haircuts and a hint of accent. I thought, They have to be with the Mossad!

We shook hands. "Nice to meet you. Hey, Bob, could you join me for a minute in the back room?" Bob looked baffled as I closed the door behind us. "Hey, Bob, do you have any idea who those two really are?"

"Yeah, Ray, they're really good contractors who've always done a good job for me."

"I bet they have, Bob. Do you write their reports for them too?"

"What are you getting at?"

"Jesus, Bob, these two reek of Mossad or Israeli military intelligence! Look at them! When is the last time you met a contractor who does this kind of work who isn't speaking Spanish or sporting a spare tire around his waist? And, by the way, Bob, if you listen closely, you'll pick up that hint of an Israeli accent."

"You think so?"

"Bob, I would bet next month's pay on it. OK, so now Ivan has a full dossier on file in Tel Aviv. Guess things could be worse. We have to get this job done over the next two days, or we've lost the opportunity. Have them do their thing. Don't share any more information with them, then go back to your office, and have that background check run again on this little company they work for."

Bob mumbled as he walked back into the room. He knew I was probably right, and I think he was embarrassed. He should have been.

Once the meeting dispersed, we all headed out the door to take care of our piece of the operation. I mentioned to my partner that I had stupidly left my keys inside my Tahoe and that I needed to find a strong coat hanger to try and unlock the door. Shlomo overheard me and eagerly offered to help. "I will meet you downstairs in the lot, Mr. Ray."

Before I could respond, he headed down the stairwell. My partner and I quickly exchanged knowing glances, and more than a little curious, I headed off to meet Shlomo. We arrived at my car at the same time, and Shlomo was carrying a "Slim Jim" tool designed for entering vehicles. He smiled, nodded, instantly slipped the paper-thin metal device between the window and door, and, with one stroke, pulled it back out to the clicking sound of the door unlocking. Case closed—he was a real pro—but I'm sure he didn't make his living working for AAA.

During the time that I worked these euphemistically called "national security matters," the man in charge of my division, or that branch of the New York office that handled CI and counterterrorism, was John O'Neill. An outspoken Irishman, John could be hard on his managers. His workers loved him, though. John remembered your name and would wrap his arm around your shoulder, inquire how you were doing, and make you feel that he meant it. His family was from the Atlantic City, New Jersey, area, and he had joined the bureau as a clerk, rising to the position of special agent in charge. Always dapper, he was a bit of a throwback to the old Hoover days, regularly holding court at his table at Elaine's, the star-studded Manhattan restaurant. Stories abounded of how John would wine and dine the heads of friendly intelligence services until almost dawn and then head to his uptown apartment where he would shower, shave, throw on a fresh shirt, and head into another fourteen-hour workday with relish.

One afternoon, while preparing my regular bimonthly report on my operation with Ivan, I sat in the rear of the office as two of my managers, men who seldom took any interest in my operation other than trying to catch me in an accounting error, tried to brief John on what we were doing. I watched as John stared down at reports and cables, reading and marking them and never acknowledging that he heard a thing. Only when my boss finished his briefing did John raise his head. He looked at me and said, "OK, Ray, now you tell me what you're doing." He listened, never once looking away. From that time forward, I would have taken on any assignment for John. I keep a picture on my desk of us shaking hands at his retirement luncheon. I believe it is the last picture ever taken of John alive.

I left my assignment with Ivan to accept an appointment as a full-time SWAT team coordinator for the New York office. The position had been part-time until this point. Amazingly, the new management team made what amounted to a sea change in our division, recognizing how critical and demanding it was to run an enhanced team for one of the bureau's busiest offices. International terrorism had become the number one threat, and the New York office had a dominant role in that fight, in part owing to the personality of John O'Neill. New York agents had obtained the indictment of Osama bin Laden in the Southern District of New York. With O'Neill's full backing, New York terrorism investigators had identified Sudan-based bin Laden as the leader of al Qaeda. It was clear that bin Laden had had his hand in almost every major terrorist attack against the United States of the previous eight years. The New York office would lead the effort against al Qaeda and Islamic extremism, and SWAT would have to reinvent itself to handle demands that now included international deployments.

I was proud to be selected as the first full-time SWAT team leader but unhappy to turn Ivan over to his new handler. I knew the agent wasn't up to the task and that his orders were simply to reign in Ivan and get him ready for retirement. The wrong people had decided that Ivan was no longer useful. Others who had worked closely with him and I believed that, with some ingenuity and hard work, there was plenty of life in him.

Eleven

Dream Job

Although my new position as the first full-time SWAT team leader didn't bring supervisory rank, I could finally apply all my energy to making the team excel and put in place my ideas about reorganizing training, team structure, and overseas deployments. New York had been designated a rapid deployment team office, tasked with reacting to terrorism attacks against U.S. interests anywhere in the world. The SWAT team, as we proved in Tanzania, was central to that capability. SWAT team members are only one element of an RDT, but they are an important component. It was clear to me that whether an RDT was activated or not, SWAT agents could provide any type of overseas deployment with a multitude of skills. Not only could they contribute security or at least a good security assessment, but also they were logisticians who were prepared to help find whatever equipment or gear the operation called for; they were investigators who were experienced enough to run down leads in bad places, conduct discreet surveillance, and work well with indigenous cops; and, most of all, they were handpicked team players. They would not complain about any assignment because they understood what teamwork meant. It was my opinion, based on solid experience, that a well-led SWAT team could be the backbone of a major deployment, and major deployments were clearly in New York's future.

Despite what certainly awaited on the horizon, I knew our bread and butter remained high-risk arrests involving "traditional" violent criminals. Further, I was reminded of this fact almost every week.

One of the FBI violent crime squads asked for SWAT's help with another group of Dominican push-in robbers. This bunch had been knocking off one target after another in the Highbridge Park area of upper Manhattan. The squad had developed an informant within the gang. A plan was set to trap the robbers. The FBI leased an apartment on the seventh floor of an upper Manhattan high-rise and instructed the informant to tell the robbers that he knew the people who lived there and that they had plenty of cash and jewelry for the taking.

My new boss was the criminal division SAC in charge of all the criminal squads in the New York office. I could tell that he was pleased to have the SWAT team under his command. It offered him an extra tool that he could call on seven days a week and on a moment's notice. I also had a hunch that he really didn't know what this tool could do. This case seemed a good opportunity to show him how we got the job done. My arrest plan had a seven-man SWAT team secreted in an apartment immediately below the seventh-floor apartment and a second team hidden in vehicles on the street that could arrest any of the gang members who waited there. The violent gang squad was also out on the street. Surveillance teams, from an entirely separate unit and assigned to cases as needed, tailed the robbers to our location.

My boss rode with me that late afternoon. I parked within sight of the building but discreetly out of view of the street. I was operating two handheld radios and my car radio almost simultaneously, directing my guys to take up positions and talking to the surveillance teams and the case agents. My boss sat next to me and took it in like an excited kid.

We'd warned the informant, "Whatever you do, do not leave the vehicle. Do not go upstairs with these guys. You don't want to be in the middle of things when we take this down."

A radio crackled. Surveillance people told me that our subjects were now in front of the high-rise. Then they said that the team's vision was blocked, but it appeared as if some of the bad guys had left their vehicle and gone into the building. Our case agents had wired our informant with a pager that was, in reality, a transmitter. Over the radio channel dedicated to the mock pager, my boss and I could hear muffled voices, then rustling clothes and footsteps up a hollow stairwell.

"Damn. He must have gone in with them!" I blurted.

My boss asked, "How could that be? He was told not to, wasn't he?"

"Well, sir, you try to prepare for every possibility, but sometimes you just can't control what happens."

The surveillance team reported, "We don't see him in the car."

My boss told me to circle the area. I could tell he was getting nervous, probably thinking this operation could damage his career and he had hardly begun to set up his new corner office. "Ray, this informant is not an agent. He's just a civilian. He could be in real danger, and we're responsible for him. We have to take this down."

"Boss, give this a minute more. We have the apartment wired with closed-circuit TV. Let's take a look and see if the informant is really with them."

"No, I want this taken down now!"

My radio crackled, "This is Mulligan. We're going in."

"No, you are not!"

Over the radio I heard a loud noise, followed immediately by shouting. Then alarms began reverberating throughout the high-rise. People gathered on the street to gawk and speculate at the bedlam as police and fire sirens wailed. I now knew that the loud noise I heard over my radio was a flash bang someone had tossed into the apartment without my authorization. It had triggered the building's fire alarm system, and every surrounding precinct was responding.

My cell phone rang. "Yeah."

"Hey, boss, this is Mulligan. We're in the apartment, and we got some news for you."

"What is it?"

"Well, I've got bad news and really bad news."

"Give me the really bad news first."

"We can't find the informant or the twenty thousand dollars in show money we left in the room. Oh, and one of them dove through the window when we flash banged the room."

"Is there a fire escape?"

"No, he went right through the window. We're seven floors up, and there is nothing in-between him and the concrete."

The informant was gone, twenty thousand dollars of government money was missing, one of the criminals probably killed himself, and we had pissed off every police precinct and firehouse in northern Manhattan. Even though my boss was ready to explode, at that moment I couldn't worry about his career or, for that matter, mine. "Send some men down to the alley. Let's find the body, and have everyone else scour the building for the informant."

Within minutes, I got the report, "There is nobody here."

"You're telling me this guy leaped out of a seventh-story window and disappeared?"

"I don't know what to tell you, but we can't find him. We'll fan out."

There was a serious air of tension in my car by this time. Up to this point, I had been too preoccupied to notice, but my boss was beginning to collect himself, and I was sure he was getting ready to channel his rage at me. The cacophony of multiple emergency responder sirens was tapering off. Fire engines crowded the boulevard in front of our building, and police cruisers had cordoned off the area.

Then we heard, "Boss, this is Steve. We found the cash, and the surveillance people have located the informant."

The Dominicans had taken the informant's transmitter upstairs with them and had left him in the car. He had hunkered down out of sight, hoping to survive the brawl he knew was coming.

Then another transmission: "Boss, this is Murphy. We found the bad guy who tried to fly."

"Where was he?"

"An ambulance driver happened to be cruising by a block away when he noticed this guy crawling up the sidewalk with a couple of broken legs. Our boy tried to claim he tripped over a garbage can, but the driver figured it might have something to do with the police activity that's going on here."

In a flash, we had gone from goats to good guys in our new boss's eyes. He was on the phone, proudly reporting our success to the new assistant director of the New York office. I never knew how the coin would land, but whenever things began to unravel, I knew it was best to take a deep breath, clear my head, and focus.

Driving home late that night, I had a curious thought. These big, bad push-in robbers from upper Manhattan weren't so big and bad when they had to deal with someone their own size. A couple of years earlier, one had committed suicide by diving into the Harlem River when we cornered him. Now another had tried to kill himself by jumping out a seventh-story window during our raid. Maybe the answer was in the nature of what they did, posing as cops and beating up the weak and the elderly? Then I reminded myself, they were just classic bullies who didn't like it when someone hit back.

▪ ▪ ▪

There was always plenty of work for my squad. One of the more traditional SWAT team roles in the bureau is to protect VIPs. Again, it seemed as if management just assumed there was little we couldn't do. A job that involved breaking down doors with rams, then wrestling bad guys to the ground before they could get to their guns wasn't exactly the same as wearing our best suits, keeping our calm while driving through horrible traffic, and holding the door for some important person who barely acknowledged our existence. The common denominator was that we were a close group, proud of our performance. We ate up any challenge as if it was cereal, and the bosses knew it.

We provided security for important persons just as the Secret Service does for the president and vice president. A typical security detail in the boroughs of New York City would require somewhere around a dozen men during the day and only two or three after the "package" went to bed. I had almost fifty men on the roster, but at any one time a dozen might be committed to trials or critical casework. Then I might have another group doing surveys, or checking out locations, for pending arrests. So usually I would have to juggle two dozen operators so that we could cover twelve-hour shifts for two and sometimes three days.

When we were out on the street running our VIP motorcade, I would always deploy a vehicle with two advance men who would check out our next destination and warn us of any traffic or parking issues. They would go into restaurants and other destinations before we arrived with the VIP and his or her entourage. I was in charge but couldn't be there 24/7, so I would try to be present when the schedule was the most demanding. At other times, I would assign one of my senior SWAT guys, usually a squad or section leader, to take charge.

These jobs were lose-lose assignments. Most dignitaries assumed that government employees existed to satisfy their every whim, so they considered it routine if we whisked them all over Manhattan and the metropolitan airports without delay or discomfort. If we did everything perfectly, the VIP wouldn't complain, and the bosses generally heard nothing. But if one thing went wrong, if one street was suddenly blocked because of an unforeseen emergency and our package fell just a little behind schedule, we could count on our boss getting an earful. Aside from the chance to wear dark suits, lapel pins, and telltale ear mikes and to stand in the back of fancy Manhattan restaurants, watching the important people dine, we didn't enjoy these assignments. However, we never dropped the ball.

We protected Attorney General John Ashcroft, a true politician who wouldn't miss a chance to kiss a baby or shake a hand. He likened himself to Harry Truman, both being from the Show Me state of Missouri and both self-reliant, independent, and fundamentalist God-fearing men. Ashcroft had a reputation among his staff and others who worked around him for also being thrifty. He always seemed to be distracted whenever the dinner bill arrived. He was a decent man, however, who appeared out of his element in New York City.

I remember the day we took him to David Letterman's set to tape a show. I was a little apprehensive, knowing that Letterman liked to toy with guests and that the AG was a little naive, especially about New Yorkers. As I stood just behind the stage curtain, I could hear Letterman ask the AG about his musical talent. Ashcroft was an excellent pianist, another similarity to President Truman. Letterman began to coax the AG to sing a patriotic ditty that he had written titled "Let the Eagle Soar." In typical Letterman fashion, he kept goading him to play and sing the song. I breathed a sigh of relief when, at the very last second, Ashcroft appeared to get what was happening and declined to sing.

▪   ▪   ▪

On a number of occasions we were ordered to escort the UN Special Prosecutor for War Crimes Carla Del Ponte. She was the chief prosecutor in the trial of former Serbian leader Slobodan Milosevic. We particularly disliked the assignment, but she was a friend of then FBI director Louis Freeh, so we couldn't complain. She'd worked with Freeh on the Pizza Connection case when he was an AUSA. Daily, she would pick up the phone in my presence and call the director. It was her way of saying that we'd better give her what she wanted or else. She looked down her nose at us as knuckle-dragging security lackeys. The United Nations provided her with Swiss bodyguards to accom-

New York SWAT security detail with Attorney General John Ashcroft.

pany her wherever she went. She had received death threats from Milosevic's supporters. The bodyguards were good men and appreciated our help. She didn't. Her bodyguards would arrive armed, and I'd invariably have to pull them out of a lockup at Kennedy Airport. No matter how I prepared the Port Authority police and the U.S. Customs inspectors, word never got through to the right people, and they'd detain our Swiss friends while Madame ranted and raved about our incompetence. It was always a security nightmare, and I was responsible for all of it.

Madame would arrive at her hotel, and it usually only took a few moments before she would look at me quizzically and say, "Hmmm, now what do I want to do tonight?" She'd continue, "I must see a play. What is good?"

I always knew what was coming, so I planned for it. Fortunately, my friend was the concierge at the special prosecutor's hotel of choice and would arrange prime seats for Madame within minutes. We would then "red light" Madame and her staff, which included her executive assistant, one or two other administrative types, and her security guards, to the play. After depositing her at the theater, one of my men and I would wait outside with her Swiss guards, enjoying the break and taking in the sights of Broadway. I tried to savor the respite, but it was almost always short lived. Most of the time, her highness would become bored and would walk out early, thinking aloud again, "Hmmm, now what do I want to do?"

After three days of squiring her to meetings at the UN, lingerie shopping, and long dinners at swank places, my jaw would hurt from gritting my teeth. It was a great relief when we could finally deposit her back at the airport. My only satisfaction throughout the assignment was that my men performed as true professionals. They always made the FBI look good.

Then there was "Number One." FBI directors have their own full-time security detail based out of headquarters. Director Mueller would usually bring the detail supervisor and one or two of his men when he visited New York City. Our SWAT team then provided the bulk of the security detail. There is no question that some of my men looked forward to being around the director. Agents are not immune to the lure of celebrity. As for me, I could have lived without it.

FBI Director Robert S. Mueller III, a decorated Vietnam War veteran, is taciturn and serious—a no-nonsense person. He was always cordial and would shake my hand, but he wasn't much on small talk. We got him around town and made sure nobody got too close. Always punctual and professional, we worked well with his staff and protection detail. We always reviewed his itinerary in advance, and my men would reconnoiter all routes and locations the day before he arrived. If we had failed to anticipate the inevitable traffic tie-up in Manhattan or if one of our lead or chase cars was in a collision, Director Mueller would have had a front seat. When he boarded the bureau helicopter at the South Street heliport to catch his return flight to headquarters, I could feel that hundred-pound sack on my shoulders get lighter as the Huey grew smaller over the harbor.

▪　▪　▪

The New York team's size and structure changed over the years. When I came on board, there were three separate teams: New Rochelle, Manhattan, and Brooklyn-Queens. Each had about fifteen men, give or take. Everyone had two jobs—the regular bureau job and the SWAT team responsibility.

Clint Guenther was the Manhattan team leader when I joined. Mike Henehan, one of the original apprehension team members, had appointed Clint to take over Manhattan when Mike decided to call it a day. When Clint retired, Kirby Scott became the head of the Manhattan team. Under Kirby, and Geoff, the new coordinator and my C-25 supervisor, the three teams were reorganized into two sections—blue and gold. Kirby appointed me blue section leader, responsible for approximately twenty-three men. Every second month, each section served as the primary response element. Usually that rotation worked; however, if a major takedown arose or multiple SWAT team–supported arrests occurred at the same time, the stand-down section was called out. The whole SWAT team numbered approximately forty-five to forty-eight men, supported by medics and communications technicians.

Just as the nature of the threat confronting America was expanding, so were the mission of the FBI and the responsibilities of field SWAT teams. As the year 2000 (Y2K) approached, everyone was spinning over the cyber threats that terrorists and kooks proclaimed would rain down like Armageddon. American security organizations prepared for predicted problems associated with Y2K and warnings of an imminent al Qaeda attack. Senior policymakers—the National Security Council, the Joint Chiefs of Staff, and the White House staff—who were privy to information they couldn't share with people on my level had concluded that there would be an attack against America somewhere in the world, if not at home. Highly sensitive information, such as overseas numbers derived through the National Security Agency's monitoring, information from foreign intelligence services, or human sources in dangerous and sensitive places, was shared with few people below the director's level. In the New York office, only the top managers, people such as John O'Neill and certain case agents working the specific threat, would be informed. The rest of us just read about it in the newspapers or sensed something was up when we noticed an unusual number of closed-door meetings taking place and the bosses wearing serious expressions.

Since the New York office owned the al Qaeda investigation, the SWAT team was directed to send two members to Ramstein, Germany, the headquarters for U.S. Air Forces in Europe, where they would serve on the Federal Emergency Support Team (FEST), which would stage there. If there were a terrorist attack as the millennium dawned anywhere outside the United

States, the FEST (subject to the host country's consent) would deploy from Ramstein to the attack site. The FEST would set up a command post there and pave the way for an incoming RDT.

At that point the newly formed RDTs were stationed in four major field offices: New York, Miami, Washington, and Los Angeles. My former team leader, Clint Guenther, who was managing New York's RDT program, and I were selected to represent the New York office. With close to ninety other government personnel, we departed from Andrews Air Force Base in Maryland on a fully loaded C-5 shortly before Christmas 1999. It was clear to us that something big was brewing. Being part of the lead element, we were assigned to prepare for a response to a terrorist attack. Once on site, we were to assess the situation and define for our bosses back in New York how the RDT should be configured for a deployment to our location, wherever that might end up being. I had to pack for any kind of climate.

On arrival at Ramstein Air Base, the FEST took over an entire three-story barracks. Each organization set up its own command post and maintained constant contact with its home office over the next two weeks. Several agents from HQ and an agent from the FBI's Critical Incident Response Group (CIRG) based in Quantico joined Clint and me. Germany was dark and cold, and it felt as if the sun would never appear. As New Year's Eve approached, we sat glued to the television and our radios, watching as midnight arrived hour by hour around the globe. It was a great relief when morning came on the West Coast of the United States and we realized we had dodged the bullet. We would find out soon enough how close we had come to deploying.

We would shortly learn that just before the millennium, an alert U.S. Customs agent had grabbed an Algerian named Ahmed Ressam at Washington State's border with Canada. The agent sensed something was wrong when Ressam began to perspire under routine questioning. When she looked in the trunk of his car, she discovered bomb-making material—he was planning to bomb Los Angeles International Airport on the millennium—along with a windfall of "pocket litter" that helped the bureau identify his accomplices in Canada and Brooklyn. When Clint and I left for Ramstein, the New York office was already swarming the identified Brooklyn location. On December 30, New York SWAT, supporting the FBI-led Joint Terrorism Task Force, was at the Brooklyn apartment of Ressam's accomplice, Mokhtar Abdelghani

Meskini. Kirby Scott gave the green light for the breachers to take down the door. My old friend Paul Sutherland was one of the first agents into the apartment at 944 Newkirk Avenue and stopped Meskini before he could destroy incriminating evidence. Meskini turned out to be a member of the Algerian terrorist organization called the Armed Islamic Group and had trained in Afghanistan with al Qaeda. Four Middle Eastern males were taken into custody. While two were released later, Meskini turned out to be a key facilitator for Ressam. His job was to supply the bomber with false documents, a cell phone, and transportation after he had attacked the airport. Meskini eventually cooperated against Ressam, who was sentenced to life in prison.

Little known to most of the world, other dangerous millennium plots had been afoot. In late December, terrorist plans to create mayhem in the Middle East went awry owing to a combination of great investigative work and luck. A plot to destroy hotels in Amman, Jordan, and Tel Aviv, Israel, had been disrupted with the assistance of the CIA and the FBI. An attempt to critically damage a U.S. warship, the USS *The Sullivans*, in the distant harbor of Aden, Yemen, had failed after the near sinking of the suicide attack boat in rough water.

Storm clouds were gathering everywhere. Only a few knew the extent of the danger and how vulnerable America was. I was not one of the few, yet.

Twelve

The USS *Cole*

Almost two years had passed since the destruction of our embassies in Nairobi and Dar es Salaam, and we were settling back into chasing regular criminals. It was a good October morning, not too cold, yet crisp, and cloudless in the Hudson River Valley.

Good weather means a good day for training. The team was at firearms practice when we received the early reports. We heard that terrorists had driven an explosive-laden boat alongside a U.S. Navy vessel moored in the Yemeni port of Aden, nearly sinking our warship and killing seventeen sailors. I wondered why anyone would detest America enough to plan and execute a complex attack in such an obscure corner of the world. I still did not fully appreciate the deep hatred that Osama bin Laden and his followers harbored against the West. Bin Laden's name had surfaced numerous times in connection with failed and successful attacks during the 1990s, but with the exception of a committed group of New York terrorism investigators, the rest of us were going about our routine business. "The Base" was the last thing on our collective minds. Sure, we knew about Ramzi Yousef, who had had a role in some faraway plot to take down airliners over the Pacific, but we still believed that the World Trade Center and Landmarks plotters were just a group of disgruntled immigrants who hated us because they didn't feel as if they fit in. Not until the 1998 embassy bombings in Africa did we get a good handle on bin Laden and al Qaeda. They had failed in their 2000 attack on the USS *The Sullivans* but succeeded less than a year later in damaging the *Cole*. That attack showed us just how big a problem we faced.

Within two days, SAC John O'Neill and a group of young investigators, an explosives forensic team from the lab at Quantico, and bureau scuba divers departed for Aden, along with virtually the entire FBI Hostage Rescue Team, in an ill-considered start to what would be a protracted and draining effort. Agents who had never deployed outside the United States were going to a Third World nation. I was baffled that the HRT was pegged to protect the New York investigative team, since New York SWAT had previously deployed for an extended period to Tanzania, where it had performed well, and the Thirteenth Marine Expeditionary Unit (MEU), which had trained and was equipped for just such a mission, was on its way to Aden. I arranged to have one of my men, Dan Fethiere, brief O'Neill and his people before they board-ed the military transport out of McGuire Air Force Base. A former ranger, Dan had participated in Operation Desert Storm and had some knowledge of Middle Eastern ways. He spoke passing Arabic, and that skill had landed him a position as an adviser and liaison to a Saudi Arabian infantry unit during the first Gulf War.

Dan admonished the young female agents, "You can't wear shorts or sleeveless blouses in Yemen, and do not sit so that the soles of your feet are exposed to a Middle Eastern man." He emphasized, "And whatever you do, do *not* use your left hand to shake with."

"Why?" asked one young female agent who could not have been much older than twenty-five.

"Because they don't have toilet paper in the desert, and they use only one hand in its place."

Dan had told me many stories that taught me not to make any assump-tions about the people from that part of the world. There was the one about the Saudi infantry unit he was with. "Even after all their training, they were incredibly bad shooters." Pride and keeping face are critical to Middle Eastern men. They will do most anything to protect it. When the Saudi general came to see how his troops had improved after their basic training, their American trainers had to do something to help them. "We planted remote-controlled explosives in the targets they were supposed to fire on and destroy, and once the drill began we detonated them to make it appear that the Saudi troops had their shit together."

We understood little about the culture, yet the FBI was ready to roll into Yemen with the equivalent of a heavily armed combat platoon. I wondered how NYPD commissioner Raymond Kelly would feel if the Saudis landed thirty or forty heavily armed Bedouin warriors in lower Manhattan after an attack against their mission to the United Nations.

When John and his team first arrived, the Yemeni government tried to hamstring the operation. Its representatives told the FBI to stand back and that they would interrogate the suspects and share any information they garnered with the FBI. Of course, John O'Neill wasn't going to buy that idea. John was used to getting his way, and he was furious. American kids were dead, and he was going to call the shots.

He was about to go a number of rounds with the U.S. ambassador to Yemen, Barbara Bodine. Ambassadors are the final American word wherever they serve. They do not accept another U.S. official telling them how things will happen within their principality, unless that official is the president or the secretary of state. Bodine would be no exception to the rule.

She had known O'Neill when both worked counterterrorism in Washington for their respective organizations. I think their animosity was deepseated and maybe personal. From where I sat, it smacked more of vendetta than mere rivalry.

Justifiably, Bodine seemed afraid the FBI would undermine her relationship with the Yemenis. In the ambassador's defense, more sensitivity would have helped the situation. When the first wave of FBI personnel disembarked from their military transport in Aden, the tone was set. Heavily armed, the bureau's contingent joined with the already present MEU to secure the damaged USS *Cole*, conduct a massive crime scene investigation, and lay out demands. The FBI asked the U.S. Embassy for assistance with matters vital to its investigation, such as entrée to specific sites, access to particular Yemeni citizens for interview purposes, setting up secure locations for communications, obtaining translators, safe lodging, transportation, other logistical support, and so forth. It was the embassy's job to line it up or procure it for us. South Yemen had not seen such an invading force since North Yemen and Osama bin Laden overran the region. It was overkill. To make matters even worse,

South Yemen had been under the Soviet sphere of influence for many years. Every Yemeni official from that region was sure that America had a bigger agenda than just solving a major crime.

During the 1960s and '70s, Moscow brought many Indian Ocean states, including South Yemen, under its umbrella. The Soviets wanted to build a presence there to gain control of the Indian Ocean. Pursuing an alliance with South Yemen allowed them to secure a crucial fueling and supply port in Aden's harbor. From there, they could also more easily monitor the movement of U.S. and allied shipping through the Suez Canal.

Although the Yemeni civil war ended with the defeat of Soviet-controlled South Yemen, many Yemeni communist sympathizers, trained by the KGB to spy and counterspy, remained. It was not a healthy environment when the FBI arrived. Some Yemeni officers undoubtedly believed that the Americans, just as the Soviets had, wanted to control Yemen, while others saw us as non-Muslim infidels. Then, of course, there were many within the government who were outright supporters of al Qaeda.

Several weeks after its arrival, the HRT decided it had more important things to do and began packing up to leave. Other than a courageous effort by the evidence response people under harsh conditions, the balance of the O'Neill team had made little progress in the six weeks since its arrival.

Back in New York, I got the call from my boss. "HRT is packing up. You need to get some SWAT people ready and head for Yemen," he said, as if this mission was little more than a trip to New Jersey.

I asked, "Oh, so the entire HRT contingent, all fifty-five, is leaving? How many can I bring in to replace them?"

"Ambassador Bodine won't let you bring in more than three. I was also told to let you know that she doesn't like weapons or at least Americans with weapons."

We were going from the HRT's small army to three SWAT people protecting the bureau's investigation. Either the threat picture had dramatically changed or someone figured New York SWAT was one helluva team!

My small contingent married up with Jay, the new FBI on-scene commander, and several fresh terrorism investigators and arrived in Aden after a two-day flight on the bureau's G-5 jet. From the air, the port looked almost as if it were in the Caribbean, but as the G-5 descended, I could make out the relatively primitive state of Yemen's most important southern city.

On the beach of the port of Aden, where the failed attack on the USS The Sullivans occurred.

The first day, Carlos, one of my young but reliable people and a former Marine, met with the captain in charge of the thirty-man MEU element. The Marines patrolled in and around the hotel proper, but they had received strict orders from the ambassador not to leave the hotel grounds. We were on our own when we ventured outside the hotel's perimeter. The ambassador had reassured the Yemenis that we would respect their sovereignty. She faced a difficult balancing act trying to do her job of keeping the admittedly dysfunctional relationship between Yemen and the United States alive while also attempting to assist the Department of Justice and the FBI in solving the murder of seventeen American sailors. She knew better than anyone that the odds were virtually nonexistent that President Ali Abdullah Saleh would allow any Yemeni citizen to be taken and tried in a U.S. court or that Yemen would mete out any real justice to its own. But she was under pressure from Washington, and she had to at least give the appearance of helping O'Neill and the FBI investigate the attack.

Threat intelligence spiked routinely while we operated in Aden. We received word that terrorists planned to crash one or more VBIEDs into our motorcade during our daily run to interrogate prisoners at the Yemeni Politi-

Author overlooking the port of Aden, where the USS Cole *was struck.*

cal Security Office (PSO), which was somewhat akin to a combination of the FBI and the CIA. Our hotel was also a likely target. The Gold Mohur Hotel had been attacked years before when U.S. Marines stayed there temporarily on their way to Beirut. In emblematic Yemeni terrorist fashion, they had launched a suicide attack the day after the Marines left and no Americans died. Here we were, though, offering these idiots another chance at us. We sealed and guarded every entrance and stationed Marines on the roof with sniper rifles. We made an attractive target because every major U.S. intelligence agency had people in the hotel: the FBI, the CIA, the State Department, and a few other U.S. organizations that would deny having been there. The place was a security nightmare, and destroying it would have been a major coup for al Qaeda.

Despite the ambassador's edict against any U.S. military leaving the hotel grounds and her overriding concern about insulting the Yemenis, I worked something out with the Marine captain. We set up a radio check system so we could communicate with the Marines at predetermined, coded points along our daily routes. The captain assured me that the Marines would support us in an ambush. I knew their word was good.

▪ ▪ ▪

We hired four drivers from northern Yemen. The State Department had made some effort to check them out, though I cannot attest to the level of the vetting process. How could we run any kind of inquiry on a native in Yemen other than to check with a few people he might have worked for? We put our lives in the hands of four smiling Yemenis who, for all we knew, were second cousins of Osama bin Laden's dad.

They drove four unarmored, or "soft," SUVs, which constituted our motorcade when we traveled through town to reach the interrogation site. When running the motorcade through tunnels the Russians had helped carve through the mountains, we were sitting ducks for an ambush. Alternate routes were indirect and still treacherous, snaking through small towns and congested marketplaces, where we were greeted with glares.

I instructed our driver, "If we are ambushed, I want you to drive straight through at full speed. Don't brake. Just go. If the road is blocked, I want you to make a three-point turn and get our asses out of there as fast as you can."

Our drivers were from the far north of Yemen and appeared to be entrepreneurs with a history as tour guides. They were relaxed about their Muslim faith, even smoking cigarettes. They joked and laughed. They appeared to enjoy and value life. I did not sense any feeling of resentment or anger, and I relied upon the instincts I had developed over years of investigating criminals. I made a calculated guess that these fellas didn't want to die any more than we did. On top of that, I always followed my "miner's canary" rule when I placed myself in the hands of a foreigner in his own land: locals, or those who live among the locals, as our men did, will have their ears to the ground better than any intelligence service could. If our regular drivers became nervous, appeared distracted, or became suddenly "sick" and didn't appear for work one day, or if the local police abruptly disappeared from the streets, or if the coffee shops were unusually empty, then it was time to take the day off.

Under the guise of offering us protection, the Yemeni troops surrounding our hotel kept an eye on our movements. Just like most of their male countrymen, including President Saleh, the Yemeni guards chewed khat every afternoon. A mountain-grown plant with a drug-like effect, it has replaced Yemen's once proud coffee industry as the primary, if not only, agricultural product. Although khat is classified as a stimulant, the chronic user becomes

The author (far left) in Aden with his security team. Al Qaeda in Yemen terrorists attacked this very spot in 2010.

extremely lethargic after developing a tolerance, which is just the posture we wanted our security force to assume when terrorists were stalking us with big bombs! It wasn't uncommon to find our checkpoint guards sitting in chairs with their chins resting on the muzzles of their AK-47s, their eyes closed, and their cheeks bulging with khat while the juice dribbled down their chins.

After a bomb exploded near a church only a mile from our hotel, we supplemented our perimeter defenses with a bomb-sniffing dog. The handsome, big-boned German shepherd was inseparable from his U.S. Navy explosive ordnance disposal (EOD) handler. Anytime a vehicle drove within the perimeter, the dog investigated. It was comforting to watch that animal work. One night a delivery truck arrived right after a shift change, and the handler, following protocol, approached the truck with the dog. The Yemeni officer on guard, who was new to us, became indignant and started yelling at our man, refusing to allow the dog to check the vehicle. The handler responded, "The vehicle is not coming in," and a screaming match erupted. The Yemeni officer shouted something, and suddenly a crew-served machine gun mounted on a nearby truck spun around and threatened the handler. All the nearby Yemeni guards came alive and raised their weapons, ready to open fire at the slightest provocation.

Someone interceded at the last minute, but the Marine sniper with the night vision scope on the hotel roof later told me, "I had put my crosshairs on the Yemeni machine gunner, and if his muzzle had moved another six inches, I would have killed him." Had that happened, we would have had a firefight that would have resembled Beirut during its civil war. The Yemenis had machine guns mounted on trucks all around us, ostensibly for our defense; however, the guns always faced us.

Moments of levity occasionally relieved the pervasive tension. One day the regional security officer told us that the Yemenis had found a body in the harbor that appeared to be Caucasian. I was directed to take a team and investigate, so I gathered our two medics and my two SWAT guys and headed to the coroner's office in downtown Aden. We arrived to find a small crowd gathered at the entrance of a dilapidated building. It smelled of a trap, and I warned my guys to look out for an ambush. "OK, you have thirty minutes to do what you need to do, then get your tails out here fast." We tried to blend in, but that wasn't going to happen as the medics climbed into protective gear that included special gloves, masks, and Tyvek suits. Just then, a man in a T-shirt, old shorts, and sandals came out of the building. Apparently, he was the coroner. Looking something like Mohandas Gandhi, the thin man watched the medics prepping themselves and walked back inside. Moments afterward, he reappeared wearing a light blue pair of latex dishwashing gloves.

Approximately thirty minutes later, our two medics reappeared. One had turned ashen gray. "Hey, you OK?"

"Whoa, I'm about ready to blow my cookies!"

"What happened?"

"Well, the crypt keeper there tried to be helpful. The torso has been feeding the fish for more than a few days, and it is a mess! We got some photos of a tattoo—looks Cyrillic—and then we asked to see the back of the body. Well, our coroner back there reaches on to the table and grabs this rotten mess in a bear hug, like he's gettin' ready to dance. He flops it over, and parts splatter everywhere!" I don't recall seeing either one of the medics at chow that night

Then there were the infamous "shower cobra" stories. Our hotel had its own power generator, a huge diesel monster that kicked in sporadically. It was so powerful that we could hear or feel its ominous sound whenever it started, no matter where we were in the hotel. The hotel's water pressure spiked

I knew the U.S. Marine Corps force protection in Aden wouldn't leave us stranded.

within thirty seconds of the engine starting. We learned soon enough that if we were in the shower when the generator turned on we'd better stay clear of the showerhead. As in most European or Middle Eastern countries, the shower hose was mounted high on the wall and we could remove and hold it in our hand. Nobody warned new arrivals about the shower cobra. Everyone let them learn for themselves.

I was introduced to it the day I arrived in Aden. Anxious for a hot shower after a long, hard trip, I had just lathered my hair when I heard a humming sound, which quickly transitioned into a squeal. Suddenly, the hose with its heavy metal showerhead lurched free of its mooring and began to thrash wildly about the bathroom. It smacked me in the forehead, causing me to tumble backward and out onto the floor. I went down to dinner that night with a red welt on my head. As one veteran walked past for a second serving, he muttered, "Met the cobra, huh?"

▪   ▪   ▪

It took the FBI a long time to undo the damage caused by our initially heavy-handed response to the attack on the *Cole*. Once everyone lowered their weapons, the bureau's next challenge was to collect evidence at the crime scene. We sent divers to the bottom of the Bay of Aden to find what was left of the attack boat and its crew and interviewed available witnesses. Afterward, the investigation expanded to include nurturing a relationship with the Yemeni investigators that, after many months, had slowly begun to swing away from outright enmity.

In time, thanks to the skills and professionalism of both FBI and Naval Criminal Investigative Service (NCIS) investigators, we made some progress. Most of the remaining tension came from Ambassador Bodine's continual intrusions. Of course, she wanted to be the one to feed details of our progress to Washington and to be able to call the State Department and relay to the secretary, "We made a major breakthrough. We identified one of the key conspirators." Then when things had started to settle down, she insisted both that the FBI pass every interview question through her people and that the Yemenis have control over the content and style of the questioning. John O'Neill, having returned to New York, could not abide it. When he threatened to return, Ambassador Bodine blocked him, declaring him persona non grata on the basis that he was disruptive and interfering with the State Department's work in Yemen. For the first time in U.S. history, an American ambassador had barred an FBI official from a foreign country. I had moved on to the graduate school of egos and turf wars.

The ambassador was determined to micromanage the bureau at every turn. She finally stopped insisting her people be present during all interviews when we reminded her that those employees would have to testify in any ensuing trials. Having lost that battle, she worked harder to drive us mad over the smallest of issues. Her "spies" would report us if a gust of wind tossed our shirts open and revealed our holstered handguns. She was outraged that we would expose our weapons in public, even though the locals routinely carried AK-47s and sported the large Yemeni knife, the *jimbaya*, on their belts. We would wrap our M4s in small carpets or towels every time we climbed in and out of our vehicles in order not to "offend the sensibilities of the Yemeni people."

After my return to the States I received a call from my boss that one of our replacements had been accused of sexual harassment by one of the female State Department employees working in Aden. I was called in to a video-conference later that day between John O'Neill and the FBI on-scene commander in Aden.

The senior agent informed John that the ambassador was flying down from Sana'a, the capital, to take a statement from her female employee concerning the agent's alleged conduct.

"What do you mean, 'Bodine is flying down from Sana'a tonight'?" John blurted.

"She says she wants to take his statement regarding a sexual harassment complaint one of her people has filed against him."

John roared, "That broad runs around playing volleyball with a bunch of sex-starved Marines and agents in her short shorts, and she wants to file a complaint against one of my guys for showing his tan line? Tell him I want him on the next plane out of Yemen."

The FBI was in Aden for the better part of six months, working the investigation side by side with NCIS. New York SWAT team members rotated in and out every couple of months, providing protection for all the team's vehicles that traveled outside the hotel that served as our compound. Months into the deployment, additional information substantiated that we were at risk in Aden. This development gave Bodine the excuse she needed to insist that we relocate. She now had a pretext to move our team to Sana'a. Once in the north, far from the crime scene in Aden, she would have an easier time watching over the FBI's every move. With her hovering over our investigators and attempting to manage our movements, the FBI's position became untenable. We decided we were wasting our effort in Yemen as long as Ambassador Bodine was there. In the spring of 2001, we pulled everyone back home, ostensibly because of the elevated threat level; however, the ambassador was the reason we left. We promised ourselves we would return as soon as her tour was over.

We did not leave empty handed, though. Our investigators had developed good intelligence and many leads. There was evidence that the attack had been planned and directed from outside Yemen and that some threat intelligence had been previously received that indicated U.S. ships entering Aden's harbor were in danger. Someone then chose to ignore that intelligence, and someone had directed the USS *Cole* to refuel there on that fateful day in October 2000. Whether the decision was made based on a desire to pump

My wife and I by New York harbor on a beautiful day.

money into the Yemeni economy is unclear; however, within only a few short months of our temporary departure from Yemen, we would learn just how shortsighted our government institutions had become and how costly our refusal to heed the obvious warnings would be.

Thirteen

Yemen and 9/11

The call to morning prayer rose over Sana'a in northern Yemen. A rolling chant competing for Allah's ear erupted from the countless mosques, a cacophony reminding believers of their primary obligation. The early morning breeze transported the first of five prayers that would flood the room daily. In this part of the world, not much had changed in fifteen hundred years. In the bed next to mine, another agent snored with a rhythm of his own.

It was late August 2001, and the FBI was back in Yemen after a three-month hiatus. When Ambassador Bodine's tour ended, John O'Neill sent us back to restart the USS *Cole* investigation. Edmund Hull would replace Bodine and would arrive in September. While we knew little about him, we assumed that after Bodine we could work with anyone.

The day Bodine left, our plane touched down in Sana'a. My entire team of sixteen—investigators, case agents, and SWAT operators—flew in on the bureau's Gulfstream V. We connected with our new State Department Diplomatic Security (DS) partners. I was the FBI's second in command and shared responsibility for our team's protection with a senior DS agent named Gunner.

Dan Fethiere was my number two. I picked him from among forty-eight agents because he was one of my best men and his knowledge of Arabic would prove invaluable. Another more critical reason was that Dan was rock solid, someone who would not place his partner at risk.

My boss John O'Neill and I at his retirement luncheon. Two weeks later, on 9/11, he would die in the World Trade Center.

One of the four FBI case agents was Ali Soufan, a handsome and charming Lebanese Muslim who was wise beyond his years. He was one of O'Neill's protégés. John had spotted him soon after his arrival in New York and recognized his talents. John was perceptive enough to take Ali under his wing immediately, to the consternation of others who envied Ali's instant stardom or who wished they could draw on Ali's considerable abilities.

Ali had played a major role in helping the Jordanians disrupt the millennium terrorist plot to blow up hotels, border crossings, and Christian holy sites throughout the region. He had accompanied Jordanian security agents on a raid of a farm in search of bomb-making material. Ali had located a stockpile of fifty-two hundred pounds of nitric acid stored in the basement of a farmhouse and explained to the agents that it was the principal ingredient of one type of powerful bomb. Rapidly, his skills became nearly legendary.

His work ethic was amazing. He was akin to a bloodhound on a trail, working until he was ready to collapse. Ali and I did not know each other well since our careers, up to this point, had taken us down different paths. Now we would become close allies and friends.

The threat level had remained extremely high since our last time in Yemen, so I wanted to set up our living space with optimal protection. First, I would have to come to terms with Gunner. The State Department technically has first say about security arrangements for any American overseas. A DS expert who had been sent ahead to ensure our security had not done his homework. Since the charge d'affaires was not inclined to find space for us inside the embassy compound, the security expert planned to put us in a block of rooms in the only Western hotel in town, the Sana'a Sheraton. Weeks before our arrival, DS sent us the security plan, including photos of our rooms' locations. I read the plan and took one look at the photos before storming into the assistant director's office. "Sir, I wouldn't use this plan for toilet paper. I was in Nairobi and Dar es Salaam, sir, and I've seen what a truck bomb can do to a large building. If you look at these photos, they've placed our entire team in the rooms immediately above the truck loading dock, and that's just the beginning."

I told him that I alone was responsible for bringing all my people safely home. I respectfully drove home the point that he, my boss, would be the one who would deliver bad news to my team's families if things went awry, so we should control our own security destiny while in Sana'a. He understood and gave me his full support. I arranged a meeting in Washington, with the head of the State Department's Diplomatic Security Service.

I brought Dan along to the meeting. Accompanied by an FBI HQ terrorism boss and in a room full of State Department people, I laid out my analysis of the DS security plan point by point, identifying the problems.

When I was done, the DS boss looked over at me and commented, "You present some pretty good arguments, Agent Holcomb. Are you a lawyer or something?"

"Yes, sir, I am, but I don't like to admit it."

"OK, I think we can work through your issues. You will have equal authority over security matters in conjunction with our senior agent on scene."

Dan and I left the meeting and met an agent who had driven up from Quantico with a box full of Glock pistols with extra magazines, ammunition, holsters, and magazine pouches. We had requisitioned enough weaponry to outfit everyone with the latest bureau-issued 9mm. I was adamant that everyone in our party had to carry the same gun for complete interoperability of ammunition and parts. We headed back to New York with our truckload of supplies and the agreement we wanted.

Tim, an experienced assistant special agent in charge (ASAC) who understood management's ways, headed our team. Following last-minute briefings with Assistant Director Barry Mawn and SAC O'Neill, we left New York on August 28, 2001. After an overnight in Athens, we landed in Sana'a on August 30 and immediately had to deal with a confused Yemeni customs official. To be fair, no customs official at any nation's border would have known what to do with a bunch of heavily armed foreign officials. Although the issue had purportedly been resolved days in advance, I was not in the least surprised that we were having a problem. The senior customs official had a heated discussion with the native Yemeni facilitator the U.S. Embassy had sent to make our entrance as easy as possible. We were allowed to bring our pistols, M4 semi automatic rifles, and thousands of rounds of ammunition into Yemen; however, we had to leave our four handheld walkie-talkies with the official, who would seek further direction from his superiors. OK, I thought, that was not a bad deal. We'll keep the guns, and the Yemenis can hold on to our radios for a while. We drove to the Sana'a Sheraton, which was a short walk from the U.S. Embassy.

Following my instructions, the DS expert booked a floor of a wing farthest from the hotel's loading dock and front entrance. Even a massive truck bomb could not reach our rooms with deadly effect. The first day, Dan and I walked the grounds, paying particular attention to a delivery gate. The pole of the security gate pointed straight into the air, and an elderly Yemeni sitting barefoot in a nearby chair let every truck enter without inspection. I thought, This is not going to work.

"Dan, can you ask this guy why the gate is not lowered?"

"I'll try." Dan did his best, and after a stuttering but highly animated exchange, he said, "He says he has no rope to pull the gate down."

I needed to recalibrate my thinking. I sent an embassy employee out on the local market to buy durable nylon rope. With some effort and additional local security guards from the embassy, we soon had the hotel staff taking a much more serious approach to our safety. Every truck was being inspected, and we convinced FBI HQ to send us two bomb technicians to train the local security personnel in identifying VBIEDs. Until our arrival, the guards had been using flashlights and vehicle inspection mirrors to look for bombs under truck chassis, but we were more worried about big drums of diesel fuel and ammonium nitrate or Soviet-issued C-4 explosives. We brought in Jersey barriers that had been stockpiled by the embassy to form a serpentine approach to the hotel's main entrance, installed locks and closed-circuit cameras on all entry points to our hotel wing, fashioned a command post in one of our rooms, and established a communications plan with the embassy and its Marine security guard.

▪ ▪ ▪

Within two days of our arrival, we had created a reasonably secure base of operations. Yemeni security forces protected the hotel perimeter, and Gunner, my DS counterpart, and I developed relationships with the Yemeni officers. The DS group had only three veterans. The other four members were right out of college and seemed to be far more comfortable with a personal digital assistant (PDA) than with a weapon. Three of them were women. They got annoyed when I suggested that it might be wise to conceal their long hair when we were on the streets of Sana'a, one of the oldest cities on the Arabian Peninsula and where women wear traditional black cover and are never seen wielding weapons.

Since a Yemeni colonel from the PSO was in overall command of the host security force, I politely negotiated a joint security plan. I had seen how poorly prepared the Yemeni security forces were to handle a terrorist attack and concluded that we did not want their help defending against an attack should any of the bad guys gain entrance to our part of the building. On all matters of security, Dan and I worked closely together. I trusted his insight more than anyone else's. Sometimes we engaged Gunner. He was tough to deal with at first, but eventually we worked well together. We devised an intruder reaction plan for our little security element. In the event of an attack, an air horn alarm would trigger a series of maneuvers; those not on the reaction team would stay locked inside their rooms. Two-person teams would defend predetermined areas. No one would leave his or her room until we announced the code word for "all clear." We also developed a suspicious package procedure with the hotel staff to ensure that bombs were not delivered to our rooms.

Our security squad ran practice motorcades through the center of Yemen's crowded, ancient capital, settling on a number of possible routes to the Yemeni prison. All our routes were color coded, and we sent an advance car to scout ahead to ensure against surprise. If anything looked suspicious, our advance team would call out a new color, and we would adjust our route immediately. Yemen, the homeland of Osama bin Laden, was notorious for its cottage industry of kidnapping, as well as regular running gun battles between tribal fighters and government forces, so we had to be alert at all times.

Mid afternoon on September 11, after surveying alternative routes to the PSO prison, I sat down, exhausted, in our break room. I wanted to close my eyes, for I was still adjusting to the eight-hour time difference. I heard footsteps rushing down the hallway in my direction, then Dan's voice, "Turn the TV to BBC World, Ray! Something's happening in New York!" I flipped the channels until I saw the World Trade Center and the smoking black hole two-thirds up one of the towers. It was a clear day in New York, and I knew lower Manhattan well enough to realize this destruction had to be intentional. I couldn't tell how big it was and thought out loud, "Someone flying a small private plane committed suicide." Then the second plane blurred across the screen and slammed into the South Tower.

I prioritized my security concerns: Is this part of the world going to rise up en masse? Are there attacks planned throughout the Middle East? Where are my people? We need to get them back here immediately.

Initial reports were that forty-two thousand Americans were dead in the WTC and that another aircraft had hit the presidential retreat Camp David in Maryland. Tim, our on-scene commander, called the New York office. He was told that John O'Neill may have died in the attack. John had retired just days before we deployed to Yemen, and he had taken the job as head of security for the World Trade Center. The irony was almost impossible to grasp.

Hastily, the charge d'affaires called an emergency action committee meeting, in State Department parlance, and informed us that things were bad at home. His information was vague and turned out to be inaccurate, but we all knew that our situation in Yemen, a conservative Islamic state, was tenuous.

FBI Headquarters directed us to return to the States on the next flight out of Yemen, and the Yemenis promised us a military escort for the long ride to the airport early the next morning. I decided that we had to move our investigative team from the Sheraton into the U.S. Embassy. America had just been viciously attacked. No one knew the full extent of the damage yet. We would not allow those watching us to see any panic or fear. We would be calm and we would be deliberate. If we were to leave Yemen, it would not be as scared, retreating Americans but as Americans returning home to help our country recover.

We gathered our people inside the embassy. A very good guy, Tim had a tendency to be temperamental. With so much coming at him all at once, he directed me to get everyone over to the hotel so that they could gather their belongings and check out. I disagreed, arguing that only a few of us should return to the hotel under cover of darkness, pack up everyone's rooms, and pay all the bills. Otherwise, I explained, our withdrawal would look chaotic, draw attention to our large group, and possibly expose everyone to danger. We had a closed-door, heated discussion, and he saw my point of view. I said, "I'll take several of my men and the embassy truck back to the Sheraton after dark. We'll check everyone out and collect all their belongings, and we'll do it quietly."

Soon we learned that we wouldn't be able to move once it was dark after all. Tim received an urgent call to meet with Yemen's minister of the interior that evening. Our move would have to wait until after their gathering. We didn't know why the Yemenis wanted a meeting, but it wouldn't have mattered. We were, essentially, hostages in Yemen.

There was little conversation during the drive through old Sana'a. Everyone was thinking of home and what must be happening there. Sana'a is high in the mountains, and it had already begun to get cold. The town was bedecked with the Yemeni signature touch, strands of bright carnival lights hung from the buildings and over the bazaars, marking the start of the Muslim Eid ul-Fitr season. The lights, which contrasted starkly with the bleak buildings and landscape, reminded me of Christmas and had me wondering what the season would be like this year.

The streets were uncharacteristically vacant. My canary theory reminded me that it might be time to worry. We arrived at the fortresslike compound of the minister, our eyes trained on every rooftop. The Yemeni guards were nervous and kept fidgeting with their weapons.

The minister's aide greeted our team at the foot of the stairway. He motioned Tim, Steve, Robert, and Ali inside. Dan and two of the DS agents, who had accompanied us, took up positions around our vehicles. The Yemeni guards who encircled us, armed with AK-47s, were a handpicked hard bunch who belonged to the minister's tribe. All "big men" in Yemen and other Third World nations surround themselves with relatives. Yemen is as tribal as it was a thousand years ago, and just like the rest of that part of the world it will take another two hundred years to change that. A nation in name only, it is bound by largesse—hefty payouts and government construction projects that President Saleh doles out to the more cooperative tribal heads.

Suddenly there was a loud crack. I know the sound of gunfire and found cover at the base of the empty pool surrounding the courtyard fountain. In earlier trips to the palace, I had noted that the defunct fountain would make a good bunker. I always looked for and stored that kind of information. My gun's safety came off before I hit the ground. In these situations, calculated reasoning takes a hike, replaced by instinct and training, and I stepped outside of myself, watching potentially lethal events unfurl in slow motion. I didn't know who fired the shot or why and waited for the barrage to begin.

There was nothing after the crack but dead silence. I stole a look from my "foxhole" and saw that everyone had drawn down on everyone else. In what resembled a scene out of Quentin Tarantino's *Reservoir Dogs*, with guns pointed in every direction, bedlam seemed inescapable.

I don't know that I thought it through, but I let out a huge bellow of a laugh followed by a loud "Jeeeeeessuuuuzzzzzz!" The guards wouldn't know English, so yelling "Freeze!" or "Stand down!" would probably only have gotten me shot. Yemenis are not inclined to laugh, so I think I was striving for the startle effect, letting out the loudest burst of nervous laughter I could draw from my lungs. As the guards turned and stared at me, even my own people looked at me as if I was nuts.

It worked, though. In those few critical seconds, everyone regained some composure. Weapons came down slowly as Yemeni bosses burst from inside, shouting orders to their people. A few guards took a boot to the backside and a hard slap across the head. We learned, to no one's surprise, that one of Yemeni's finest had accidentally discharged his weapon into the ground.

Dan walked over to me and put his hand on my shoulder. "What the fuck?" he asked.

Tim, Steve, Robert, and Ali exited the palace, somber and anxious to leave. Once inside our SUV, Tim asked me, "Everything OK?" He'd assumed the gunshot was nothing more than another Yemeni wedding celebration. I didn't bother telling him what had really happened, because now it seemed irrelevant. With matters under control, at least for the moment, my adrenaline rush had subsided. In its stead I felt an overpowering fatigue, and all I cared about was getting everybody back to the embassy safely.

As it turned out, the purpose of the meeting had been conciliatory. The minister wanted to convey President Saleh's condolences to America and expressed his regret over such a horrific event. I think he was really trying to assess what America would do in response. He had seen American might during the Gulf War, and he wanted to make it clear whose side he was on, at least for the time being.

The streets were still vacant on the ride back to the hotel. People in this part of the world are so attuned to danger that they can tell when to lie low. Unlike most Americans, they live with it from the time they are old enough to cross a street.

Around midnight, I took two of my men with me in an embassy truck and returned to the Sheraton to collect everyone's belongings and move them into the embassy. The embassy's "Inman design" made it practically impregnable. The threat of terrorism had drastically altered America's overseas identity. After the terrorist bombings in Beirut in 1983, stringent new security rules were established. They came to be known as the Inman standards, after Adm. Bobby Ray Inman, who headed the panel that authored a 1985 report calling for sweeping changes in embassy location and design. For new construction, standards mandated a security setback of a hundred feet from streets or passing vehicles, sites of fifteen acres or more, locations far from downtown, and a reduced use of glass. A ten-foot-high wall topped with razor wire encircled the U.S. Embassy in Sana'a, and to gain entry we had to pass through a double-gated portico with a steel delta barrier that dropped only after a thorough inspection of each vehicle. Yemeni soldiers patrolled the outside perimeter, and a ten-man U.S. Marine guard force, backed by trusted local guards, controlled the interior's grounds.

We paid off everyone's bills, packed up their belongings, and left for the embassy. Before I climbed into the truck, a Yemeni major who had been part of the security detail at our hotel approached me and held out his hand. I hesitantly grasped his, and he clutched mine with both hands. With tears in his eyes, he said in broken English, "I am very sorry for the deaths of your countrymen."

When the move was complete, some of my men slept for a few hours. My mind was racing as I thought about all I had to do. If we made it out of Yemen, there'd be plenty of time to sleep on the extended flight home.

Before dawn on September 12, we took off in a heavily armed motorcade to Sana'a Airport, which, as a large billboard proclaimed, was under renovation by the Bin Laden Construction Company. We drove at breakneck speed, encountering only a few decrepit dogs in otherwise empty streets. Many Muslims, because of proscriptions in certain religious literature, would never keep dogs as pets and will not allow them in their homes. Most Yemeni dogs are directly descended from ones the English had brought with them. They resemble diluted English terriers, are undomesticated, and live off the land.

In the airport's VIP waiting area, I leaned back in my chair and closed my eyes. I heard Ali Soufan's cell phone ring. He was one of the few in our group with a working international phone. "Yes, uh huh, yes, I will tell Tim. We are doing OK."

Ali turned to Tim, "Tim, that was headquarters. They have reason to believe that the Yemenis have certain individuals in custody who know about the attacks, and we need to talk to them. They want four of us to stay behind."

Tim called me over. It was a given that I would remain. As a senior agent and second in charge of the FBI team, I never would have thought to leave once I learned suspects were in custody. Tim would stay too. Another certainty was Ali Soufan. Headquarters wanted him to stay, and Ali was ready, willing, and able. Ali specialized in terrorism and, in particular, al Qaeda. For a number of reasons, not the least of which were that he was Muslim and that he spoke Arabic, he was one of the best terrorism interrogators the FBI had at that time.

Nobody else volunteered.

Two of my guys were big and rugged, about six foot two or three, and single. Ironically, before the tragedy I had nicknamed them the Twin Towers.

I asked, "Which one of you is staying?"

After some foot shuffling and mumbling, they decided to flip a coin. These big, rugged SWAT operators were smack in the middle of the VIP lounge at the airport, and a crowd began forming around us. As they flipped a Yemeni coin, calling heads and tails, it dawned on them that neither had a clue which side of the coin was heads or tails. Now they started squabbling over whether a laurel wreath or a mountain, the two sides of a Yemeni coin, stood for heads or tails. Reluctantly, I looked over at Dan. He had a wife and kid back home so I would have preferred not asking him, but I needed him and I knew his answer.

■   ■   ■

We were in for a surprise when we returned from the airport. The events of 9/11 had dramatically transformed our Yemeni hosts' attitudes. Their concerns about the United States headed in a different direction after the worst terrorist attack on U.S. soil. Some of the senior Yemeni intelligence officers had become enamored of the charismatic John O'Neill during his time in Aden. When they heard that he had died in the attack on the World Trade Center, the other side of the world did not seem as remote to them.

Then there was the other concern. President George W. Bush was pounding the war drums, and everyone in the Middle East knew what was coming. With the memory of Desert Storm still fresh, his message was, You are either with us or against us. Afraid that the United States would retaliate against Arab countries that showed any sign of collaborating with al Qaeda, the Yemenis began to give us unprecedented cooperation. They told us that we might want to talk to a few people they had under arrest, Yemenis who had spent time in al Qaeda training camps in Afghanistan. For months, our hosts had "forgotten" to tell us that they had these men in custody.

Fourteen

Hoarding Information

The U.S. Embassy in Sana'a was at full capacity, so we requisitioned mattresses from supply and slept on the floor of the main conference room. I doubt the embassy staff had seen anything quite like it. Our six-days-a-week routine of extended night shifts wore on us, and we took on a disheveled, distant look. We would stagger out of our "bunk room" around 9 a.m., about the time that embassy operations were in full throttle. With a towel over the shoulder, toilet kit in hand, clothes wrinkled from sleeping in them, and eyes still swollen almost closed, we shuffled through the hallways to use the restroom. The staff knew who we were but not what we were doing. People would steer a path around us and hardly ever made an attempt at conversation.

We agreed that it would not be wise to travel outside the embassy during daylight, unless it was imperative, and that we would handle all interrogations at night. The Foreign Service nationals—reasonably trusted Yemenis employed by the embassy—shopped for us, buying the peanut butter and canned Yemeni tuna that became our staples. The fish, straight from the Indian Ocean and processed in a southern Yemeni plant, was dark, replete with bones, and tasted like, well, fish. The one item we relished was the local traditional flatbread. The embassy employees procured it for us every night, hot and right off the pan, from the kiosk-like souks around the corner. We'd splatter peanut butter and tuna all over it for our protein intake. The other perk was the embassy's Marine gym where we worked off our frustrations.

After several weeks of confinement, I began to understand what prison must feel like. I realized that we had no idea when our mission would end and that the bosses back home had more important things to worry about than our morale. I found myself walking around the embassy courtyard in circles and could feel a sense of desperation seeping in whenever I had time to myself.

The threat level spiked again when we received intelligence suggesting a strike against the embassy. The Marine contingent was small, no more than fifteen men, and the embassy had a substantial perimeter. The gunny, or the senior noncommissioned officer (NCO), called the FBI SWAT and DS agents into his office. "Here's the deal, folks. I need you to be part of our defense force if this attack materializes." If we had to battle alongside the Marines, we were ready. We could have only staged a delaying action, and if the Yemeni military showed some fight, we might have been able to hold off the attackers long enough. If the Yemeni government forces were slow to respond or, worse, fell in with our attackers, then no one else was over the horizon who could have gotten to us in time.

Whether targets for kidnapping or murder, we were a valuable commodity to the bad guys, so we always worried about ambushes as we made our way to the prison compound and interrogation center on the southern edge of the old city. As in Aden, each day we reviewed and updated our plans of alternate routes and the use of advance, or scout, teams. Unpredictability was our greatest protection. Any security expert will tell you that it is the single most important countermeasure to being attacked. We would send a lead car out with a Yemeni translator. The occupants would drive a half mile ahead, keeping their eyes open for anything suspicious. If they saw something that looked like trouble, they would call us, and we would alter our route instantly, communicating through handheld radios, "OK, we're going to blue now."

During the following months, Ali Soufan, supported by Robert of the NCIS, worked in his incomparable fashion. Our DS partners and Dan and I kept them safe and helped wherever we could. Unquestionably, though, Ali was the man.

Every night we waited for Ali and Robert to finish the grinding interrogations, which usually lasted from around 9:30 p.m. until well after midnight. Sitting in our SUVs, we stared at the desert sky, wondering what was going to happen next, whether America would strike back, and who or where it would target. We all believed that this time America had to do more than throw missiles into mountainsides and pharmaceutical plants. Even from our isolated part of the world, we could feel the beginning vibrations of the war machine.

Understandably, the Yemeni compound guards were uncomfortable with us. Here we were, armed to the teeth, sitting inside their maximum-security prison. I couldn't imagine the U.S. Federal Bureau of Prisons allowing eight heavily armed Yemeni soldiers routine access to one of our federal prisons.

When Ali and Robert finished their interrogations, they usually left the building in the company of their Yemeni counterparts. It was apparent that they had developed a genial relationship with the Yemenis. Ali could do that wherever he went, and Robert was an impressive sidekick.

During the drive back to the embassy, as Ali and Robert prepared their interview notes and logs for transmission back to the States, we listened to them discuss the night's progress and setbacks. Robert would regale us with stories of how Ali had "worked the crowd that night." Ali might smile and occasionally add something, but he never blew his own horn.

Ali had a certain style. He immediately went to work developing relationships with the prisoners, who often accepted him because he spoke their language and he seemed sincere. He could be humble, he enjoyed humor, and he treated his elders, in the way of the Middle Eastern male, with respect. He was nothing short of brilliant in his approach, bringing a dimension to the FBI's counterterrorism capability that, heretofore, did not exist.

His tools were many. He was an educated, progressive Muslim who was so well versed in the Koran, he could have held his own in a debate with most imams. He punctuated his generally calm demeanor with occasional bursts of laughter. He was empathetic and shrewd. If he felt increasing resistance from someone he was interrogating, he'd back off and spend hours discussing irrelevancies. He would almost dutifully pack a small offering of snacks before our nightly visits to the prison compound. As in dealing with children, he rewarded cooperative prisoners with candy, a warm smile, and a hug, and he'd punish the recalcitrant with aloofness. His modus operandi was ideal for the Middle East.

The Yemeni prisoners we targeted had almost no access to the news. These particular prisoners had been in virtual solitary confinement and didn't fully understand what Ali and Robert were trying to learn. They did not know the details of what had occurred on 9/11, and nobody was about to share those bits with them. It wasn't long before Ali, with Robert's help, had these guys boasting about their time spent in al Qaeda's training camps in Afghanistan. They claimed to be firearms instructors and bodyguards for bin Laden, and Ali encouraged them to talk of their exploits. Ali's interrogation style worked like a charm. There were evenings when the chatter flowed so nonstop that Robert had a hard time keeping notes.

Within a week of 9/11, Ali and Robert devised a plan. We helped them collect a classic police photo spread, a dozen or so pictures of young Middle Eastern males, all having approximately the same appearance. It was a photo spread that would have made Quantico instructors proud and would have stood up in any U.S. court of law. Pictures of three of the suspected 9/11 hijackers were mixed in the array. The New York office had collected the flight manifests from all four aircraft involved and tracked down visa photos for everyone who might fit the suspects' profiles.

Well into the night's interrogation, when the mood was close to perfect, Ali casually nodded toward the pictures on the table and asked, "Have you ever known any of these men?" As the prisoners sipped fruit juice, they scanned the photos. They paused before scrutinizing some of them, and it became apparent that these few were of particular interest to them. Following their exchange of chatter and nods, they turned to Ali and announced proudly and without a scintilla of doubt that two of the men in the photos—two of the six we suspected—had sat at bin Laden's side. We understood that they didn't get to sit next to bin Laden unless they'd been singled out for some important assignment. We knew Ali and Robert had clinched it. We now had precisely what the president wanted—the identity of two of the hijackers and confirmation that they were members of al Qaeda. World opinion would not fault America for unleashing its dogs of war on the Taliban and al Qaeda. In police or FBI language, we had developed the probable cause; however, in this case, it was justification for more than just an arrest warrant or a wiretap. It was for a military invasion of Afghanistan.

We returned to the embassy early the next morning, and Robert and Ali immediately readied their report for secure transmission to the New York bosses. The FBI had a strict chain of command at the time. If you worked for a field division, such as New York, you reported directly to the management in that division. Those managers took that information and did their own review before channeling it to FBI Headquarters. In Washington, after clearing another multilayered bureaucracy, the report would find its way to the director's desk, assuming, of course, someone close to him decided the report was worth the director's time.

Tim, the FBI's on-scene commander, told us that the bosses in New York were excited about what Ali and Robert had accomplished. Our nightly sojourns continued unabated. We caught up on backlogged administrative items on Friday nights and Saturdays, since the Yemenis, like most Muslims, will not work on their Sabbath. It wasn't as if we could go out for a night on the town. We still remained in a lockdown status, with the only concession being an occasional lunch over at the Sheraton. Otherwise, we made the best of things, hanging out in the Marines' quarters, watching movies, or swimming in the pool with our DS comrades and the other ex-pats huddled in and around the embassy.

Following his big score, Ali deftly convinced one of the prisoners, a former bin Laden bodyguard and al Qaeda weapons trainer, to describe every weapon al Qaeda possessed and trained with in Afghanistan. Dan, himself a weapons expert, recognized that this disclosure was another huge home run. American and Coalition forces were ramping up to invade Afghanistan. Everyone knew that it was coming, and we had a chance to lay out the entire Taliban–al Qaeda arsenal. Dan went down the hall to visit the defense attaché and borrow his copy of *Jane's Infantry Weapons*, the world-renowned British resource. He handed it to Ali and told him to pore over it page by page, with his new best friend. Since Ali had no military experience and little exposure to Soviet Bloc weaponry, he had Dan give him a primer each night and make sure he got the terminology right. This collaboration resulted in a huge windfall.

Ali was having a field day. He now had the former bin Laden bodyguard describing in detail not only every weapon the Taliban had but also how many of each, how much ammunition they had stockpiled, where these weapons were primarily located, and how competent the Taliban and al Qaeda were with them. When the defense attaché heard about the intelligence breakthrough, he was beside himself. He would stand at the embassy door every night, waiting for us to return so that he could write up his report and send it to the Pentagon right away. Suddenly, he was a fan of the FBI and, in particular, of this young Muslim agent.

I don't believe many intelligence collection efforts in the past fifty years superseded what our tired little group of FBI and NCIS people, sitting out on the edge of nowhere, accomplished during those months in the fall of 2001. With our backing and protection, Ali and Robert had positively identified some of the 9/11 hijackers and gleaned mountains of detail on the weapons that our troops would confront. Before Operation Enduring Freedom kicked off weeks later, America and its allies knew in detail what they would face when they hit the ground in Afghanistan.

We sent information nightly to the New York office. We wouldn't go to bed until our New York counterparts confirmed receipt and we'd answered their follow-on questions. We felt that our little group was taking the offensive and hitting back, helping the U.S. military machine prepare to kick the hell out of the people who had attacked us. We were confident and proud, expecting a pat on the back from Director Mueller and a grateful U.S. government.

We would work until we couldn't stay awake any longer. Our nightly routine usually ended with a few beers or a glass or two of scotch. Then one by one, we would stagger downstairs to our bunk/conference room in the embassy. Drinking alcohol was in violation of embassy rules, but we were working harder than most and had been going at it for a long time. Many nights, Robert would lie on the floor of the conference room, utterly exhausted, with a glass of scotch on his chest. In the dark, we'd talk about the night's interrogation, our families back home, and what we hoped to accomplish the next day. Then, eventually, we'd drift off to the sound of ice cubes clinking in Robert's glass as his chest rose and fell.

▪ ▪ ▪

About ten days after 9/11, I was up early and in our small work space, cleaning up the beer cans before the Marines came through on a security inspection. I heard the click of the secure fax machine, the incoming message rolling out of its mouth. Ali had just entered the room, and I handed him what appeared to be a surveillance photo. He reacted, "Holy shit, I know these guys!" He went on, more for his own benefit than for my education, "These are surveillance photos taken in Kuala Lumpur, Malaysia, by the CIA. This was a meeting between some suspected al Qaeda types, one of them Yemeni, and the JI." I knew the Jemaah Islamiyah (JI), or the "Islamic Group," was an Indonesian-based Muslim extremist organization with an agenda similar to that of al Qaeda.

Ali continued, "It happened a few months back. I know about this. They [the CIA and an FBI analyst working with them] showed these pictures to some of our people [New York–based FBI case agents working al Qaeda] in New York but refused to give any details to our criminal guys. To make matters worse, some bureau headquarters people were with them and threw up that Chinese wall crap, claiming that the law barred our criminal guys from access to FISA [Foreign Intelligence Surveillance Act] information."

"Come on! You mean they showed these pictures to the guys working the case but wouldn't tell them anything about what went on at the meeting in Malaysia or who these people are?"

"Yeah, I wasn't there but I heard about it, and I'm seeing these pictures for the first time. Holy shit, I recognize this guy! He's one of the guys that hijacked the planes! He's one of the guys the Yemeni prisoners ID'd!"

Over the next days, we received more disturbing news. The National Security Agency (NSA) and the CIA were always hesitant to share information with the FBI. They neither trusted the FBI with their secrets and worried about compromising covert operations nor wanted the FBI to know exactly how they acquired the information. The CIA could operate away from the watchful eye of the inspector general, free of merciless congressional scrutiny, and out of range of Freedom of Information Act (FOIA) requests and whistleblowers. The FBI could not.

The NSA and the CIA had critical intelligence before 9/11. Through intercepts and sources within friendly foreign intelligence services, they knew that the JI was meeting with al Qaeda members in Malaysia and that two al Qaeda members at the meeting received cash and traveled to the United States through Thailand. Although I don't think anyone knew the meeting's objective, this discovery was still crucial since it was one of the first pieces of irrefutable evidence that the two major Islamic terrorist groups cooperated.

They had also identified a terrorist safe house in Sana'a that was owned by an old man whose son was one of the terrorists who planned the attack on the USS *Cole* and was closely associated with bin Laden. This location had served as a "switchboard" before 9/11, patching twelve calls from al Qaeda through to at least one of the hijackers—Khalid al-M'idhar—when he was in the United States. To anyone checking, it would appear as if the calls to the United States were from Sana'a, but they actually originated in Afghanistan and elsewhere.

The CIA and NSA knew all this before 9/11 but shared little with the FBI. Had the CIA and NSA given this critical intelligence to the FBI—especially the information that linked the switchboard house with bin Laden—the FBI would have thoroughly investigated any phone numbers contacted through the hub. What would have happened from there is anyone's guess, but even the most blockheaded bureaucrat in FBI HQ would have had to recognize that calls originating from a key terrorist overseas to someone inside the United States could not be ignored. NSA was intercepting the calls and was hesitant to share that information with other agencies, including the CIA and FBI.

▪   ▪   ▪

On the morning of September 23, I staggered down the embassy hallway to get to a bathroom so I could brush my teeth and then hunt down some coffee. The building was filling up with neatly starched embassy personnel who, as usual, avoided making eye contact, probably because they were embarrassed for me. I'm sure I looked like a homeless vagrant.

I shuffled into our congested work area to perform my regular scan for obvious security violations before the Marines came through. The secure telephone rang, and I picked it up. "Good morning, Sana'a," said a female voice on the other end.

I cleared my throat, "Good morning. Who is this?" She told me she was the lead analyst assigned to the 9/11 case out of headquarters and politely asked me how our team was faring. I said that we were OK and expected her to say something like, "The president and the director want you to know how impressed we are with the information you've acquired. America owes you a debt," and so on. What I heard instead almost put me on the floor.

"We were wondering, agent. Have you fellows developed any information from those prisoners you've been interrogating? We haven't seen a report from Sana'a for some time."

"Could you please repeat that?"

She did, and I realized what had happened. The New York office owned the case. The carnage had taken place in its backyard. New York management did what it was trained to do, that is, run a major case investigation. The managers had decided to develop their case, just as they would any other criminal investigation—step by step, cross-checking facts and making sure everything was right before updating FBI Headquarters. When the time was right, New York would present the director with a tight package that was ready for the grand jury and then a big press conference. The New York office needed the time to ensure it had all the answers. When face-to-face with the director, agents needed to have the answers at their fingertips.

Director Mueller had been attending daily briefings with the president. It is possible that at some level in FBI HQ some official had some knowledge of what its little New York team was accomplishing in Yemen, but again, if that was the case, it wasn't getting to the top.

I had a lot of experience preparing photo spreads that held up in criminal prosecutions. The photo spread that Ali and Robert used in Yemen was every bit as good as any I had seen. It was solid evidence that at least two hijackers were hard-core al Qaeda. There was no reason to keep that from anyone at the top.

The president could have told the nation only ten days after the worst terrorist attack on American soil that we had a breakthrough, that we had a positive ID on some of the al Qaeda suicide hijackers. Someone in the FBI bureaucracy, however, was holding back the information. The motives, while probably well intentioned, were misguided.

I was seething. As loyal to my field division as any agent, I knew how managers operated and the prism through which they often viewed things. But even I understood that the al Qaeda specter spread far beyond the borders of the New York office or any FBI division for that matter. We weren't dealing with local Mafia dons or the Bloods and the Crips. This group was involved in international terrorism, and New York wasn't going to stop it on its own. In a read-between-the-lines tone, I managed to control the fury that I felt building and suggested, "You had better call New York because there is a lot that you need to know."

■　　■　　■

For urgent personal reasons, I had to return to the States. Dan and I left when our replacements came, flying from Sana'a with stopovers in Dubai and London. It took us almost four days to get home.

On our final leg from London aboard a British Airways 747, our flight attendant asked if we were armed; our official passports, flight itinerary, tactical bags, rumpled cargo pants, and military desert boots gave us away. We told her we weren't. Then I thought there might have been another reason for the question. Many were still terrified to fly, and those who managed to get on planes were warier than ever. I asked her to pass my business card to her captain, assuring her that Dan and I would be happy to assist if there were any problems on board.

Fifteen minutes later, the chief steward approached us with two bags, each containing a bottle of good brandy and a selection of fine food from the galley. In the manner of a retired senior NCO in the British military, he shook both our hands and snapped to attention, "Acknowledgments from the captain and crew, gentlemen. Now go get those bastards!" Several of the flight attendants gathered in a small group facing us and began to clap. Passengers seated nearest to us smiled, nodded, and gave us the thumbs-up sign.

It was the first time anyone had acknowledged Dan or me since 9/11. It was a little overwhelming. I had kept a lot bottled up inside for a long time. I felt my bottom lip begin to tremble. I bit down hard, took a deep breath, and reminded myself I was in public and people were watching. Save it for a private moment, I thought.

Fifteen

Getting in the Fight

On a late November morning, some of my SWAT guys picked Dan and me up at Kennedy Airport. These normally exuberant men were silent as they drove our Suburban along the Belt Parkway toward downtown Manhattan. The moment we entered the Battery Tunnel, I detected a smoldering, smoky odor; it was a potent blend of burning metal, wood, fuel oil, and plastic. I knew that mixed in with the noxious stink was the smell of the flesh that had burned and that every time I breathed the downtown air, I inhaled death. It was almost two months after 9/11, and as we surfaced from the tunnel, I saw the empty hole in the skyline. Instead of the Twin Towers, which I had grown so accustomed to passing during many years of working in the city, I was look-ing at a contorted steel wreckage that resembled the rotting skeletal frame of some giant prehistoric creature.

"Those fucking bastards."

Without the WTC and with no one slamming on a car horn, downtown Manhattan was eerie, hardly recognizable. People in the streets were quieter than usual, wearing strange expressions. My office of almost fourteen years was in shambles, and my former boss John O'Neill had died in the attack. America was preparing for war as we all looked over our shoulders, wondering when, how, and where the terrorists would strike next.

Immediately following the attacks, lower Manhattan had become practi-cally inaccessible to anyone not searching for victims and evidence. Debris from the WTC's collapse clogged the air ducts of the FBI's New York head-quarters, which were only a few blocks from the towers. The entire FBI team moved out of Twenty-six Federal Plaza and set up a temporary command post uptown in a building that used to house an auto dealership. To a person, FBI employees responded like patriots. Despite the transportation chaos caused by the attack, they found a way to get into work from the suburbs, and some slept on the floor rather than go home. The SWAT team handled security, positioning snipers on the roof and around the perimeter. It took on the feel of wartime London during the Blitz.

Much of America wanted revenge and expected the government to re-taliate. Of course, no city in America felt the hit as New York did. Only the residents of Washington, D.C., and Northern Virginia could truly understand what we felt. Flight 93 had gone down in an empty field in Shanksville, Penn-sylvania, where there is hardly a community. The media had not yet begun its orgy of recrimination and finger-pointing, and Congress had only begun its blame game.

It was surreal, but I couldn't dwell on it. In my absence, my wife had been tending to a recently widowed mother, helping her deal with the loss, and my brother was beginning treatment for a virulent form of cancer. The one good note was my daughter had been preparing for her wedding. I was away when all of it took root and mushroomed. It was time for me to step back into their lives.

I returned and resumed my job as head of the SWAT team. We continued to train and assist the investigative squads whenever an arrest warranted our skills. While attending a funeral service for the father of one of my SWAT op-erators, my boss called me. He told me to rally the SWAT team and meet him in the office as soon as possible. I activated our call-out tree, an established system that makes every operator responsible for contacting the next team member on his roster. Then I headed up New Jersey's Garden State Parkway using my lights and sirens.

I arrived in downtown Manhattan in good time, but it was already getting late. My SAC called me into his corner office and introduced me to several detectives with the Maryland State Police, as well as a senior U.S. marshal. On October 30, Kofi Orleans-Lindsay, a minor drug dealer, had killed an undercover Maryland State Police officer in northeast Washington, D.C., during a drug rip-off. Law enforcement agents do not take the murder of their own well, and they expect the fellowship of cops to help them until the killer is caught.

The murderer had relatives and friends in Brooklyn. The U.S. Marshals Service, specialists in tracking fugitives, had a technical unit that was monitoring the killer's use of a telephone calling card. They saw calls coming from Brooklyn, so it was a good possibility the killer was there.

When cops—I use the term generically here to include sheriffs, city and state police, and federal law enforcement officers—commit considerable sweat equity to an investigation or the development of an informant, they become protective. They feel they own it. It's normal. When the time comes that they can use some help, it's difficult to admit it. Sometimes it's about personal glory, but often it's simply not being able to accept that after all their time and effort, they just can't close the deal on their own. The FBI is no exception to that rule and neither are the U.S. Marshals. Everyone wanted to be the first to find the cop killer.

We decided that if the killer were in Brooklyn, we would flush him out with a massive effort. The story aired the next night on *America's Most Wanted*. Volunteers, policemen, and FBI agents all manned the phones. I organized my two SWAT team sections and set up a rolling twenty-four-hour schedule so that as soon as one section came off a twelve-hour shift, the other came on and kept moving. Within hours of the episode's airing, the public began calling in leads.

Things started to churn. "I'm pretty sure I saw the guy leaving this spot in Bensonhurst." Another said, "I could almost swear I saw him in Sheepshead Bay near Lundy's."

As soon as we learned of a new location, I sent over a squad. We were working round the clock and wearing a little thin, having been up the better part of forty-eight hours. Whenever possible, I would give my people a break, but no one wanted to go home.

On the morning of the third day, the marshals were nowhere to be found. Even my boss didn't know where they had gone. It turned out that they had left for Boston in the middle of the night without telling us, following a hot lead. The subject's phone card was used in Boston, so they were heading that way to bag him before anyone else knew what had happened.

I had activated the entire SWAT roster of almost fifty men for the case. On such a big case, the office would activate surveillance squads and surge whatever resources were needed. Along with surveillance teams, radio technicians, and fugitive squad agents and detectives, we had at least seventy people out working the streets of Brooklyn round the clock, and the Maryland State Police were with us every step of the way.

At one location, a relative of the killer admitted that he had just been with Orleans-Lindsay and that Orleans-Lindsay had taken his car. Now we knew exactly what we were looking for. It was around 2 a.m. when I went to an impromptu meeting on a Brooklyn curb with my boss, the head of the surveillance team, and one of the Maryland troopers. We were running on sheer adrenaline. Like many, I hadn't slept for two days. The surveillance squad's supervisor started to brief us when a white Lexus cruised past. Even Brooklyn streets quiet down at that time of the morning. "Jesus, that was him! Let's go!"

What followed was not in accordance with the plan. Four cars, three full of managers, men who are largely at a stage in their careers that qualify them for "noncombat status," took off after the car. Fortunately, our radios worked, and years of training kicked in. Our four-car pursuit fell in at a discreet distance. We didn't want to start a wild car chase through the borough if it could be avoided. We were looking for a way to pin him into a tight intersection or dead-end street when it became apparent that he had made us. The winding streets, however, never allowed him to get up some real speed. With almost uncanny instincts, the surveillance supervisor announced, "I'll cut him off at the next sharp turn. Next two cars pin him in."

Within seconds, we had executed a classic Quantico-taught car stop: one car angled in front to block him, another pulled up parallel, and the third pinned him from behind. Everyone exited from his vehicle on the safe side (away from the suspect's car) and took cover in the right place, not behind the trunk or an open door, but behind the engine, the only place that provides reasonable protection from gunfire. I thought, I should remember to give the bureaucrats more credit next time; they were doing pretty well for desk jockeys. Street agents and the SWAT team train regularly for this kind of situation, but I didn't expect my bosses to perform so well.

The surveillance agent with the best view into the subject's vehicle commanded, "Turn off the engine and show us your hands!" I had the vehicle blocked from behind and my sights dead on the driver's head. There was no response to the initial order, and I thought I saw the subject shifting in his seat. My finger closed on my trigger; the instant a gun came into view I was ready to take him out.

"Show us your hands now!" Then one of the bosses stepped out from cover. In an awkward movement with his weapon trembling and held out in the general direction of the subject's vehicle, he started moving toward the car.

"Jim," I screamed, "get back here!" He stopped, realizing what a dangerous cross fire he was walking into, and did a Groucho Marx squat walk back to his car. I thought, There you go, just when I thought these guys were pretty good! Seconds later, our killer came to his senses and gave up. Had he hesitated a few more seconds and had his movements appeared aggressive, bullets would have been flying and Jim would have been right in the middle of it.

Later that evening, the FBI's Fugitive Task Force, having taken over custody, transported the killer to the downtown Manhattan federal building. As a member of the task force, Paul Sutherland was one of the agents escorting Kofi Orleans-Lindsay. As they exited their vehicle, Paul saw one of the Maryland State Police detectives standing among the waiting crowd of agents and bosses. Paul asked a nearby agent to take control of the killer, walked over to the Maryland detective, reached out, and took the briefcase from the detective's hand. Paul said, "He's yours, detective. You take him from here." The detective hesitated for an instant and then gave Paul a subtle nod, acknowledging what Paul had done. The Maryland State trooper would now have a role in processing a killer who only seventeen days earlier had executed one of his police brothers. Only a cop would fully understand how important Paul's gesture was.

There was a press conference the next morning to announce this high-profile arrest. After processing, it was time for the media event during which law enforcement escorted the perpetrator from the FBI building to the nearby federal courthouse for arraignment. Just before they left the building, a throng of bosses nosed their way into the photo op. I stood back and watched the circus that I had witnessed many times before. Bosses who a day or two earlier didn't know your name or what you did became your best friend when the cameras started rolling. Paul never got that big picture on the front of the *New York Daily News*, something that would have made the folks back home proud, but what he did get was much more important—the lasting respect of those who saw and understood what he did, as well as the respect of the Maryland State Police.

I'd like to think that there are men and women in the Maryland State Police who still remember how the FBI stood with them. The stories of discord and jealousy get told. There are many more good stories, such as this one, that don't.

▪   ▪   ▪

Although we had been trying to resume our normal routine in FBI New York, it was clear that things would never be the same.

In the midst of the devastation, New York valiantly tried to run the investigation of the 9/11 attack. It made sense, not only because New York took the biggest hit, but because the Southern District of New York, based on years of hard work by FBI investigators, had indicted Osama bin Laden and had successfully prosecuted al Qaeda members for the first WTC attack and the bombing of the U.S. embassies in East Africa. The SDNY had proven it knew how to deal with terrorists.

FBI Director Mueller, now fully aware that managers of FBI regional offices routinely held critical information back from headquarters, had swiftly taken steps to alleviate the immediate problem. CIA Director George Tenet was not going to scoop Director Mueller anymore at daily White House briefings. Mueller moved the 9/11 investigation from New York to headquarters. Next he would have to make sweeping changes affecting the very core of the FBI and the way it had done things for almost a century.

So why did Director Mueller choose to transfer the 9/11 case, along with a number of New York investigators and New York Special Agent in Charge Pasquale "Pat" D'Amuro, to the Hoover Building in Washington? I believe he recognized that in the matter of international terrorism, the bureau's system was dysfunctional. Before 9/11, Director Mueller thought that he knew what was going on in the field. He could never get real-time information, though, and when the information did reach him, it was rarely the full story. High-level managers often omitted or distorted distasteful details to leave a good impression. We used to joke that the director had no clothes on but that he believed the people around him who told him he was well dressed. The system was stuck in the 1950s.

Director Mueller couldn't continue to rely upon distant, semiautonomous field divisions, with onerous management layers, to decide when and whether he would receive critical information. He couldn't brief the White House and Congress based on what experience confirmed could be delayed, filtered, or slanted reports. The menace was now global, cunning, and highly dangerous, and the FBI would have to pool its meager resources to confront it. What had started in New York as the TWINBOM case—an acronym for *Twin* Towers *bom*bing—was renamed PENTTBOM, for the Pentagon bombing. The double *T* was a concession to the Twin Towers of New York.

The Eastern District of Virginia now owned the investigation. An unprecedented attack had warranted an unprecedented move. For the first time in modern history, an investigation was being run directly out of the Hoover Building. I was not surprised. I had been at the eye of the tempest the morning the headquarters analyst called us in Sana'a and requested "any information" on what we were doing there. I was incredulous that my field office, regardless of its array of talent, seemed to think that it alone could track down and bring all the planet's terrorists to justice. In addition, a schism had grown between the FBI New York office and the NYPD, which had determined that it would fight terrorism virtually independent of the FBI. Its detectives were acting with little or no authority all over the world, hoping to catch bin Laden and his thugs and haul them to New York City for a trial in front of a state judge. The field offices were still not sharing information well. In the FBI, old habits died slowly and painfully.

The FBI was created in another era; its purpose was to address regional criminal concerns. Hoover gave his SACs considerable autonomy in tackling problems unique to their locale, and that arrangement made sense then. It allowed the FBI to adapt and counter escalating criminal elements without the bureaucratic meddling from headquarters that most other federal agencies faced. The setup didn't work for combating international terrorism. Widespread international threats required centralized efforts and a single effective point of coordination and direction.

Ever since I took that phone call in Sana'a, I'd been figuring out where I fit in the post-9/11 FBI. Even though I was back at work in Manhattan, I had trouble regaining focus, distracted by a sense that it was in the nation's capital, and not in New York, that I might make a difference in the fight against terrorism.

I volunteered for a temporary duty (TDY) assignment with the new PENTTBOM squad. TDYs were normal in the bureau whenever the need arose to surge additional personnel to a major investigation for a limited time. When the TDY ended, agents would normally return to their field offices and resume the same positions they had left. It usually meant a welcome change of routine, and the bureau paid a per diem for lodging and meals. In this case, they had rented a block of efficiency apartments in a nice building in Alexandria, Virginia.

I wanted the TDY transfer despite what I'd heard about the working conditions in headquarters. Crammed into windowless basement rooms where everyone sat elbow to elbow and had to share computers, the highly motivated agents on this case worked long days and weekends without complaint.

My new assignment came with a promotion, but that wasn't meaningful. I had reached the maximum pay scale for a street agent, a GS-13 step 10. To move further up, an agent must join management by becoming a GS-14, or a supervisory special agent. In an organization where most fight to stay on the bottom, moving into management is often thought of as entering purgatory. The difference in pay between a GS-13 step 10 and a GS-14 supervisor is in many cases modest and not worth the resulting morass of bureaucratic responsibility. In my particular case, since the New York cost of living adjustment is the largest in the bureau, my paycheck as a new headquarters supervisor actually decreased. In any event, my new job came without the usual management baggage. I would not be responsible for anyone's work but my own.

Weeks into the investigation, several of us were assigned to building a prosecutable case against Zacarias Moussaoui, the so-called twentieth hijacker. Now that the media had exhausted personal interest stories about the victims and heroes of 9/11, it went into attack mode. Investigative reporters learned that immigration officials had arrested Moussaoui before 9/11 for remaining in the United States on an expired visa. He had actually come to the attention of the FBI office in Minneapolis because he was taking flying lessons and, according to his instructor, was not at all interested in learning how to take off or land. A Minneapolis FBI agent found a way to arrest him for overstaying his visa and asked headquarters for a warrant to search his personal effects. FBI HQ turned down the request to pursue a warrant, saying that a visa overstay did not justify that type of search. No one denies it was a bad call by bureaucrats whose reading of the law was too constricted. This decision was typical for headquarters personnel who were concerned about career boards and promotions. They didn't get into trouble if they didn't push the envelope.

The issue didn't die there. Another Minneapolis special agent and office legal adviser Colleen Rowley, soon to become *Time* magazine's 2002 Woman of the Year, went to the press right after 9/11 and claimed whistleblower status. She exclaimed to all who would listen that FBI Headquarters had dropped the ball by failing to follow up on the Minneapolis agent's search warrant request, which she had personally approved. I knew Rowley when she was an agent in the FBI's New York office. She had worked some counterintelligence matters and then transferred to the legal counsel's office. At a time when the FBI was struggling to recover and rebuild, Rowley became a celebrity by trumpeting the bureau's bungling of the search warrant and by giving interviews to any media outlet that asked.

Yes, there had been critical mistakes prior to 9/11. Risk-averse managers and a lack of imagination at all levels played a major role in the failure to protect America. We all knew that, and many of us were working hard to do something about it. I reached a point where I couldn't take her grandstanding anymore, and I wanted to set her straight. I told her over e-mail that, from her legal adviser's perch in Minneapolis, she had no idea what the FBI had been doing in the international terrorism arena. I reminded her that agents were putting themselves at risk daily all over the world and that she was undermining those hardworking and effective people. If she truly had believed that Moussaoui's computer held the key to stopping a terrorist attack, I said, she would have fought much harder to win her case. She could have gotten on a plane, walked into the unit chief's office, and raised some hell. Agent Rowley responded with a subdued, almost humble reply that she was sorry and didn't mean to negatively impact the hardworking men and women of the bureau.

Eventually, the inspector general's office issued a report that Agent Rowley had failed to pursue all the avenues at her disposal, did not push the issues hard enough when she had the chance, and was Monday morning quarterbacking. This finding, of course, hardly made any of the media outlets. How could they criticize the Woman of the Year?

I learned eventually that once Moussaoui's laptop was accessed, along with his other belongings, nothing was discovered that would have led investigators to the 9/11 plot. The FBI case agent in Minnesota had every reason to be frustrated and even angry. A good investigator with honed instincts, he knew that Moussaoui was planning something bad. The reality is, though, that Moussaoui's personal effects disclosed neither the plotters nor their plan, and he would not have talked, even if "enhanced interrogation" techniques had been employed. I watched him in court and am convinced that he would have died rather than divulge anything he knew; moreover, what he knew was limited because his al Qaeda bosses had recognized, long before the attack, that Moussaoui was a loose cannon. Although he didn't know the particulars, he did know that there was a plot to fly aircraft on suicide missions..

My primary job, along with a captain from the New York–New Jersey Port Authority Police detailed to the PENTTBOM squad, was to review all of the emergency phone calls made by World Trade Center victims, the cockpit recordings from all of the hijacked aircraft, and every private video taken of the World Trade Center after the strikes. I was told to pick the most shocking and disturbing audio and visual recordings to support the prosecution's argument for the death penalty.

This assignment would influence the balance of my FBI career. I listened to the cockpit recordings and all the 911 calls from inside the hijacked aircraft and from the burning towers. One was from a young pregnant woman, choking on smoke as she called an emergency operator and pleaded for help. In the background I heard shrieking, moaning, yelling, and the reverberation and thud of furniture against glass as victims tried to break shatterproof windows. The woman was saying, "The smoke is black. It's getting so thick I can't breathe in here."

The operator already knew that an entire section of the building below the caller had vanished. She had to know the girl was going to die. "It's OK, honey," she said, "firemen are coming. You are going to be OK."

There was also the man who called to say, "I'm in the stairwell. There's got to be hundreds of people here. We're on the fifty-eighth floor, and the floor beneath us is completely gone."

Hundreds of calls, pleas for help that was not coming, were logged, and people in droves leaped to their deaths. Some jumped and tried to hit a small awning over a kiosk in the plaza below, desperately deluding themselves into believing that it would break their fall from sixty stories above. People were jumping sometimes three or four together, holding hands. Even more horrifically, they would literally explode when their bodies struck the concrete. The gore was inches thick around the buildings when they finally collapsed.

I went by instinct. When a piece of evidence bothered me more than some of the others did, I put that in the pile for the jury. One particular conversation stood out from all the rest for me. A mother in Pennsylvania received a call from her son who was in the back of the plane on United Airlines Flight 93. He asked her to call the police about the hijacking and find out what the passengers should do. This mother had already seen on TV what had happened to the Twin Towers in New York. Her daughter-in-law, eight months into a pregnancy, was screaming hysterically in the next room.

I listened to the recorded conversation between the dispatcher at the local police station and the mother. He was confused and having a hard time following the conversation. Here was a man from a small Pennsylvania town dealing with a situation the likes of which he never could have expected.

"Excuse me, officer, but my son is on a plane that has just been hijacked."

"Excuse me, ma'am?"

"He wants to know what they should do. The passengers want to know what they should do."

"What do the hijackers look like, ma'am? What flight number is that? What are they demanding? Well, I'll get back to you on that, ma'am. I'm not quite sure."

In an effort to calm the dispatcher down, the mother said, "It's all right, son. Just take your time. It's OK, it's all right."

During the entire time that this conversation was taking place, the daughter-in-law continued to shriek in the background. The mother was trying to handle that, too, intermittently telling her, "Calm down now, sweetheart."

This mother knew that the plane was going down with her son on it. I don't recall hearing panic in her son's voice as he spoke to his mother. Maybe that's because the passengers didn't yet know the story. Maybe they still hoped that it was a typical hijacking and that they would land someplace where the hijackers would start making their demands.

His mother told him, "We think, or the police think, that you should probably try to take back the aircraft."

"OK. Is that what you think?"

The daughter-in-law was still sobbing and moaning, and the mother said, in a tone that was peaceful and powerful, "Get on the phone now and make your husband strong. You make him strong."

In the cockpit recording of Flight 93, a flight attendant seemed to be choking on something and groaning, "Oh, my God." There was pounding, two men in the cockpit talking in Arabic, and then a crashing sound as the passengers attempted to break down the locked cockpit door. It was apparent that there had been a big fight. The passengers had overcome one of the hijackers and were trying to get into the cockpit.

I heard one terrorist ask another, "Is this it?"

"This is it."

Then they chanted, "God is great" several times.

We had matched flight simulation software to the cockpit voice recordings, so we knew that the hijackers were manipulating the plane side-to-side, trying to throw the passengers off their feet. When they realized that the cockpit door was coming down, they turned the plane upside down and slammed it into the ground. I knew there were heroes on Flight 93 long before "Let's roll!" became a national call to action.

I was present during the interview of a flight attendant who had been married to one of the pilots of the hijacked planes. It had been a second marriage for both. She had heard the press's hype and media accounts of how the FBI had messed up, that the bureau could have stopped the attacks. She sat there, very poised, and toward the end of the interview she said, "I finally met the love of my life. I knew he was the man I wanted to grow old and die with." She looked at me, "You didn't know about this before it happened, right? You didn't know they were going to do this before it happened, did you?"

I said, "No, ma'am, we didn't know."

What I did know was that we needed to make sure that threat information was never withheld again, that every organization responsible for protecting America worked together for one purpose, that risk-averse bureaucrats should step aside and allow risk takers to start making people and organizations think "outside the box." Until these things were accomplished, America would remain vulnerable to a repeat of those horrible events.

■   ■   ■

When it was time for Moussaoui's trial, we wanted the families to have unhampered access to the trial proceedings. We arranged for closed-circuit TV coverage at protected locations across the nation. We could not permit the press to harass them or the curious to bother them.

I attended two preliminary hearings and sat right behind Moussaoui. I had learned something about the personalities and machinations of terrorists. Many misconstrued Moussaoui's ravings and stratagems as that of a mad man. He was a fanatic, but I knew he was not crazy. He just wanted to be perceived that way. It was part of his plan.

I was livid as I watched him toy with the judge and equally disturbed by the judge's bewildered and ineffectual response to his ranting. I realized then that our trial system may not be well suited to deal with fanatical terrorists who, if they are unsuccessful at killing nonbelievers, want nothing less than a public forum from which to rage against our way of life. I still am not sure of the solution. Greater minds than mine have struggled with this issue. While as a nation, we continue to debate the question of how to treat terrorists justly, I'm sure that in the highest reaches of al Qaeda, they shake their heads in astonishment and plot to take full advantage of our discord.

Sixteen

The Fly Team:
Super Squad for Terror

Influential voices were calling for the reinvention of America's counter-terrorism effort, and the "experts" clamored for a British MI5-type security organization staffed with highly trained, specialized terrorist sleuths instead of the FBI. (MI5 is Britain's domestic counter-spy organization, responsible for internal counterintelligence, whereas MI6 works outside the country.) This plan would have resulted in disaster. MI5 specializes in tracking spies. Its agents have no authority to arrest, so they have to enlist local police departments or Scotland Yard to handle it. There is often friction between the cops and the MI5 officers. The Brits themselves, when they are candid, will say they dislike their system.

As the FBI took its blows, the CIA, America's premier intelligence collection organization, hunkered down in classic CIA style, steering clear of the tempest churning around the FBI. Director Mueller set out to save the FBI from almost certain dissolution. Even without another attack on the homeland, it was teetering and could crumble under the weight of anti-bureau sniping any day.

My boss at headquarters, Pat D'Amuro, was battling many fires, so he spoke plainly when we talked in early March 2002. "We're forming a Fly Away Team, Ray, and we think you're the right man to get it off the ground. The director wants his eyes and ears at the scene. He wants headquarters to get firsthand reporting from the scene as soon as possible. You'll serve as the acting unit chief until we can find someone with the required management experience to take over. In the meantime, it's up to you to start building this thing."

In what was another sea change, Director Mueller and his "West Coast" advisers resolved to form a counterterrorism rapid response team based at headquarters. Mueller had been the U.S. attorney in Northern California and had dealt with the FBI frequently in that position. He came to know some of the senior agents out there and brought some of them with him to headquarters. Just as all leaders do when they establish new regimes, in business or in the government, he had gathered around him those he knew and trusted. Pat D'Amuro, a veteran New Yorker, was the exception. To Mueller, Pat held the keys to understanding the New York office, the division with the biggest store of al Qaeda knowledge.

As for the Fly Away Team, I envisioned gathering experts and investigators who were familiar with the enemy and preparing them to deploy out of headquarters on a moment's notice to any location, domestic or international, wherever America's interests were in peril. I thought it should be something of an investigative SWAT team, with one significant difference: instead of being equipped with high-tech weapons, these operators would possess in-depth knowledge of the enemy.

I fully understood that we couldn't effectively fight the battle from disparate field divisions and offices with widely different pools of talent and experience. We had to do it from a central site close to the seat of authority and import the right people from the field and anywhere else we could find them.

Field agents thought that they did all the crucial work and that no one from Washington should interfere. I know. I had been one of them. What they were missing was that unless their director looked good at the White House or in front of incessant congressional committees that wanted nothing more than to pummel the head of the FBI on C-Span, then the bureau's authorities, funding, and credibility would be diminished until it was nothing but a balkanized shadow of itself. In D.C., only those with quick answers survive.

I told my bosses, "If this is going to work, you have to start by getting some of the best terrorism investigators the FBI has, a unit of senior, respected veterans; otherwise, it will have no credibility. And these guys are going to need it when they are out in the field telling other agents that the rules have changed; that from now on they will be reporting to and cooperating with FBI Headquarters. But this is the problem: we have to offer them a reason to come, and it can't just be patriotism or an ambition to do the right thing. These guys have to go home and sell this to their wives. Give me something they can take home, like, 'Hey, honey, I'll be making a lot more money.' Or, 'If we do this for two years, I'll be given my office of choice.' These are things you can sell to your family. Say, 'Hang in there and do this with me, sweetheart, and this is the reward we will get.'"

One of the first hurdles I knew I had to overcome was the prohibition against "take home" vehicles. By law, federal officials working in Washington may not drive government vehicles to and from work. It is understandable considering the huge number of government employees in the D.C. area. I argued that the governing statute exempts "emergency responders" and that these agents should fall within the exception. It took months of inane wrangling before I could get even that issue resolved. No case agent with the requisite skills I needed would have given the job a second thought if he or she had to drive his or her own personal car into downtown D.C. every day. At the time, Metro service was more limited and the areas serviced were too close to the District for an agent, especially one married and with a family, to be able to afford to live.

Income mattered. I knew I also couldn't draw the necessary experience and talent from the field if it meant having to move to D.C. on a GS-13 salary, no matter how excited some agents were about the team's concept. I made a case that the Fly Away Team members also needed some rank since they'd be rubbing elbows with high-level military officers and State Department personnel, in addition to field division bosses. Filling GS-14 supervisory spots meant having to use an arcane promotion system known as the Career Board. At its best, it is a bureaucratic mess that takes forever to resolve. Anyone who can write can get lucky with the board, but I didn't want to rely on the roll of the dice when building my program. I resolved, for the time being, that my only option was to try and fill the GS-13 positions with quality people while staffing two or three supervisory spots (GS-14s) with top-notch counterterrorism veterans who would serve as role models for the less experienced agents. Once we were staffed at our approved level of thirty personnel, we would need some supervisors, which I hoped meant internal promotion opportunities.

The first reaction from the field to our recruitment efforts was not encouraging. I needed some real inducement, so I pushed for a policy that would allow my people the chance for an early transfer to an office of preference (OP), which is the place every agent thinks he or she wants to spend the end of his or her career. The bureau already offered this incentive program to the Hostage Rescue Team (HRT), and it seemed fair in our case since we would expect our Fly Away Team agents to spend a good part of the year in some unfriendly parts of the world. In the FBI, OP transfers are usually based on seniority. An agent requests a place on a particular list for a particular office and waits to move up. Depending on the office, it can take an entire career before an agent can even get close to the dream transfer. It wasn't a surprise that my proposal generated a firestorm from the FBI Agents Association, which saw the idea as another threat to the sacred OP system. I did understand how difficult it would be for agents to spend fifteen years waiting on a list to get the transfer of their dreams only to be bumped at the end by a young agent with a quarter of their time in the bureau.

Nothing would be easy. Politics, self-interest, and the resistance to change would get in the way.

As false information swelled, bureau adversaries of the Fly Away Team accumulated faster than al Qaeda procured recruits. The rumor was out that the Fly Away Team would inspect or second-guess other agents' work and take business from the field division squads that already had some piece of overseas terrorism investigations. The extraterritorial squads worried the Fly Away Team would usurp their roles. The job of an ET squad is, in the main, to track down traditional criminals who are outside U.S. territory. These squads were not created to assist inexperienced field divisions start terrorism investigations. They had plenty to do without embedding people in military units in virtual war zones, analyzing the terrorism threat in regions of the world, and jointly conducting preemptive terrorism investigations for extended periods in very inhospitable places. The ET squads had their place. Most important, the Fly Away Team was not going to report to a field division's management. It was going to report directly to the new international terrorism sections that were being created at headquarters, and they were reporting to the director daily. Finally the FBI was centralizing the effort to combat terrorism. Field divisions would continue to run their cases, but no division would bear full responsibility for stopping al Qaeda and all of its quickly multiplying franchises. Still, many just didn't get it.

I sat in meetings where the director ordered senior FBI officials to devise an incentive plan to attract qualified counterterrorism agents to Washington. The officials nodded while having no intention of following through. They knew from experience that if they ignored a directive long enough it usually went away or they'd receive a transfer before anyone would ask what progress they'd made on the matter.

After months of political infighting, an agent who was helping me construct the Fly Away Team tried an unorthodox tactic. She approached Director Mueller as he played golf on a Sunday and asked him for a wiretap authorization. Then she proceeded to advise him of the problems I was having building the Fly Away Team because I couldn't get an incentive package past first base.

She must have caught him after a good putt. The next day, he contacted the head of the administrative division, which handles all things dealing with human resources. He tasked the assistant director with making some form of recruitment incentive happen. Once more, heads nodded in vigorous agreement. A month later, the division head transferred out of headquarters to his dream job, and the idea was lost again.

When I reached out to a senior counterterrorism manager in the Hoover Building to plead and grovel for help, I was told that some in the highest circles did not view the Fly Away Team as a priority matter. I would therefore have to wait in line to have my needs addressed.

I personally lobbied a number of field agents whom I thought would be right for the squad. I kept getting similar responses: "I will do what I can for my country, but I have a wife and kids to take care of. Why would I move to D.C. unless I can offer the family something?"

When Pat D'Amuro was promoted to executive assistant director of the bureau, the man who assumed his duties was well suited for the job, and I had renewed hope. Larry supported my efforts to develop the team. I'd worked with him at the 1996 Atlanta Olympics, when he was sent down as a CIRG representative. Earlier in his career, he had been a member of the HRT, so he appreciated my challenges better than most executives did. He also knew Director Mueller from the days when they both worked on the West Coast. He seemed to have the director's confidence.

Larry had to rebuild and reorganize every facet of the FBI's overseas capability, including the Rapid Deployment Team's manual of operations, which hadn't been updated since the program's inception in the mid-1990s. The RDTs, in their purest form, were "soup to nuts" stand-alone operations consisting of every conceivable element required to set up camp in the middle of a desert and support a long-term investigation. The manual was in drastic need of revision. For some inexplicable reason my bosses had lumped RDT oversight into my new unit, the Fly Away/Rapid Deployment Team Unit (FA/RDTU), so it fell on Douglas, the administrative assistant who made up the other half of our team thus far, and me to handle it. I did see how it would all fit together, however. The big, lumbering RDTs would deploy, host country permitting, within two to three days of an event and run an investigation for their respective divisions; that is, New York's RDT would run an investigation on behalf of a New York terrorism squad and would report back to New York bosses.

My Fly Away Team, meanwhile, would be a small and responsive group that might already be working in a nearby part of the world when a crisis arose. Arriving quickly, Fly Away Team agents could immediately coordinate with the local legal attaché and the host country's security services. They could flash immediate reports back to headquarters and to the director and advise the incoming RDT how to structure itself to deal with the realities on the ground. Once the big RDT arrived, the Fly Away Team agents could introduce everyone, bring the new investigators up to speed, possibly hang around to help with the transition, and then, after filing their last report with headquarters, return home or head to the next assignment. It all made sense to me, but I had a hard time selling it to people.

Fortunately, Douglas had been involved in drafting the first RDT manual, so it was familiar territory for him. It was a tedious task. For one thing, the call-out procedure—the system for determining which of the RDTs to activate in response to an incident—was nearly broken. Other critical sections dealing with worldwide territorial responsibility and logistics and with tracking the whereabouts of FBI personnel were incomplete. As Douglas and I left Larry's office, he stopped us and in his straightforward style stated, "I want all the details ironed out, and I need it soon. We're going to explain to the field offices once and for all who has what region of the world."

Whoa, I thought—we've finally got someone who is going to rein this thing in. All we have to do is fix this two-hundred-page manual in a few days and build the Fly Away Team. No problem. I was looking forward to working for Larry.

We no sooner managed to pull all the disparate parts of the manual together into a cogent and field-usable format when management advised the FA/RDTU (Douglas and me) to devise a systematic procedure for handling a terrorist attack against a U.S. interest anywhere in the world. The Terrorist Incident Response Protocol (TIRP) spelled out clearly who would attend the high-level meetings, how the information would be digested, and who would make the deployment calls. The TIRP fell in our laps for logical reasons; we were responsible for the two crisis response elements—that is, the Fly Away Team and the RDT program.

A terrorist attack against American interests anywhere in the world typically meant every FBI RDT would ramp up and lobby to become the first in the air. On at least one occasion the bureau launched a trimmed-down version of an RDT from Ramstein Air Base only to have the host African nation deny landing privileges. That was in fact the problem—given the competition and desire to be first on the scene, they'd be in the air before securing permission, risking being turned back and wasting time, manpower, and money. The entire team, after circling above Africa for hours, had to return to Germany and ultimately back to the United States. Our TIRP was intended to bring some sense and order to the prior chaos.

Douglas and I were running pretty hard in those early weeks and months. With a little help from our friends, we were gradually creating the Fly Away Team's structure. We had updated and upgraded the Rapid Deployment Team's manual and written a Terrorist Incident Response Protocol that the bureau's management adopted. We did it all while being shuffled from one crowded, little backroom office to another inside the bowels of the Hoover Building. In spite of it all, we were having a great time.

On an evening in May 2002, I plopped down in an armchair in my small efficiency apartment near the Pentagon, turned on the television, and began nursing a glass of scotch. My boss, Director Mueller, was on a news channel, addressing yet another in a string of congressional panels. He announced, "We've made real progress in reorganizing the FBI. Among other steps taken we now have a rapid response Fly Team operating out of headquarters." (Although the official name was Fly Away /Rapid Deployment Team Unit, within the bureau we were referring to it as the Fly Team by this point.) I almost fell out of my chair. He was referring to Douglas and me and to the occasional volunteer or two we were able to recruit. For the first few months, I was the only full-time team member deploying!

The front page of the May 15, 2002, edition of the *Washington Post* picked up the director's announcement with the headline, "FBI Director to Propose 'Super Squad' for Terror." Although mobilized on paper with a complement of forty, it was still just Douglas and me.

Back in Minneapolis, when Colleen Rowley saw the news, she wrote to Director Mueller, making certain that her letter was published in the media:

> Your plans for an FBI Headquarters' "Super Squad" simply fly in the face of an honest appraisal of the FBI's pre-September 11th failures. The Phoenix, Minneapolis and Paris Legal Attaché Offices reacted remarkably, exhibiting keen perception and prioritization skills regarding the terrorist threats they uncovered or were made aware of pre-September 11th. The same cannot be said for the FBI Headquarters' bureaucracy and you want to expand that?! Should we put the counterterrorism unit chief and SSA who previously handled the Moussaoui matter in charge of the new "Super Squad"?! You are also apparently disregarding the fact the Joint Terrorism Task Forces (JTTFs), operating out of field divisions for years (the first and chief one being New York City's JTTF), have successfully handled numerous terrorism investigations and, in some instances, successfully prevented acts of terrorism. There's no denying the need for more and better intelligence and intelligence management, but you should think carefully about how much gate keeping power should be entrusted with any HQ entity. If we are indeed in a "war," shouldn't the Generals be on the battlefield instead of sitting in a spot removed from the action while still attempting to call the shots?

We would prove Ms. Rowley wrong.

Seventeen

Terrorists in Our Midst

According to one of our sources, something was developing out of the Buffalo, New York, office that had the director's personal attention. Six young Yemeni Americans had become radicalized. They had trained at the al-Farooq camp near Kandahar in Afghanistan just prior to 9/11 and were receiving guidance from a more senior al Qaeda member overseas. The first homegrown terrorist group identified after 9/11 was conspiring to commit violent jihad against America.

Lackawanna is right outside Buffalo and home to a large Yemeni population. Not unlike other immigrant communities, it is generally averse to cooperating with authorities and difficult to infiltrate. The director was not comfortable with what he didn't know about the case. He told Pat D'Amuro, who had grown up in Buffalo, to send his Fly Team there to offer assistance and provide Washington with some reassurance that things were under control.

My Fly Team was going on the road.

Pete Ahearn was the Buffalo special agent in charge. I remembered Pete from the days when he ran a drug squad out of the FBI's Newark field division and my squad, the Manhattan-based C-25, regularly bumped up against his people. Back then, neither group fully recognized the Hudson River as a borderline. Pete was an aggressive crime fighter, not a bureaucrat who worried more about his career than about taking risks to get a job done. I hoped he remembered me because it's not easy for a new supervisory special agent to walk into a SAC's office and announce, "Hi, I'm from headquarters, and I'm here to help!"

I hurried around the Hoover Building from briefing to briefing, wondering how I could track down people with the skills and knowledge that Buffalo could use. First I snatched one of the sharpest analysts from a fledgling al Qaeda unit, a woman who had been monitoring the Buffalo case. I made some calls to find an FBI attorney who understood the Foreign Intelligence Surveillance Act of 1978 and the concept behind the infamous wall that would garner so much attention during the hearings of the National Commission on Terrorist Attacks upon the United States, aka the 9/11 Commission. Agents in the field were at a loss over what they could share with each other without being subjected to criminal prosecution. It was a mess.

The act grants agents targeting foreign intelligence officers or state-sponsored terrorists the right to listen in on the conversations of these targets. The burden of proof—the quantum of preliminary evidence required to justify a FISA warrant—is lower than the traditional level of proof required for a criminal, or Title III, wiretap. A special, secret court known as the Foreign Intelligence Surveillance Court was created to hear requests for such warrants. Safeguards were put in place to ensure that investigators pursuing criminal matters did not obtain warrants to intercept conversations under FISA that they could not get from an ordinary criminal court judge. Because FISA warrants were arguably easier to obtain than Title III warrants, there was a fear that agents denied criminal warrants would gain information through the back door from their fellow agents working under FISA.

Of course, Justice Department lawyers and the FBI's Office of the General Counsel all interpreted FISA in the strictest sense. The word was out that law enforcement officers who shared information derived from FISA with the criminal investigative side of the house could find themselves in deep trouble.

After more than three thousand Americans died on 9/11, steps were taken to adjust the legal interpretation of how FISA really worked. The Uniting and Strengthening America by Providing Appropriate Tools Required to Intercept and Obstruct Terrorism (USA PATRIOT) Act was passed in October 2001, and the wall was taken down. It had taken the loss of over three thousand Americans to bring common sense into the equation. As Director Mueller stated in testimony before Congress, "There are no neat dividing lines that distinguish criminal, terrorist, and foreign intelligence activity."

I tracked down the supervisor in charge of the bureau's translation section and pleaded on Buffalo's behalf for help. Every office was screaming for the few Arabic translators working for the FBI shortly after 9/11. I convinced the technical people to send an information technology (IT) expert to Buffalo and help the office monitor Internet communications. Finally, I contacted a Detroit agent who had a solid reputation for developing informants within the Middle Eastern community. He understood the culture, and I hoped he could share his insight with the Buffalo case agents.

Our small unit went to Buffalo on the Fly Team's first deployment. Pat D'Amuro had been promoted, and Andy was now my immediate boss. On Pat's orders, he flew to Buffalo before I did to meet with Pete and pave the way. Andy wanted to reassure Pete that it was what the director wanted. Pete was the kind of FBI manager who knew how to lead. He loved his work and his enthusiasm was catching. Most important, he understood what the mission was really about.

That afternoon we gathered in the main conference room and brainstormed. Our attorney explained how FISA had been reinterpreted and how terrorism agents could now use FISA-derived information without fear of going to jail. I offered to place a request into headquarters for more translators, and our IT genius went to work, helping Buffalo wring the most information possible from their wiretaps. He showed the Buffalo technicians how they could stand down extra surveillance teams that were on the point of burnout from working 24/7. They learned technical secrets, such as discerning if a subject was home by the energy levels emitted from his computer or how to determine when someone was using computer-based voice-over-Internet protocol, a relatively new development at the time, to have a real-time conversation with little fear of being monitored. Headquarters eventually redirected its limited translation resources to support Buffalo as a priority, and additional surveillance teams and assets were deployed there from surrounding FBI divisions.

In September 2002, the Buffalo office arrested five members of the first Islamic terrorist cell discovered in the United States. Other members of the cell were overseas when their U.S.-based coconspirators—all later named the

Lackawanna Six—were caught or otherwise brought to justice. The suspected ringleader, Ahmed Hijazi (aka Kamal Derwish), was killed in a Hellfire missile strike in Yemen along with one of the conspirators responsible for the attack on the USS *Cole*. The sixth conspirator, Mukhtar al-Bakri, whom we located with the help of another agency, was arrested and returned to the United States. He and his five brethren pleaded guilty to supporting terrorism. In return for their cooperation, each member of the Lackawanna Six received sentences ranging from eight and a half years to ten years.

This achievement was the first big success for the post-9/11 FBI and an indication that, similar to a fighter who'd been staggered by a hard left hook but has had just enough time to shake it off, we were rebounding. The Lackawanna headlines boosted morale inside the newly reorganized Counterterrorism Division at headquarters, but not for a moment did the pace slacken or did anyone think we were even close to having gotten our act together. The Buffalo case underscored that if a cell could coalesce in upstate New York, it could breed in any city in America with a Middle Eastern population. We weren't even worried yet about non-Arabic Americans becoming radicalized. That problem would come later.

Only a few days back from Buffalo, I found myself immersed in equipment and logistical problems. From the first day that we stood up our "Potemkin village" team, Douglas and I agreed that if we were going to send our people into bad places around the world, they would at least need to have the best body armor and communication equipment available. But nothing the bureau had would stop a round from an AK-47, the terrorists' weapon of choice, and word had come down that FBI agents from other divisions were being deployed alongside military units fighting in Iraq and Afghanistan. The armor issued at the time would only protect against lighter handgun fire. The military was only beginning to acquire state-of-the-art level IV armor for its combat troops, and the demand far exceeded the supply. While I was away, Douglas had gone to work trying to get our team funding for both the armor and the Iridium satellite phones that would provide communication from virtually anywhere in the world.

The bureau, in typical knee-jerk fashion, had sent numerous New York agents and some Joint Terrorism Task Force cops into Afghanistan days after the invasion began to assist with prisoner processing and interrogations. The bureau's management was famous for ordering missions without a passing thought for the logistical issues. Most managers have never run difficult investigations themselves, and they didn't have a clue about what was involved. They were spoiled by the efficiency and ingenuity of good agents who were accustomed to making it up on the fly and getting the job done with minimal assistance from management.

Carlos, whom I was trying to recruit for the Fly Team, was at Bagram Airfield, which U.S. forces had just captured from the Taliban. Somehow he was able to get a call through to me. "Ray, can you express ship some body armor, helmets, and gas masks to us? We have nothing over here." Even though Quantico's Critical Incident Response Group was responsible for logistical support for this overseas deployment, Carlos had called me because he knew I would give the matter special attention. I was his former SWAT team leader from New York, and we had a bond. He thought if he tried to reach someone at CIRG in Quantico, it might have taken days to fulfill his request. Douglas and I could make it happen in hours.

"Carlos, I hear you guys [the U.S. and Coalition forces] just captured the airfield there. Are you sure FedEx is delivering?"

Douglas called over to me from his cubicle, "Hey, Ray, they're [the FBI's Finance Division] giving us twenty thousand dollars for the armor. I've got a guy who'll pull fifteen sets out of the production line and set them aside for us. He says he'll call, and we can go over to Virginia and pick them up."

I thanked Douglas, who always knew better than anyone in headquarters how to get things done. I thought, What a way to run an elite counterterrorism unit—by the seat of our pants.

Back on the line with Carlos, I said, "There's a mil flight heading your way in a couple of days. We'll get the gear on board. Keep your head down."

During every spare minute, I worked the telephones, trying to recruit for the Fly Team, with virtually no help from the human resources people. In spite of the director's repeated orders, I still couldn't get any support inside headquarters for some kind of incentive package to draw new agents to the team. At the same time, I'm sure Director Mueller was being reassured that his Fly Team was healthy and growing.

In times of crisis and with the backing of Pat D'Amuro, I would reach out to the New York office and borrow good agents such as Ali Soufan and George

Crouch to help me on a temporary basis. Since Pat was slated to return to New York and technically still their boss, it was easy to get them on loan. Plus they really liked the pace we were running and the chance to get out of New York City.

I knew Soufan well from our months together in Aden and Sana'a. We had developed something of a symbiotic relationship during our time overseas. If anyone in the bureau could get information from a Middle Eastern male, it was Ali, and he knew that with me he didn't have to worry about who was covering his back, no matter where we were. It was good to work with him again.

I didn't know George well, but one story in particular told me something of his mettle. When he was still probationary with the bureau, having less than twelve months in service, George was sent to monitor a wiretap on an island off the coast of Africa. The target was a known terrorist facilitator. The host service didn't have a budget, and its monitoring equipment was almost nonexistent. With some bureau help, a crude tap was run from a hard line on a telephone pole to a shack that accommodated the recording equipment and monitoring agent. With little to no supervision, George went to the jungle to ensure the full and legal monitoring and recording of incriminating conversations. Since George might have to swear in court that he never lost custody of the original recordings, he would regularly turn off the equipment, grab the tapes, and race to a country road to meet an agent from town who would, in turn, both assume the tapes' custody and drop off a bag of groceries. George was worried that every time he met the agent on the country road with the tapes, he would miss recording a good conversation between the bad guys, so he would literally run back and forth.

One day during a particularly violent electrical storm, George stayed at his post with the recorders running and his earphones on. Suddenly he heard a loud crack, and the entire shack shuddered, followed almost instantly by the smell of smoke. Lightning had hit the wires, traveled into the shed, and destroyed the recorders while George was listening. He laughed about it, "I guess my rubber-soled sneakers saved me."

One morning in October 2002, Andy called me. A bomb had ripped through a crowd near a U.S. military base in the southern Philippines. First reports indicated American fatalities. "Ray, can you get someone over there and find out what happened?"

"I'll try, Andy."

Douglas and I had just been squeezed into another temporary space in the Hoover Building, and we hadn't had time to unpack our boxes. "Doug, where's George?"

"I'll get him. He's somewhere in the building. I don't think he's headed back to New York yet."

We eventually found George walking in the hallway. I asked George if he was willing to deploy to the Philippines as soon as possible to find out what had happened. He didn't hesitate to accept. I told him to track down a bureau explosives expert, check in with the legat in Manila, and then get on a plane. "Look, George, I'm trying hard, but right now the only thing I can offer you is a brand-new Level IV ballistic vest. Aside from the usual overtime and Sunday per diem pay, I've got nothing more to offer. We're trying. We just submitted another proposal to give Fly Team members a promotion to GS-14, but I can't hold out any real hope. Sure you're OK?"

"Yup, I'll let you know when we get there." Two days later, he was meeting with senior police officials and military officers and sending us detailed reports. He was precisely what the Fly Team needed, but I would not be able to land him because the bureau could not come up with a plan to offer him and his family a good reason to move to Washington. But I'm sure the director still believed we were doing fine.

Right next door to us, they were creating another new unit, the Military Liaison and Detainee Unit, from the ground up. Responsible for military liaison matters, which in the post-9/11 world meant almost anything, the agents were overseeing FBI personnel embedded with military units throughout Afghanistan and later in Iraq. I walked over and found one of them on two phones simultaneously. I arranged with them to get the equipment Carlos requested from Quantico and have it loaded on the next military flight to Bagram. Never before had the bureau committed so many agents to work side by side with troops on the ground. Agents were helping the military to process the battlefield detainees into Bagram and other detention centers throughout Afghanistan. They knew how to fingerprint, take mug shots, and capture important confessions or statements.

Suddenly the FBI was everywhere.

Within two months of the arrests in the Buffalo case, Pat D'Amuro called me back to his office on the executive floor of the Hoover Building and laid out my next assignment. "Ray, we've got a problem brewing with a boss out in the Portland, Oregon, office. They have a good case developing. Another Buffalo deal. This time it's mostly Americans converted while in prison. They've been buying into the hate program at a local mosque. The Portland Terrorism Task Force has proof that they've been training with weapons out of town at a private farm, and a couple of them have tried to get into Afghanistan, or someplace over there, to fight with Osama.

"Real problem is, the boss in Portland is about to retire, and he seems to have gone a bit rogue. He's making noises that he's decided, against our strong objections, to go out and arrest everyone on whatever charges can be found—expired driver's license, probation or immigration violations, failure to pay child support—you know, anything to get these characters off the street.

"We've got a great chance to place a bug inside a very sensitive location. Touchy stuff, monitoring some of these protected professions, but [the Department of] Justice thinks we have enough grounds here to justify it and they think the attorney general will approve it. But Chuck doesn't want to wait. He wants to take it down now, and he's telling the director, in so many words, to go pound salt.

"You are to deliver a message to Chuck: either join the team or pack up your desk."

I was to let the Portland SAC know that the director and the attorney general were not pleased about plans to take down the Portland case prematurely. The bureau was already taking heat from some in liberal circles that the Lackawanna Six were merely kids "playing at killing infidels." This time DOJ agreed with the FBI that the investigation should mature before people were arrested; therefore, no bleeding heart could cry entrapment or claim that the federal government was profiling Muslims.

Chuck had a different view of things. He was worried that this group of self-styled mujahideen could walk into a synagogue any day and start killing people. When I explained to him that my first assignment had been in Atlanta during his time there as a supervisor, he became slightly more cordial, but he didn't seem inclined to change his attitude about how the investigation should culminate. In the end, though, I had nothing to do with the decision to let the case develop further in Portland. I would imagine that the U.S. attorney for the District of Oregon might have made it clear that he alone decided who would be prosecuted in his judicial district and when those people would be prosecuted. But I'm just guessing.

Ultimately, five of Portland's American mujahideen were convicted of conspiring to support terrorism. Six tried to hook up with their al Qaeda brethren in Afghanistan but were unable to pass through China. Five returned to the States, but one stayed behind and eventually found his glory when he was killed in Afghanistan almost a year later. Another cooperated and pleaded to a lesser charge.

Now the bureau had two field divisions, Buffalo and Portland, that knew how to handle a terrorism investigation with international implications. We were working against time, but we were getting the engines running.

I did have a major success in Portland. I met a young case agent who really seemed to be what the Fly Team needed. He asked me if he could buy me a beer and I accepted. Later that evening, after we became more familiar, he looked at me almost pleadingly and said, "Mr. Holcomb, please help me get the hell out of here. I've had enough of this place. Half of these people don't even think 9/11 really happened." Just as my first SAC in Atlanta had said to me many years earlier when I pleaded for a job back in the Northeast, I told him that there was only one job I might be able to help him with. He eventually became one of my best Fly Team members. The trip had been well worth it.

Not long after my return from Portland, Pat had more news for me. "Looks like something is brewing in Albany; maybe another homegrown cell like Buffalo. Borrow Soufan from New York and head up there. They've got a new SAC. I'll call him and let him know you're coming."

I grabbed an analyst from the al Qaeda unit, arranged for Ali and two other New York agents to meet me in Albany, and headed upstate. The Albany office was small, and many of the agents there tended to work bankers' hours. It had a reputation as a retirement office for agents escaping from New York City.

The new SAC was young, having risen up the career ladder quickly after catching the director's eye. We arrived in Albany late that night, sat down together, and reviewed the case. It looked as if a local Muslim imam was the real deal. He was a terrorist threat and had made suspicious movements, such as placing suspicious phone calls overseas and contacting local ex-cons who, sources indicated, had become radicalized while in prison. The case followed the same pattern we saw in Portland.

To the Albany boss's credit, he admitted his ranks were thin when it came to counterterrorism experience. He also conceded that he had virtually no experience with it himself. I told him, "It looks like you may have something serious here. You've got a guy who is calling a number overseas, a number that comes back to a known terrorist. Your guy also had a visit before 9/11 from a very radical cleric who is also a known supporter of terrorism. On top of it all, he is showing your surveillance people all the signs of being wary, and he seems to be trying to spot them with classic countersurveillance moves. "

The SAC summoned his agents into a conference room for a strategy discussion. Twenty mature-looking agents and a smattering of new ones flanked the table. I said, "It looks like you have landed the next important case. It's conceivable that by the end of the month there could be a dozen or more FISA wiretaps up and running on your suspects." I expected a little emotion from the room, but most of the agents were expressionless. A few kept glancing at the clock; it was almost 5 p.m.

"OK, then, anyone have a question?" Not even a comment. Then one by one, they rose from their chairs and headed out the door.

I thought, These are the same folks that hate headquarters because it meddles and tries to tell them what to do. We're going to have to get some fresh blood in here. Fortunately, a young case agent—a bright, motivated kid who had spent time in Japan as a Mormon missionary—was up to the task.

I told the agent in charge how I could help and called Pete in Buffalo. His office had earned bragging rights as one that could successfully work a terrorism case. Pete said, "No problem, Ray. I'll call the SAC in Albany tomorrow, and we'll give him whatever he needs. We'll walk him through the paces and help him line up the assets."

When I called the supervisor in Portland and asked her about helping Albany, she was also willing. "We'll try to do whatever we can, and we can sure show them how to avoid some of the land mines along the way."

Buffalo sent nine people to Albany to help the agents there get up and running. That kind of commitment, without direct orders from headquarters, was unprecedented. Buffalo wasn't a big office and didn't have people to spare, but the Buffalo folks really got it. They understood the importance of supporting other field offices in dealing with terrorism. Eventually, the Albany subject was arrested trying to buy shoulder-launched, surface-to-air missiles or man-portable air defense systems. In rapid succession, with a little backing from Washington, three field divisions had rolled up wannabe mujahideen before they could hurt anyone.

Eighteen

Interrogation in Kabul

Between the Portland and Albany cases, we were having another frustrating day crammed into our undersized temporary quarters. The *Washington Post*'s "Super Squad for Terror" was still largely a fiction. Douglas and I continued to borrow agents from New York and elsewhere whenever we needed someone for a mission. I could not have continued with deployments while struggling to build the Fly Team if it had not been for Douglas.

Douglas charged into the room, tripping over one of the boxes that were strewn everywhere. "Pat and Andy want to see you right away." He seemed concerned. "And it looks like somebody is in trouble."

OK, I thought, which bureaucrat have I insulted today? It was becoming almost impossible to do our job, whatever we thought that job was in the chaos following 9/11, without upsetting some prima donna in headquarters. "Where are they now, Doug?"

"I think they're with the director. They hustled up to the seventh floor without explaining anything except I heard Pat say, 'Nobody past you and me gets briefed on this!'"

I went up to Andy's office. "Boss, you want me?"

"Hey, Ray, this is the deal. I need you to pack your bag, a light bag; get Ali Soufan; and be out at Dulles by tonight. You're going to the Middle East. Can't tell you where, and I can't tell you who, but the director wants you two to join in the interrogation of a really big one. We've finally nailed one of those

221

bastards, a top guy. Now the biggest problem is not getting him to talk, but getting the CIA to let us have access."

Andy was very excited so I let him roll on. At least ten years younger than I, he was still exuberant. He hadn't been in headquarters long enough yet to have that beaten out of him. I said, "Boss, you're telling me that Soufan and I are heading for the other side of the world tonight, on an important mission, and I can't know who it is we'll be interrogating?"

"Sorry, Ray, Pat's orders. You know how this thing will explode if the press gets it. America needs some kind of good news. The agency had a role in grabbing this guy, and if there is a leak, they'll be even more reluctant to deal with us. This news really needs to come from the U.S. government, not some police blotter reporter in New York City."

I liked Andy a lot, and I wanted to believe that he really knew I could keep a secret. If it had been somebody else, I would have taken it as an insult. Andy said that Soufan, a couple other young agents from New York, and I would be boarding a private flight out of Dulles that night.

"OK, boss, but I have to ask you: don't you trust me?"

"That's not it, Ray. You know better than anyone that when Ali starts packing his briefcase, those cops on the New York Joint Terrorism Task Force will do anything to find out where he's going and why. It will be a headline in the morning edition of the *Daily News*, and there will be no one—not the CIA, not the Pakistanis, no one—who will deal with the bureau again." He was right, but it still bothered me that I was good enough to start up the director's Fly Team but not good enough to be trusted with a name.

Then I reminded myself, What was I thinking? This trip sounded as if it would be the first big break. We had just kicked the Taliban and al Qaeda out of Afghanistan, but we had only captured one other major al Qaeda member, Abu Zubaydah. Ali and I had the opportunity to get our hands on somebody big, and my feelings were hurt?

I called Ali. "Ali, pack your bag. The director is sending us to the Middle East tonight. They caught a big one."

By now, he had taken to calling me "uncle," which I knew was a sign of respect. If anybody else called me that, I would have known it was a jibe, but in his case he meant it in the best way.

"Who, Uncle?"

"Don't know, and they won't tell me."

"You are fucking kidding me, right?"

"Dead serious, man. You know—*Daily News* paranoia."

"Fucking unbelievable! OK, I'll get on a flight to Dulles this evening."

"Good, I'll meet you there; just don't give your fiancée a time line. We have no idea how long we'll be gone."

"You got it, Uncle. I'll call when I'm en route."

▪ ▪ ▪

I drove to Dulles early that evening and picked up Ali and two other young terrorism agents from the New York office. We then met the group we'd be traveling with; they had gathered at the private hangar. They were less than cordial and obviously not happy that we were joining them.

The private jet held thirty people comfortably. We crammed in thirty-five and headed out for somewhere. Ali and I talked in low tones as the jet cruised well above forty thousand feet. "Hey, Uncle, I know who we're going to meet."

"You do? How did you find out?"

"The CIA briefed the NYPD yesterday, and when I ran into the office this morning, my boss was being briefed by a police captain!"

"You're kidding, right?"

"Since Cohen left the CIA and came over to the police department as Kelly's best friend and deputy commissioner in charge of intel, he has been scooping the bureau on everything that happens, whether in the Five Boroughs or overseas. His contacts in the agency still feed him information and then take shots at the FBI for leaking classified information whenever they get the chance."

"If it leaks to the New York papers, you know the cops will claim it was the FBI. Pretty slick, and the bureau doesn't win."

"Yeah, Cohen hates the bureau, and he uses his buddies at the agency to stick it to us every chance he gets. Anyway, it's Ramzi bin al-Sheib, you know, the guy who helped KSM [Kahlid Sheikh Mohammad] plan the whole 9/11 attack. Very, very big catch. He has to have the keys to the whole AQ [al Qaeda] organization and its future plans."

The aircraft was not configured for a good night's rest. Normally leased out to private entertainers, it had bench seats and tables. We had no place to lie back, at least not in the section allotted to us.

Aside from the few FBI agents sent to process intelligence from the raid site and my small team, the rest of the plane was packed with strangers who didn't want to meet me or anyone else on board. The CIA folks were a cold, taciturn group, very different from what I had become accustomed to in the FBI, where backslapping, crude jokes, and in-your-face frankness were the rule instead of the exception.

We touched down in Cyprus to refuel and arrived in Karachi, Pakistan, late the next day. We'd been traveling for nearly twenty hours, and not one of the other passengers ever said a word to us. So much for the new spirit of cooperation. They had obviously been instructed to be cautious around us.

Over the next weeks, I would come to realize why. Their modus operandi differed from ours, and now we were moving into their territory. Although we had good reason to believe that the agency made end runs around the bureau inside the United States, we had little idea how the agency ran things overseas. Frankly, it didn't really matter much to us before 9/11, as long as it didn't involve spying on U.S. citizens. It's illegal for the CIA to conduct intelligence collection on U.S. citizens unless it does so in concert with the FBI.

The sun was bright and the hot air thick as we stepped down on the tarmac. Beret-wearing Pakistani troops and nervous-looking Americans were everywhere, most of them scowling at us. Fuck it, I thought. We'll do our job if we just get a little direction and support from our headquarters. I had heard that some bureau managers were prone to being conveniently away from their phones when it came to making hard decisions or strapping on some balls and taking on the folks at Langley.

A number of black vans rolled in and prompted some activity. We went to the FBI legat's house for a quick briefing. The Pakistanis had raided a location, and the agency was sifting through a treasure trove of intelligence. FBI Headquarters had asked for access, and the agency had agreed, reluctantly and with limitations. Their agents would only let FBI analysts near documents, computer hard drives, and cell phone records after they had reviewed them. The legat told us that bin al-Sheib and his friends were being moved somewhere else later that day, and we had better be ready to hustle or we would be left behind. "Whatever the folks back in headquarters have been telling you that they've worked out," he continued, "well, forget about it. Those deals don't stand up over here."

I threw some water on my face and dashed for a seat on the van heading toward the embassy in Islamabad. We had just sat down for a hot cafeteria meal when there was a flurry of activity and muffled conversation followed by people heading for the door. The legat said a few words to one of them and returned to our table. "Take a swallow, fellows. You're heading for the airport."

Only two hours after landing, we were turning around and heading somewhere else. We didn't have a cell phone that would work in that part of the world, and the lone satellite phone I had grabbed on my way out of headquarters was packed deep in my duffel. As I boarded the minivan I asked the legat to call and update Andy back in Washington.

"Man, good luck wherever you're going!"

With my empty stomach gurgling, I nodded and tried to grin, reminding myself that the younger agents might be watching. Some of the agents who had flown over with us—the document examiners and computer experts— stayed in Karachi to haggle over access to the seized documents and computers. At this point, few in the CIA or White House were thinking about prosecuting terrorists in the United States or anywhere else. Legal issues focused around evidence, chain of custody, discovery, and detention were not on anyone's mind outside of the FBI. Understandably, most were focusing on gleaning critical intelligence pertinent to another attack.

We arrived at a military air base. Pakistani orderlies in turbans, carrying burnished platters with linen napkins draped over their arms, offered us soda and grape juice.

We sat there for hours. The sun was setting by the time aircraft engines reverberated, and a darkened C-130 Hercules aircraft taxied into view. The engines fluttered and quieted and the plane's tailgate dropped down. Black vehicles rolled in and men who appeared to be Americans started leading figures up the ramp of the plane. The five male figures had chains on their legs and hands and black hoods over their heads. A man stuck his head through the terminal door, "Everybody who's going, get on board!"

We hauled our duffel bags, which were becoming heavier by the hour, out to the tarmac and lined up to board. I deftly stepped over and around the dark-hooded figures chained to the floor of the aircraft. We strapped ourselves into four basket seats hanging from the wall. The men seated across stared at us, patently signaling that we were unwelcome. As the C-130 lifted off, the five hooded figures on the floor sat cross-legged, possibly trying to pray or so fatigued that they were asleep sitting up.

After about an hour and a half we started our descent. Ali told me, "We're en route to Afghanistan, Uncle." He knew there was only one place we could be landing within an hour from Karachi. "Ray! This guy is big. He helped KSM plan 9/11. He has to know what else is on the planning board. He knows a shitload of stuff!"

I was impressed that Ali could muster so much energy after two days without sleep, but I had come to know that this work was what he lived for.

We landed on a blacked-out runway on the edge of Kabul—the Taliban still roamed the adjacent countryside—and vehicles dashed across the tarmac to the plane. After men with red lens flashlights—red light is not as visible from a distance—created a rough perimeter around the aircraft, the five hooded prisoners were removed.

We'd had almost no sleep for days and little food, and it was cold in Kabul. Everyone looked ragged. Even the newly energized, young Ali had dark circles under his eyes and a three-day beard that made him look much older.

When a female in her thirties arrived with the CIA greeting party, she and Ali realized that they knew each other from another mission. That was reassuring. Up until now nobody would acknowledge us, let alone provide us with any help. The CIA was not happy we were there, but I could tell that she and her compatriots recognized, respected, and thought they might make use of Ali's skill set.

The road into town was pockmarked with bomb craters. There was little light in downtown Kabul, but we could still discern the outlines of people stirring in the alleys between run-down buildings. We went to the compound, which had been transformed into a virtual fortress, enclosed by sandbagged walls and sizable steel shipping containers crowned with loops of razor wire.

The guards at the complex were an amalgam of trusted Afghans and former U.S. special operations types who were now working as private contractors. To blend in, the Americans had grown beards and wore the traditional, Afghan pie-shaped hat and long pajama-like shirt. With weapons slung across their chests and ammunition magazines strapped everywhere, they were bad-looking dudes, betrayed only by their black Oakley sunglasses.

The senior officer was less than gracious, telling us there were no beds at the inn. "You'll have to make do with whatever you can find."

The FBI had a two-man contingent there in an office the size of a walk-in closet. Both agents hailed from small midwestern offices. They'd volunteered for the assignment and were hanging out in Kabul and picking up odd jobs. The nearest legat, in Islamabad, didn't appear to have a clue or care about their mission. I did know they were handling some counterfeit U.S. currency issues and providing limited training to the fledgling Afghan police, mostly firearms instruction. Other than that, I couldn't figure out why these two were there.

That first night, despite a lack of sleep, Ali was anxious to question Ramzi bin al-Sheib. Ali and another FBI agent, Stephen, had previously questioned Abu Zubaydah. At one point, Zubaydah was head of military operations for al Qaeda and had a key role in the millennium plot to bomb the Los Angeles International Airport. After a shootout and his capture, the CIA secreted Zubaydah at a location outside Pakistan. There were no qualified CIA interrogators available, and he was in bad shape after taking rounds in the stomach, testicles, and thigh. The doctors thought he would not survive the night. Under normal circumstances, the CIA agents wouldn't have let the FBI near their captive during an agency operation. Because Zubaydah seemed near death and Ali spoke Arabic, the CIA grudgingly afforded Ali and Stephen access. The agents told both of them to get whatever they could out of him before he died.

Ali and Stephen changed the dressings on Zubaydah's wounds, gave him water, spoke calmly with him about normal things, and developed a relationship in a brief period. Zubaydah survived the first few days and gradually gained strength.

Before deploying, Stephen copied pictures of the fifty most wanted terrorists off of the Internet. One day, on a hunch, Stephen started showing Zubaydah some of the pictures. One was of Khalid Sheik Mohammed, who we suspected was a key player in just about every major terror attack against the United States over the previous ten years. Zubaydah, impressed with Stephen's preparedness, referred to KSM as "Mukhtar" during a passing comment.

Bingo! For months, every American intelligence agency had been trying to find out who the mysterious Mukhtar was. The name had repeatedly come up in intercepted messages. Now we knew that Mukhtar was another name for KSM. Ingenuity and hunches often reaped results. Coupled with Ali's talent and painkillers, Stephen and Ali now had Abu Zubaydah talking a blue streak.

The information they garnered went straight to the CIA people running the detention site, but initially only these two FBI agents were in that room with the hardened terrorist. Langley and the White House received their daily progress reports. Whether senior CIA officials learned that these two FBI agents were pulling off one of the most successful interrogations in recent memory is subject to debate. The issue has been aired so there is no dispute that a CIA specialist showed up and started instituting a much more aggressive approach to questioning Zubaydah. Soufan made it clear that he would have nothing to do with the new approach. But he had no authority to interfere. He was in a CIA facility in a foreign land. He could verbally object but if he tried to do more than that they would remove him.

Reports to the White House outlined how "enhanced interrogation measures" had been successful in gleaning critical information from Abu Zubaydah and others. Whether waterboarding or other extraordinary measures were credited with getting some or most of the information that Soufan and Stephen obtained through more subtle and cunning techniques is an interesting question. Perhaps the reports misled the White House or maybe the so-called extraordinary measures were successful, as some within the CIA claimed. Ali left. Stephen stayed on for a while longer but did not participate directly. He was not in the room with the CIA when the CIA took over the questioning but may have been allowed to pass questions through to Zubaydah. Only those present really know.

It is reputed that when George Tenet learned that two FBI agents were debriefing Abu Zubaydah and having some success, he was not happy. I am sure he and his senior staff wondered why an organization with a budget that dwarfed the FBI's tenfold or more was not handling one of the most important interrogations in some time. In any event, the agency's man took over, and Soufan and Stephen stepped aside.

Now in Afghanistan, we were running out of steam. Ali was anxious to get out to the detention facility immediately, but he soon realized that it made little sense since the subjects were in worse physical shape than we were, and we were dead tired.

"Ali, you will be wasting your time with these guys. They probably don't even remember their own names right now. Let's find a corner on the floor, curl up, and try to sleep."

We found two sleeping pads in the FBI office. The room was so small I had to place my pad under one of the desks. Our two partners went to a filthy, old bunkroom for some fitful rest.

It was still dark when we rode out to the detention facility, a warehouse converted into a prison. The interior contained two to three dozen cells and rudimentary latrine facilities. Tajiks—Afghan tribesmen who were, at least for the time being, siding with U.S. and Coalition forces—provided security. The building, surrounded by a high wire fence, was nondescript on the exterior. Guards walked the perimeter casually, Kalashnikovs slung from their shoulders. None spoke a word of English.

■   ■   ■

Early the next morning, well into the fourth day since we had left the States, we were given access to the prisoners. As the senior FBI agent, I was responsible for guiding my group, keeping everyone safe and on track. The problem was a lack of clarity; we knew only that the CIA and FBI were going to conduct a joint interrogation of the prisoner. Great, I thought, easy for them to say back in Washington. I'm sure that over a cup of coffee at Langley, one of my bosses was given complete assurance that we would be allowed to do our job, but we were on the other side of the world and weren't welcome here.

At this point, I was the only armed agent. The two FBI agents back at the compound had an extra pistol, and they lent it to me along with three full magazines before we left that morning.

A CIA employee escorted us out to the prison, and together we inspected the men we had brought in the previous night. In some cases, when they appeared to be too tight, I removed the flex-cuffs binding the prisoners' wrists. We made sure that each prisoner was relatively healthy, fed, and given water, and then the CIA employee headed back into town.

As he walked away his only comment was that he would see us later. There was no furniture in the room that my small team could use, just some native

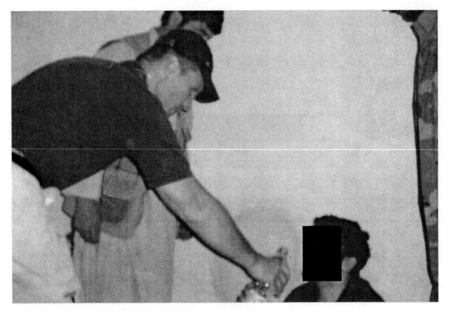

An al Qaeda detainee and the author somewhere in Central Asia.

blankets on the concrete floor. Ramzi bin al-Sheib, as with the others, was in solitary confinement somewhere in the vast building, and the Tajik guards watched our every move. Ali wanted to get right to work, but no one in our group spoke even a smattering of any Afghan dialect so we couldn't converse with the men who had the keys. We believed that someone from the agency would be joining us soon. Hours passed but no one arrived. They were making it clear that they were in charge of the interrogation. I wondered if it was just the old CIA-versus-FBI thing, or whether Ali's role in the Abu Zubaydah interrogation was coming back to bite us.

The Tajik guards were there to ensure no one would help the prisoners escape. These guards were the toughest I had ever met, hard physically and mentally. The nights had turned very cold. They wore sandals and squatted around their small cooking pot at meals and teatime. At night, they'd wrap their shoulders with a shawl and disappear into the frigid dark, watching, just watching. As there was no plumbing, I cautioned my team to make sure that when they stepped outside to relieve themselves at night, they did so right by the door where there was a small overhead light. I told them to avoid any sudden movements since many sets of eyes would be locked on them from somewhere out in the dark. As the day turned late, the guard commander—six feet five, bearded, and green-eyed—realized that we had gone without food for some time. He motioned to us to join them, and they shared their tea and soup, nodding and grinning throughout the meal. After almost a day of waiting, it was the first thing we'd eaten. Although comforted by the fact that the food seemed well boiled, I would have eaten just about anything.

Late in the afternoon of the following day, a car pulled up outside. We heard some chatter between a new voice, clearly an American, and the guards. Finally, we might be able to get something going. Then in walked a small man, balding, in his forties, and wearing black tactical clothing similar to what my SWAT team had worn in the mid-1990s. He had a slight accent. "Hey, guys, how's it going out here? Hi, Ali. I think we've met before, can't quite remember, though. I'm going to go check on the boys, and then let's have a talk. Be right back."

He had barely acknowledged anyone but Ali. Wide-eyed, Ali stood, for the first time since I had known him, speechless.

Ali shook his head, bemused and frustrated. "Ray, I know this guy. This is who they send to interrogate bin al-Sheib? Incredible! He's Jewish, and bin al-Sheib will figure that out right away. He's not stupid. There is no way he will give important information to a Jew. What are they thinking? The biggest catch since Zubaydah and this is their A team?"

"Hey, Ali, maybe it's some kind of mind-screw. You know, try to mess him up psychologically?"

Ali didn't even answer.

The CIA interrogator returned in a little while with a number of others who must have been with his organization. They didn't introduce themselves. He took Ali and me aside. "OK, guys, this is how I'm told it will work. You give me your questions and I'll ask them for you. I'll give you the answers after each session with him. Those are my orders."

We were miles from anywhere, and our sole means of communication was a satellite phone. We couldn't call headquarters and explain that there was virtually no collaboration. We were somewhere in northern Afghanistan, and it wasn't clear what instructions our Tajik guards had been given should we try to leave. As far as our hosts knew, we were cut off from home, we were not comfortable, and we were bound to wear out fast. I'm sure they figured we'd be out of their way soon.

I was fuming, sick of being jerked around. We had spent the previous night trying to sleep on the floor, but I had been awake most of it with my pistol nearby, thinking anyone could slip in at any time and slice our throats like Afghan goats. Yeah, everything's been worked out with the CIA. Just get there and do your job. I had fought back chills as I lay on the cold concrete floor. Now I was beyond angry and beyond tired.

During the time we spent at the "facility," I saw some amateurish attempts at scaring the prisoners but nothing even resembling torture; instead, they were more like bad Halloween pranks. Some of these prisoners had fought against the Coalition's invasion of Afghanistan. The older ones might have fought the Russians. Some had taken cover in mountain caves while American bombers dropped tons of explosives on them for days. They had trained and fought alongside Afghan and Pakistani Taliban, by far some of the fiercest fighters in the world. Here we had Americans just a few years out of graduate school who thought they could intimidate the prisoners.

The second morning, I decided to fire up the satellite phone, pacing the prison yard until I found a four-by-four-foot area where I could get weak reception. Each time I thought I was getting a call through to headquarters in Washington, I'd lose the connection. I reached the legat in Islamabad on his cell phone, explained our circumstance, and asked him to relay our situation to Pat D'Amuro in Washington. Hopefully he could read between the lines of my message and do something to help us.

I told Ali, "Well, we're not going to be seeing the cavalry over the horizon any time soon, so it's time for the great escape." Ali agreed.

The guards seemed relaxed with us now. We casually peered into the few vehicles parked nearby and noticed that one old Pathfinder had keys in the ignition. The problem was that the steering wheel was on the right side and the manual shift was to the left and on the floor. That's the least of our problems, I thought. We'd only driven the route from the compound in Kabul to the detention center once. "Ali, gather up the guys. We're out of here. By the way, do you remember how to get back into town?"

"I don't remember how to get back, but I can drive this wreck if you navigate." We gathered up our gear, and looking as official as we could, we drove out of the compound, the young guard at the gate smiling and saluting as we bucked and jerked in and out of gear.

Things were still rough in Kabul. We drove down a bombed-out dirt road past abandoned Soviet tanks and aircraft that littered the roadsides and near land mines marked by white rocks. Some of the bomb craters were so big that our Pathfinder practically disappeared from view for a moment before re-emerging. The fields near the airfield were full of people bent over and probing, searching for antipersonnel mines the Soviets had dropped everywhere in their retreat, and their legacy—limbless people on crude crutches—was apparent everywhere. Nearing the city, the streets became more congested with pedestrians: Afghan women with large bundles on their heads, most in light blue or violet burkas; men in various kinds of ill-fitting military uniforms; and some angry-looking, bearded men with black turbans, the Taliban.

We saw more Afghan security posts and checkpoints as we neared the town. The night we had arrived, someone had written down the password for entering the compound. Fortunately, Ali had saved the scrap of paper. Suddenly an Afghan soldier, shouldering his AK-47, began shouting at us, his finger on the trigger. He was talking in a dialect, neither Arabic nor English. "OK, Ali, tell him what he wants to hear," I whispered while trying to smile in the soldier's direction. The password was also in an Afghan dialect, and Ali had no more familiarity with it than I. With each failed attempt at pronunciation, the guard got louder and his glare intensified. I was ten feet away, but I could see the increasing pressure on the trigger. We sure as hell didn't look like Taliban, but this guy was getting ready to blow us away because we couldn't get the fuckin' word right? On the third, and probably last, attempt, Ali got it close enough, and this furious soldier, who'd been ready to kill us, smiled, lowered his weapon, and waved us on in the right direction. Minutes later, we were in the center of town.

I was awestruck at actually being in Kabul, after watching it on TV months earlier when American and Coalition forces arrived. Afghan men and some women sported Western-style business clothes. Commerce was resuming. Some traffic lights actually flashed, although drivers generally ignored them, and the place had signs of returning energy. We worked our way down the main street, not worried about rules of the road since there were none.

Back at the government compound, we headed upstairs to meet the man in charge. The young woman who knew Ali and had met us on our arrival stopped us. "You can't have access to this area without an escort."

This interference was not a shock, although it did annoy me. I got to a phone and reached Andy back in Washington. He had already been briefed on the situation and assured me that Pat had taken the matter "across the river," meaning over to Langley. In the meantime, Andy told us to sit tight and not to go back to the holding facility until "this thing is resolved."

We slept in the compound in one of the vacated bunk rooms. Exhausted, I felt as if I were staying in a five-star hotel, even though the filthy shower with the plugged drain would have reminded most Americans of a septic tank. It would have taken a small earthquake to rouse us that night.

Andy called the following day, saying that things would now go as originally planned. The local boss, for his part, rebuffed most of our attempts to meet, preferring instead to convey pithy messages through his subordinates. "He is very busy," was their pat response, as if he had many more important things to do than interrogate the biggest terrorist leader captured since Abu Zubaydah.

The next day, back at the detention center, Ali sat close to the prisoner. Initially, Ramzi bin al-Sheib avoided eye contact with Ali. When Ali looked straight at him, greeting him in his own language, the prisoner's gaze left the floor, and he looked directly at him, somewhat startled. Within minutes, a rambling dialogue was under way. I could only identify an occasional word, but it was apparent that they were engrossed in conversation about more than the weather or the quality of the food. Bin al-Sheib was chattering more than I had heard during the previous few days.

If anything, Ali's technique had gotten even better since our days in Sana'a. Again, he employed his understanding of Islam and of Arab and Middle Eastern culture. He looked for the first opportunity to engage bin al-Sheib in a discussion of religion, almost challenging him on certain points and conversing about the meaning of the Koran. In classic law enforcement style, he used knowledge to steer bin al-Sheib subtly in the direction he wanted, just as he had done on those late nights interviewing the Yemenis, who, unknowingly, handed him the identities of two of the 9/11 hijackers.

Time and again I would marvel at how Ali deftly planted seeds of doubt in prisoners' minds. At first, they would be astonished that they were sitting across from a young, handsome, erudite Muslim American, who happened to also be an FBI agent. Then, when they realized that he could actually recite the Koran, they were disarmed and, in time, at his mercy.

Later, during trips to Guantánamo, I would watch Ali through a one-way mirror and listen through an intercom system. During other interrogations, I would sit nearby, close enough to watch and hear. I didn't speak much Arabic, but I was good at gleaning information from voice inflections and body language. Often I had a translator by my side. Ali and I always sat and talked afterward. He was good at sharing with me what he had learned. In some way I think discussing it helped him gather his own thoughts. I assisted him in any way I could to prepare daily transcripts of the interrogations and reports that would be sent back to headquarters as soon as possible. Later, we would discuss the day's results and the answers he would seek the following day. All Ali needed was time.

In this case, however, time was never in the equation. Someone back at Langley had played the FBI, and the true design was to deny us genuine access to bin al-Sheib. Only an hour into Ali's first interview of the prisoner, we heard a sudden roar of engines and gravel splattering outside the building. A string of black SUVs slammed to a stop, and a group of men dressed in dark battle-dress uniforms entered the room and hooded and shackled bin al-Sheib. Without acknowledging our presence, they practically lifted him off the floor and carried him out to the waiting vehicles.

At the last minute, one of the Americans turned to us. "They're taking him to a new location. It's been agreed that two of you can go on with him. However, from this point forward other people will do the interrogating and you will only be allowed to pass questions through a middle man. That's just the way it is. We're done here."

"Son of a bitch!" Ali complained, "I could fill a two-page, single-lined report with what he told me in forty minutes. We were just warming up!"

I'm certain that the agency's interrogator got a lot less in four or five days than Ali did in forty-five minutes, but it was the agency's parade. It wasn't going to let the FBI join in.

When we got back to the compound, I called HQ and asked for Pat. "Pat, this is bullshit. Ali was getting good information. The agency guy got squat. Then they pulled the rug out from under Ali. They're shipping the guy on to another location, and they've said that we can send two along to watch."

Pat told me he'd find out where they were taking bin al-Sheib but that he needed something from us in the meantime. "Ray, have Joe and Stan go on with the agency folks. You and Ali have to get down to Sana'a to get the bureau involved in a counterterrorism task force that is being stood up there. It is going to be a State Department–led operation, but the Defense Department will have a big say. They've asked for the bureau's participation. Get there as soon as you can."

Nineteen

The Next Attack

We followed our orders to return to Yemen and work with the new anti-terrorism fusion cell. This collection of U.S. government agencies, all with a major stake in the war against terrorism, would operate from forward, somewhat hospitable, and strategically located countries to assist cooperative governments in combating the greater terrorist threat.

We would be flying from Kabul to the former Soviet satellite of Uzbekistan and by way of Rome head to Sana'a. The night before our flight out of Kabul, we gathered in a small, popular expat bar. Soviet war memorabilia hung on the walls. Afghanistan has rarely known peace. To its men, fighting is an unrelenting inheritance.

The bar's walls were also covered with graffiti. Most expats posted comments for friends and strangers passing through, including doodles, witticisms, and even poetry by some notable former tourists. Being a fan of Rudyard Kipling, I spotted one of his most appropriate poems, which another fan had scrawled in a corner:

> *When you're wounded and left on Afghanistan's plains,*
> *And the women come out to cut up what remains,*
> *Jest roll to your rifle and blow out your brains*
> *An' go to your Gawd like a soldier*
> *Go, go, go like a soldier,*

Go, go, go like a soldier,
Go, go, go like a soldier,
So-oldier of the Queen!

History has shown that Afghanistan proves to be a graveyard for invaders. As I began to feel the effects of the Russian beer, I wondered what history will divulge fifty years from now about America's intervention in a place where the people didn't appear to have any interest in change.

We were up most of that night drinking. Russian beer reportedly contains a good deal of formaldehyde, but after what we'd been exposed to during the previous weeks I didn't think it made any difference. I was damn determined to get good and hammered. I had earned it.

I talked to some people in the bar, including one older man who was stunned that the FBI was in Kabul. "I used to be one of the guys who filled out the Taliban's shopping lists. When we were helping them fight the Russians, I was responsible for getting them the tools they asked for."

The two local FBI agents walked into the bar to say farewell. Good guys, they didn't seem to be doing a lot of heavy lifting, but then again they were in Afghanistan, far from friends and family. My impression was that neither one had had much experience with the CIA before. I was concerned that they were unwittingly putting themselves in a corner. I told them, "We're leaving at sunrise, guys. Watch your backs, and stay safe. Hey, just a thought, I'm not saying that it's a setup, but since you two, out of the goodness of your hearts, have been taking care of a lot of the routine chores out at the prison—food deliveries, paying the help, making sure things work, all that stuff—who do you think they'll be pointing fingers at if anyone should ever have issues with that place?"

I was alluding to the increasing worldwide controversy over special holding facilities and accusations of prisoner abuse and torture. It was clear from their expressions that they had never considered the possibility that they could be implicated.

Our sixteen-passenger government plane to Uzbekistan took us above a varied collage of terrain, from a corner of the Kashmir mountains to stark deserts, highways, and the cobalt-black spikes of the Pamirs, the Zeravshan, and

Our last night in Kabul was spent at a popular expat watering hole.

Kakshaal mountain ranges. When we cleared the mountains, we flew above valleys of burgeoning greenery and followed a twisting river that finally took us to the metropolis of Tashkent.

The embassy people who picked us up were mostly ethnic Russians, another irony. During the Soviet occupation of Afghanistan, we helped the Taliban slaughter Russians. Now we were hiring the Russians to run our embassy. After the embassy people dropped us off at our hotel, we walked down the street to a Middle Eastern restaurant, starving for decent food of any kind. Although the sun was setting, I could easily see that Tashkent was a head-turning mix of cultures and history, with its Muslim and Russian architecture, Orthodox Church spires, old minarets, prerevolution classic architecture, and stark, massive Stalin-era buildings. The people were a blend of Asian or Mongol and Russian blonds. It was intoxicating for me, as I had studied the history of Central and South Asia in college. We had just left one of the most deprived and precarious countries in the world and now were walking down cosmopolitan streets where women dressed in European styles and cars lined the thoroughfares. Missions such as this one kept my senses in turmoil. It was not a job for someone who needs continuity and likes to follow a regimen.

When we finally located a restaurant serving Mediterranean fare, Ali was elated. We hadn't eaten anything worth remembering for days, and he now found a taste of home. He did most of the ordering, and we tore into delicious bowls of tabbouleh, baba ghanoush, hummus, chicken and lamb kabobs, and flatbread. We ate too much, too fast; then we went back to our rooms to go to sleep.

The phone woke me around three in the morning. "Uncle, I feel terrible. Hold on." I heard Ali throwing up. "My head has been over the toilet bowl for the last hour."

"I'll be right down."

Ali was losing body fluids as though he were a fire hose. I called the embassy's emergency number and left a recorded message, asking for the medical unit. As I waited for a return call, I made him as comfortable as I could. At 8 a.m., the embassy sent over a nurse. She turned out to be not only competent but also attractive with a great personality. Her presence, along with a few liters of intravenous fluids and some antibiotics, had him feeling better in a day, and two days later we were booking our flights to Sana'a.

Her diagnosis was food poisoning. I chided Ali, asking how it was that a Lebanese kid couldn't handle the home cooking while the two young white agents from the New York office and I had done just fine. The day before Ali's and my flight (the two New York agents had flown out the morning before), Ali said he felt stronger, so we took a stroll. We explored the old section, enjoying good weather and a sidewalk vendor fair that hawked local art, exotic spices, and delicious foods. Tashkent was on the old Silk Road made famous by Marco Polo, and the fair presented beautiful silk rugs and tapestries. The town's central park featured an immense statue of a fierce-looking, mustachioed Timur the Lame atop a giant warhorse. A descendant of Genghis Khan, Timur had taken raping and pillaging to new extremes in a part of the world infamous for destructive invaders. And this man is their George Washington, I thought. I understood a little better why Central Asian tribes think of war as their regional pastime.

We had a long layover in Rome, and while checking departure times, I ran into a young-looking American with a military haircut. We struck up a conversation, and when I learned the young Marine was heading to Sana'a,

Ali and I took him under our wing. Destined to join the Marines' security detachment at the U.S. Embassy, he was from a small Midwestern state and had never been out of the country. We took an immediate liking to this wide-eyed kid and brought him to the business class lounge as our guest.

As we explained to the young Marine who we were and why we were heading his way, Ali became agitated. "Uncle, see that guy over there?" He was nodding his head toward a swarthy, Mediterranean-looking man who appeared to be in his forties. "I know that guy. I think he's a terrorist. Possibly Palestinian."

I thought Ali might be joking, but when I pressed him he seemed more confident and more convinced. The young Marine's eyes grew larger as Ali said, "Uncle, I really think we need to get the carabinieri to stop and ID him." He was so confident that I was beginning to believe him. I was about to step into the terminal and see if I could find an Italian policeman when the PA system announced that our flight to Yemen was boarding. We grabbed our bags and our young Marine and headed toward the gate, where we were surprised to find the suspect ahead of us in line, boarding our flight.

Ali's suspected terrorist sat in the front row of first class, immediately behind the cockpit door. Now if he were a terrorist, maybe he chose to sit there because he was planning on taking over the plane. There could be accomplices on the plane as well, I thought, as fatigue and Soufan's paranoia took hold of me. I had learned to trust Ali's instincts.

I pulled the Marine aside, told him about the man seated in first class, and instructed him in what I needed him to do. "If that guy or an accomplice makes a move to enter the cockpit, I will snap his neck. I need you to watch my back." I can still see his expression. He had left the States that day thinking things were going to be uneventful, and now he was in the middle of a Tom Clancy novel.

"Remember, Marine, if you see me move, watch the cabin because he'll have buddies in here, sleepers, and they'll go after me." He nodded vigorously and returned to his seat in the back of the plane.

I sat down and thought through my plan. The Yemenia Air pilots left the cabin door open during the entire flight. This practice was in keeping with the general lack of concern for security that I had observed in Yemen. I removed my trouser belt, thinking that if I subdued this guy I would need a way to cuff him.

Then I settled in for the three-hour flight, keeping a close eye on the suspect. At one point, he got up and started in the direction of the cockpit. Here we go, I thought. Then he turned into the forward galley and asked for a bottle of water. I watched to see if he was making eye contact with anyone on the plane. I looked over in Ali's direction and he was sleeping. Understandable, he's still not recovered from his problem in Tashkent, I thought. Then I looked over my shoulder to find my Marine backup out cold, too. His head was hanging into the aisle, bobbing with the air turbulence. Great, here I am watching Soufan's terrorist, I thought, and my two partners are resting like babies. Guess they have a lot of confidence in me.

An hour later our plane went into a turn, and the pilot announced in Arabic that we were landing in Sana'a. The airport approach passes right over the U.S. Embassy. I continued to watch my target intently for any telltale sign of trouble. With the screech of tires hitting the runway and the whine of jet engines settling down, Ali came to, but he didn't look good. I was worried that whatever had bitten him in Tashkent wasn't done with him.

We shuffled to the gangway, ducked, and exited into the night air. I recognized the familiar, but not necessarily pleasant, smell of Sana'a. I noticed large vehicles down on the tarmac pulled up close to our plane. Then Ali remarked, "Damn it, I was sure I knew this guy! Shit, Uncle," he said with a chuckle, "he's CIA. Really big guy in the organization."

"Wait a minute. You mean the guy you were sure was a terrorist, the guy you wanted the Italians to pull out of line, the guy I was close to strangling if he took one step in the wrong direction—that guy is a CIA boss?!"

There at the foot of the gangway, surrounded by unmistakably important people, was one of the senior counterterrorism bosses in the CIA. I saw the international headline banner in my head, "American FBI Agent Assaults CIA Official on Flight to Yemen; Read All about It!"

Things had to be cooking in Yemen for him to be there. After the usual customs hassles with confused and highly suspicious Yemenis, an embassy driver picked us up and drove us to our hotel. We stayed at the Sheraton, still the only real show in town and where we had set up operations a little more than one year ago, just before 9/11.

The head clerk greeted me with a big, white-toothed grin. "Good evening, Mr. Holcomb. It is so good to have you back."

Yeah, I thought, that's because we pay with a U.S. government credit card, and we don't treat you like servants, as the Middle Eastern guests do.

"I am so sorry you do not like your room, Mr. Holcomb!" I was exhausted and thought that I misunderstood. He continued to smile at me, "Yes, we apologize that the room is not to your liking, Mr. Holcomb."

I was getting irritated, and then I realized what he was doing. He was still smiling, nodding, trying to encourage me to think. "Yes, Mr. Patel. The view is terrible," I said loudly. "I didn't travel all the way here to stare at a garbage dump. What else do you have?"

"I think I have a very nice room for you, Mr. Holcomb."

From our first day in Yemen, we were warned that the security folks would actively try to collect intelligence on us. The Yemeni Political Security Office and Interior Ministry people were very suspicious of our motives. Mr. Patel was telling me that the room that had been set aside for Ali and me was bugged.

Early the next day we went to the embassy. It was only about a quarter mile from the hotel, which was a good thing since the driving conditions in Sana'a were awful. I had forgotten how bad the air was in town. Just as in the rest of the Third World, being environmentally responsible, is not even a passing concern. Eating and surviving the day are. The minute we stepped outside our eyes began to burn. There are no catalytic converters or air pollution regulations. The diesel engines belch black smoke, and the wide-ranging soot mingles day and night with that of burning piles of garbage. And Yemeni men love their cigarettes. A young American has to be tough to work there.

We presented ourselves to the ambassador's secretary, and she advised that he was out at a meeting. Having attended to the requisite protocol, we headed to the temporary rooftop offices of the new counterterrorism cell. One of the techies, the guys who keep communications running and generally provide access to most of the video entertainment in these out-of-the-way places, greeted us. They are often quirky people who get a kick out of things we might consider bizarre, but we learned to love them because they kept us in touch with our world. We crouched down and entered the building's "attic." It was dark, and after the glaring sunlight of mid-morning Sana'a, it was difficult to see. I immediately smacked my head against an aluminum air duct. It sounded worse than it felt but did serve to announce our arrival. My eyes adjusted, and I could make out men and women scattered among the machinery, cables, and pipes. They were huddled over computers by lamplight; papers, maps, and photos were taped all over the walls.

A stocky, strawberry blond male in his mid forties approached us. I could tell he was in charge by his bearing. You can't conceal a Marine colonel in civilian clothes, no matter how hard you try. "Welcome on board, agents. We were told you'd be coming, and we're real happy to have you here. I'm Lieutenant Colonel Smith, and I'll let everyone else introduce themselves." He had that kind of grin that says, Please, just bring it on!

Ali's reputation had preceded us. The cell needed a real-life expert, not just an analyst who has spent time in Langley sorting through someone else's reports, but someone who has gone toe-to-toe with terrorists. Ali was someone who could actually get inside their heads.

I wasn't surprised when the colonel explained that the CIA didn't have much of a team spirit. They would from time to time send someone to a meeting to observe, but generally the agent failed to contribute anything. "They don't like us being here, and the ambassador isn't sure what to make of us. He had no say in our coming, so we're a real bastard stepchild in this place. We're going to have our daily briefing in a few minutes so why don't you join us? You can look over the intel reports we just got in while you're waiting."

Ali went over to the table covered with copies of cables and intelligence reports. As he scanned them, I tried to get the dusty, old FBI computer up and running. Of course, it had no Internet connection, so I asked one of the communications techs if he could help me.

"Sure, boss, but I can tell you right now, it's going to be hard to get you any service and keep it running for long."

He took me out on the roof and, amid a jumble of satellite dishes, found a little thing that looked as if it was from RadioShack. We pushed away some garbage that the wind had tossed up on the roof and set the FBI dish back upright. I was almost embarrassed.

"Yeah, boss, this is a first-generation system. The real problem, though, is that your outfit is cheap so it leases cheap satellite time." He sure didn't pull any punches. "Well, let me try to explain this better." He knew he was talking to a cave dweller. I couldn't hide it. "OK, your agency doesn't buy good bandwidth on many satellites. It's very expensive. The only satellite you can reach passes over during a short period, and usually it's situated way over on the edge of the horizon, so you have to grab it when you can, and the best time is usually about late afternoon."

At least we had a secure phone that let us make calls. That phone was a hell of a lot better than what we had in Afghanistan.

After about twenty minutes, the colonel called everyone to join him in a dim corner at the conference table. I rose from my seat, slamming my head against an air duct for a second time and tearing my pants on a jagged piece of sheet metal. Then I heard Ali's voice in a dim corner of the attic, "I see something. I see something coming."

The colonel paused and then asked Ali to share with us what he saw.

"I believe there is going to be a seaborne attack similar to the one on the *Cole*. It is going to be soon, and it's going to be in Yemen somewhere probably near the Straits of Mandeb, the cities of Al Hudaydah or Al Mukalla." Ali had spent no more than fifteen minutes rifling through the data. The gist was that a number of people had been picked up and arrested while mostly coming through the United Arab Emirates en route to Yemen from Afghanistan and Pakistan. Ali laid out precisely how he knew who these people were and how he was sure they had a connection to those who had planned the attack on the USS *Cole*. That information, coupled with intercepts that alluded to something happening on water, convinced Ali that another seaborne attack was imminent.

There was a stunned silence in the room. Ali went on, precisely articulating the links he had discovered in the pile of papers. "These people are connected to the same people who are connected to the *Cole*. There has been other recent intelligence to the effect that they want to attack commercial shipping. It all adds up to what I think is a plan to block the flow of oil out of Saudi Arabia."

It made sense. The colonel realized that he finally had his quarterback and was getting ready to drive the ball right through the CIA and the State Department. "I'll take this to Ambassador Hull. We need to act on this."

I told him, "Colonel, Ali and I know how they planned the attack on the *Cole* down in Aden. I walked the grounds of the compound and the beach where it was launched. We can show you exactly what your people need to be looking for and just about where to look." We briefed the cell on how the men had planned and executed the attack against the USS *Cole* and how they had almost succeeded in attacking the USS *The Sullivans* the year before. It would be relatively easy to get some flyovers and look for a walled compound within two miles of the water that had a large boat dry-docked inside.

"Great, I will get clearance to put some recon teams in these cities and start looking. I'm gonna ask for a satellite to be repositioned so we can look in backyards, but that will take time. You don't just grab a joystick every time you want to move one of those things."

They asked Washington to reposition a satellite to fly over Al Mukalla, Al Hudaydah, and the Straits of Mandeb. The colonel argued for putting foot surveillance in those locations, but it was a tough request since it would have required the permission of the Yemeni authorities. The likelihood was that the bad guys would be told almost immediately.

I was told thirdhand that America's primary intelligence organization did not take Ali's prediction seriously. It is possible, though, that the agents did and were already working the issue. That's how they usually functioned. They didn't play with the team. I also got the impression that although they were willing to pick Ali's brains as they are trained to do, other intelligence organizations really didn't like him around. The truth was, Ali had the talent and the skills that few in the intelligence business could match. He was threatening to the other intelligence professionals. Good natured and inclined to view matters through a positive prism, he didn't fully appreciate that.

Within a typical government embassy, conflicts among the various agencies housed there are routine. For us, Ambassador Hull, Bodine's replacement, was much easier to deal with. He was a diplomat first and foremost. Just like most ambassadors, he had a big ego. With a government teetering toward disaster, Yemen was a hotbed of terrorism; so while diplomacy was important, the counterterrorism mission had to take prominence. Still, Hull had to resent the power that other agencies around him wielded, and I would imagine that those agencies saw the ambassador as someone who was all but working for them.

The ambassador quickly learned to set great store by Ali. I'm sure he had learned about Ali during stateside briefings on the *Cole* investigation before coming to Yemen. Once Hull arrived in Yemen, he immediately took Ali to his side, spending hours consulting with him. I believe the final nail was driven into our coffin the day that the ambassador insisted that Ali accompany him when he and other U.S. officials met with Yemeni president Ali Abdullah Saleh.

I'm told that to nobody's surprise, President Saleh was also enamored of Ali, having heard about his skill as an investigator. He insisted that the young, congenial, Arabic-speaking FBI agent sit near him during the meeting at the presidential palace. While nice for Ali, it could not have helped our relationship with the other folks who ran the embassy.

That evening back at the hotel, Ali again complained that he was not feeling well. He had the look that I had seen in Tashkent, so I took him to see the embassy doctor, a German national. Immediately the doctor proclaimed, "We will have to take him to the hospital in Sana'a as I do not have the diagnostic equipment needed here at the infirmary. I will arrange it, and we will pick you up shortly with a vehicle."

I wondered why a doctor who had been hired to care for embassy personnel had more confidence in local Yemeni doctors than in himself.

When we arrived at the hospital, we had to force our way through a crowd waiting for care. It reminded me of movies of old Bombay, where throngs engulfed the Englishmen in their white pith helmets. We were politely ushered upstairs to a "private" room without screens on the windows. We met two small Yemeni doctors wearing oversized suits with the price tags still on the sleeves, as is their custom. They conferred after reading Ali's vital signs.

The German doctor walked over to me. "It is possible that this man has spinal meningitis. I want him on the first flight out of Sana'a in the morning. I will not take responsibility if it turns out to be meningitis."

"Is that also the diagnosis of these doctors?" I asked, becoming more uneasy about this embassy doctor's inclination to disown us.

"Yes, they tend to agree that it is a possibility. They want to take a spinal tap."

"OK, let's hold on." I walked over and whispered low to Ali, "Did you hear that?"

"Yes, Uncle, but I can also understand these other two doctors, and they are not talking meningitis. I don't trust this embassy doctor."

I asked the German doctor, "Can we move Mr. Soufan back to the embassy infirmary for the night?"

"No, there is something very wrong with Mr. Soufan, and I will not be responsible. I would prefer that he stay here tonight."

"Well, Doc, I'm responsible for this guy, and I'm not feeling good about the security at this place."

"I'm sorry, but I cannot allow you to stay for the night at the infirmary. If you take him back to the Sheraton, I will, again, not be responsible. I must insist that we place him on the first flight back to the States in the morning."

This predicament was not good. We were in the center of downtown Sana'a. Ali was well known among the Yemeni terrorists. He would be a target if they knew he was in the hospital. The doctor didn't care. He just knew that he didn't want Ali sick on his watch. I asked Ali, "Do you want to fly home in the morning?

He was not looking good at all, but he somehow found the energy to raise himself on his elbows. He replied, "After all we went through to get here? Hell, no."

I returned to the German. "We would prefer to wait here until the morning to see if Mr. Soufan's fever has decreased by then."

He was adamant. "I am going to return to the embassy to book the first flight out for both of you." Then he became belligerent, "And I will obtain the backing of the ambassador on this issue!"

I had one bar left on the embassy-issued cell phone, and I was desperate not to let this guy kick us out of Yemen. I called FBI Headquarters and asked for a friend who was one of the bureau's most respected doctors. It was a stroke of luck that he was there and answered the phone. "Doc, it's Ray Holcomb. We have a medical situation in Yemen."

"Can you talk freely, Ray?"

"No."

"Okay, just give me yes or no answers." I responded to his questions concerning Ali's symptoms. He was savvy. "Ray, do you think they're ramrodding you two? They want you gone for some other reason?"

"Yes, I do."

"Put me on the phone with the embassy doctor. I'll handle it."

After a brief discussion, the embassy doctor turned to me and curtly said, "The FBI doctor has accepted full responsibility for Mr. Soufan. We will wait until tomorrow to decide what to do. Good night."

Our embassy doctor couldn't wait to leave us. After everyone had left the room, the telephone next to Ali's bed rang. He answered, listened for a moment, then hung up without having said a word. He had a quizzical expression when he spoke to me, "It was a male speaking in Arabic, and he wanted to know if Ali Soufan was in this room."

"Great," I said. "Here we are, buddy, in a rundown Sana'a hospital room. I have a dead cell phone and a SIG Sauer 9mm with thirty rounds of ammunition. Strange phone calls to the room, no lock on the door. My job is to make sure I don't put us in this kind of situation. I wish I could bust that screwball embassy doctor right in the nose! OK, Ali, get some sleep. I'll be right here. You'll be good in the morning."

"Thanks, Uncle."

His sedative kicked in, and he slept. I took a metal chair and jammed it under the doorknob. I checked the windows. There was no fire escape, and we were on the fourth floor. I settled into another chair with my gun in my lap.

Sometime around 3 a.m., I woke with a start. Someone was trying to open the door. I heard female voices. I did my best to tell whoever it was in Arabic that I would open the door. Setting the chair aside and holding my gun near my hip, I opened the door a crack to two sets of dark eyes peering out from under black burkas. Neither person was taller than five feet, and each held a medical tray. I hesitated. I should have patted them down, but that would not have gone over well.

At that time, other than the attack on the USS *Cole*, and unlike Pakistan and Afghanistan, Yemen wasn't awash in suicide bombers. Against my judgment, I motioned them in after concealing my weapon, and they went about taking the sleeping patient's blood pressure and temperature. Ali awoke for a moment, smiled, and fell back asleep. The women were whispering excitedly. I'm sure he was the closest thing to a celebrity these two Florence Nightingales had ever seen. Now for sure the world would know of his presence.

The two nurses nodded my way, then left. I repositioned the chair and settled in. I would have paid for even one of those worthless drugstore tabloids or anything to read, but there was nothing in the room. I sat and swatted insects, waiting for the morning.

CLICK! The sound was an explosion in the recesses of my semiconscious mind.

What the fuck! I thought as I sat bolt upright, trying to figure out where I was. Someone was trying to open the door again. OK, this is it, I thought. If the chair doesn't hold, then all I've got on my side is surprise. If I let the person know I'm awake in here maybe that will scare whoever it is off, or maybe it will just force the issue. A sturdy door of solid wood, it wouldn't stop bullets, but it wouldn't come down easily, either.

Ali was off to the side, sleeping. He was out of the line of fire.

There was a discernible push against the door, but the chair held. With the next shove, though, the chair started to slip. I didn't know how many people were outside. OK, fuckers, I've got a couple rounds for both of you, I thought. Come and get it. My heart was pounding in my head. There would be no backup coming. I positioned myself tight against the wall, weapon at chest level, barrel pointing toward the threat. Out of the corner of my eye, I could see Ali sleeping like a baby, and in some strange way that was nice to know.

Suddenly, there was a loud crash that sounded like a metal tray hitting the floor. Someone, maybe startled, had dropped a tray. Then I heard a deep male grunt, and the pressure against the door subsided. I waited a minute but heard nothing. I got down on the floor and could see no movement in the thin sliver of light beneath the door. So what do I do, I wondered, call the local police? I could phone downstairs and try to explain. Probably couldn't make any sense. OK, my only option was to ride this out until sunup, when the embassy people were supposed to return. There was no nodding off until I saw the first spikes of sunlight on the floor.

By morning, Ali's temperature had fallen. The embassy doctor returned, and, after conferring with the Yemeni doctor, we were able to check Ali out of the hospital. The embassy doctor recommended a couple days of bed rest and IVs. He acted as if nothing had happened the night before and never mentioned meningitis again.

I was right. Someone had wanted Ali out of Yemen.

About three months after I returned from this trip, I ran into my doctor friend at headquarters. "Hey, Doc, I can't thank you enough for helping us out in Sana'a."

"No problem, Ray. Just so happens I wanted to tell you that I was at a conference the other day with some medical personnel from another government agency, and one of them, with a very heavy German accent, came up to me and thanked me for taking responsibility for Ali when he was sick in Sana'a. Interesting, huh?"

I was confident that the German doctor was part of the mosaic aimed at getting the FBI's nose out of Yemen. Although they didn't win that round, they weren't done trying. I had to give them an *A* for determination.

■   ■   ■

The new head of the embassy's security, the regional security officer, appeared to be on the edge of a nervous breakdown. When I asked him for a driver and some protection for our nightly trips back to the old Yemeni prison to interrogate terror suspects, he shrugged off my request, saying we didn't need it. Things sure had changed in a year.

The interagency counterterrorism team in Yemen included some well-trained military people, some of whom were real squared-away war fighters and were led by a young army captain who looked as though he could take care of business. In conversations over beers, we discovered that we had some mutual friends, and clearly they had a high regard for our pursuit of the people who had attacked the USS *Cole*. The captain had overheard my conversation with the RSO and took me aside, "Ray, I'll get a couple of guys, and we'll tail you down and back. You have any weapons?"

We still had our pistols and M4s stored in the Marines' weapons vault at the embassy, so I checked out what we needed and turned them over to our new escorts. It felt good to see their car in my vehicle's rearview mirror every night. We probably broke enough regulations to get us fired, but any right-minded person would have done the same under those circumstances.

On October 6, 2002, precisely two weeks to the day of Ali's prediction, a seaborne suicide attack off the Yemeni city of Al Mukalla severely damaged the French oil tanker M/V *Limburg*. It was the same modus operandi as the attack on the USS *Cole* in Aden, again exactly as Ali predicted.

We saw the first broadcasts on CNN World and could tell that the hull metal bent inward at the waterline, indicating the explosion happened outside the ship. A crewman claimed to have seen a small, manned boat approaching immediately before the blast. We were confident that terrorists had launched a strike upon critical commercial shipping to disrupt the flow of the huge amount of oil from that region to the rest of the world.

Ali Soufan had been right, and the colonel was gloating because the intelligence organization down the hall appeared to have disregarded the idea. The colonel went so far as to post a sign in the embassy hallway: What Else Does Ali Soufan Know? If Ali's recent status as President Saleh's new favorite hadn't finished off our chances of getting cooperation with our partners at the embassy, then I'm sure the colonel's sign did.

With Yemen's approval, FBI explosives experts, along with NCIS and Diplomatic Security agents, traveled to Al Mukalla to investigate. They were able to locate the safe house where the conspirators had left behind cell phone boxes. Their serial numbers eventually led the Yemenis to most of the people responsible for the attack. It was more great crime scene work.

Fawaz Yahya al-Rabeei was caught and sentenced to death for the attack on the Limburg. One sailor had been killed, twelve were injured, over ninety thousand gallons of crude oil had spilled into the Gulf of Aden, and the environmental and revenue losses were huge. Eventually Osama bin Laden credited the attack to al Qaeda. On February 3, 2006, al-Rabeei escaped from a Yemeni prison with twenty-two others, including Jamal al-Badawi, the reputed mastermind of the attack on the USS Cole.

The colonel was right: What else did Ali Soufan know?

Although Ali was never near the Yemeni city of Al Mukalla at any time before or after the attack—he was on his way to America with me—he was later accused of causing a political uproar by insulting a Yemeni official there. Someone persuaded the ambassador that Ali was the culprit and that he had set back relations with his imprudent actions. From that time on, Ali was not allowed to return to Yemen. He was officially declared persona non grata, just as his first boss in New York, John O'Neill, had been. There is a lesson in both of their stories concerning how the various parts of America's counterterrorism "team" actually work together. I leave it to the reader to conclude what that lesson is.

On a final note, on November 3, a month after the Limburg attack, a drone missile incinerated the vehicle of Ahmed Hijazi (aka Kamal Derwish), who was the spiritual leader of the Lackawanna Six terror cell. In the vehicle with Hijazi was Abu Ali al-Harithi, another of the masterminds of the Cole attack. Both were killed.

Shortly after returning to Washington, Andy told me to attend a meeting sponsored by the bureau's victim assistance unit and meet representatives of the families of the sailors who had died in the *Cole* attack. Since I had just returned from Yemen, it made sense that I should speak to the representatives. I soon learned that these people were frustrated and angry over the apparent lack of progress in bringing justice and closure to their children's deaths. News of al-Harithi's death was not yet public.

I tried to reassure them that Americans were working very hard to locate and capture the people who had killed their children. I told them I had just returned from Yemen and that although I couldn't discuss many of the details, I asked them to accept my reassurance. Days later the story of al-Harithi's death hit the news.

The bereavement counselor at headquarters forwarded an e-mail to me from a father of a young sailor who had died. "If you would, please pass on to Agent Holcomb wherever he is . . . Thank you! Thank you! Thank you!" It's hard to describe how much that e-mail means to me.

When Ali and I left Sana'a, Stephen, the same agent who had helped Ali with the interrogation of Abu Zubaydah and who had recently joined the Fly Team, stayed behind to help establish a permanent FBI office in Sana'a. The night that the Hellfire missile took out Harithi and Hijzai, Stephen was given only twenty minutes to collect DNA from the corpse suspected to be Hijazi's.

He called the FBI Laboratory's hotline and got a forensic expert on the phone. "Well, the best spot is the femur. If you can collect from there, we'll have a good chance of getting enough DNA for comparison purposes."

Stephen borrowed a clean hacksaw blade and did what he had to do. He then carried the sample, packed in dry ice, back to the United States for analysis. The DNA matched positively with one of Hijazi's relatives, and we knew that the leader of the Lackawanna cell, the man largely responsible for leading six young Americans of Middle Eastern descent down the path of jihad and ultimately to prison, had met justice.

I didn't have a direct hand in the killing of Hijazi and Harithi, although I wish I had, but many other agents and I had a piece of that victory. If the FBI Buffalo office hadn't done its job and discovered Hijazi's role in the Lackawanna threat, his death that night would have been virtually meaningless to us.

If the Fly Team hadn't been formed and Stephen had not deployed to Sana'a at that precise moment, no one would have been available to take advantage of the twenty-minute window that the Yemeni coroner offered, and Hijazi would still be on the most wanted list. Every player has an important role in defeating terrorism. It takes a team of people and a team of organizations. That fact is the lesson of 9/11.

▪ ▪ ▪

There was at least one light moment during our second trip to Sana'a. We were there during October, when, of course, the Germans hold their Oktoberfest. Some enterprising German capitalists, in an attempt to sell expensive luxury cars to wealthy Middle Eastern potentates, decided to bring Oktoberfest to Yemen.

Try to conceive of an Islamic country, where pork and alcohol are forbidden and women are not allowed to expose any skin. Then imagine swarthy, small Yemeni men dressed in traditional Bavarian garb—yes, lederhosen, felt caps, calf warmers, all of it—with a backdrop of brass oompah music, and you have Oktoberfest in Sana'a.

The festivities lasted a week at the Sheraton. I had to hand it to those Germans. They put up a huge tent and had stunning BMWs on rotating pedestals as German music blared and Yemenis served illegal food. We could sit down and actually enjoy smuggled German beer and delicious bratwurst.

As if there was a superior plan to confound our Western senses, in the middle of this circus-like atmosphere of German songs and Bavarian impersonators, three black Land Rovers rolled in, and a Yemeni tribal chief was announced. His bodyguards, hanging over the car's hood with automatic weapons, entered the hotel first to establish the sheikh's security. The sheikh followed in flowing robes as his bodyguards took up perimeter positions with their AK-47s slung ready only yards from our Bavarian ball. He had another purpose, a meeting separate from us. He did not partake; he did not even come over to our tent.

Twenty

Taking It to the Next Level

Several months after the *Washington Post* announced the creation of an FBI Super Team, Brad and Matt came on board as my first two permanent, deployable agents.

They joined the team because the logistics worked for them. Both already lived near D.C. Brad was former air force, having been assigned to the United Nations' inspection team in Iraq that hunted for weapons of mass destruction prior to the second invasion. He was big, smart, and had a good sense of humor. His size belied the fact that he was a computer geek. He had worked the Washington sniper attacks case, and once it ended he became bored. Matt, meanwhile, was young and single, with some police experience. He was eager to learn and willing to deploy just about anywhere.

Getting two agents on board was a start, but we needed more good people. If I couldn't get experienced al Qaeda investigators, I would have to make do with agents who at least had some real-world experience. Anyone with street smarts—cops, former probation officers, returned Peace Corps volunteers who had spent time in miserable places, anyone who had been through the school of hard knocks and understood that people aren't always nice or trustworthy—could have worked. It's my strong feeling that bright young people straight out of college or graduate school are not ready to take a lead on any criminal or terrorism investigation. They might have graduated in the top 2 percent of their class, and they might have read every detail on al Qaeda and its terrorist affiliates that they could find on their computer, but they had to have some familiarity with the sordid side of human nature in order to work a case. That kind of experience only comes with time "on the street," whether that street is in Detroit or Baghdad.

We still lacked an incentive package. We had nothing more to offer candidates than a great deal of travel, most of which was on short notice and often to inhospitable places, so I was surprised that we got any responses at all. I knew that many agents hated desk jobs, but I had underestimated how much FBI agents crave a challenge and the excitement that comes with travel. We received forty-five responses.

We waded through them and found about fifteen we hoped had some valuable skills, along with some experience and maturity. We did what background checks we could, calling references and people who had to know something about the applicant. Then, comparable to throwing darts against the wall, we took a chance and offered a group of applicants positions on the team.

They were relatively new to the bureau—none with more than five years of FBI experience—but some of them had that "street experience" I was looking for. They learned on the job. As soon as each of them got to Washington and figured out how to get around D.C. and in and out of the massive, complex Hoover building, we were preparing that agent for deployment.

It was not the way we wanted to stand up the Super Squad, but we had little choice. If after a thirty- to ninety-day deployment to Iraq the new recruit remained enthusiastic, we knew we had a keeper. Some showed leadership tendencies early. We let the dynamics work themselves out. Gradually we saw the signs of an esprit de corps building. Asked to do so much more than most agents and without extra compensation, the men and women who made up our first real Fly Team roster were beginning to think of themselves as unique. Nine months after our first draft, no one had quit. I was beginning to think that we could make it work.

The pace picked up as word got out. We assisted FBI legats in far-flung places, and we sent our fastest learners to those field divisions that lacked terrorism expertise and were confronted with real threats. We were not able to offer the graybeard institutional experts I had envisioned, but I hoped that if some of our people stuck around long enough, they would become those graybeards.

With the help of Douglas and of sympathetic agents who believed in the mission but could only provide part-time help, I ran the Fly Team for the better part of nine months. While I was trying to patch together an effective unit, the FBI Career Board was slowly reviewing applications for the three other supervisory positions on the team. I needed some help in dealing with the administrative morass that inhibits the creation of anything new and effective, so I could return to the street and do what I knew best.

The rumor was that a former operator with the Hostage Rescue Team, Bill, had the inside track on the unit chief position. After HRT, he moved on and ran a criminal squad in Phoenix, which in my mind was a big plus. It showed that he had to be more than just a "super SWAT" guy. He had to understand that the core of the FBI is built on investigating cases and arresting bad people. I was anxious for Bill to arrive.

We built a training syllabus based upon a military model. Soon, team members were attending courses in interrogation, orienteering, and Middle Eastern culture.

The working conditions inside the Hoover Building didn't change, however; things remained deplorable. At one time, we were in the basement immediately next to the truck delivery docks, listening to engines running, pneumatic lift gates operating, truck doors slamming, and drivers shouting. The smell of engine exhaust was so strong that the building services' crew had to install a portable air ventilation machine to keep us from being asphyxiated. If we sat near the droning machine, we had to shout to be heard. Some elite team, I thought; I can't get an incentive package approved, but I sure can wow my people with their new work quarters. After the loading dock, we were moved upstairs to quarters immediately next to the cafeteria. It was congested and noisy, but the odor was a big improvement.

Eventually, Bill arrived from Phoenix to take over. He brought with him some quality analysts who had worked with him in the past. He also brought George Piro, a young agent who had worked with Bill in Phoenix. We still hadn't made any progress with the issue of a recruitment incentive, but word was out that the Fly Team was doing impressive things. Now that Bill was the official unit chief, I became one of the team's four supervisors. I'd never been happier over a demotion; now I could focus on working cases.

On May 16, 2003, there were five nearly simultaneous suicide bombings in Casablanca, Morocco. Forty-one people had died, and a hundred were injured. Bill wanted some experience with international deployments so he assembled several investigators and headed to the site. I respected the fact that he wanted to see firsthand what the work really involved. He walked the bloody crime scenes and returned with a true perspective of what his people would be dealing with. On August 5, 2003, a vehicle-borne IED detonated near the entrance to the JW Marriott Hotel, part of an American-owned chain, in Jakarta, Indonesia. Jemaah Islamiyah, the same group that had met with some of the 9/11 hijackers in Kuala Lumpur, claimed responsibility. Twelve people died, and 150 were wounded. The fireball literally cooked some taxi drivers in their vehicles as they waited their turn for business. The explosion used a mixture of chemicals similar to that found in the Bali bombing in 2002, where an explosives-packed van detonated outside the Sari nightclub on the resort island, killing 202 people and injuring scores more.

It was my turn to deploy. With two explosives evidence technicians, George Piro and I headed out. We would link up in Jakarta with two agents from the Los Angeles field office, whose region of responsibility included the entire Pacific Rim. They would take over the long-term investigation. It was a long flight, almost twenty-four hours, including a stopover in Singapore. We arrived late in the evening, and an obviously irritated FBI assistant legal attaché (ALAT) met us. In the presence of a mixed group of officials, he didn't hold back from expressing his displeasure with our mission, stating that we needed to get back on our plane and return to Washington. I reminded him that the director had sent us and that he was expecting our report as soon as possible. However, that information didn't seem to impress Gerald. The embassy RSO was equally resentful. During a meeting with the ambassador the next morning, he too expressed his opinion on our mission. Not mincing words, he stated that he didn't want us in his backyard. There was no spirit of cooperation inside the U.S. Embassy in Jakarta. I sensed that my problems with the ALAT were not over.

The next day we began integrating with the evidence teams working the crime scene. The government of Australia had sent its equivalent of a rapid deployment team to assist the Indonesians in their investigation. As it was a Sunday, Gerald curtly explained that he didn't see the need to pay an embassy driver overtime for our transportation to the site; therefore, we would have to take taxis. OK, I thought, this is his territory. I don't like it, but he's supposed to know the terrain.

It wasn't long after we arrived at the crime scene that we concluded the Australians had it together. Their procedures and forensic skills were impressive. The Indonesians working alongside the Aussies had the will but lacked the expertise to investigate the bombing. Unlike our American counterparts, the Australians and Indonesians welcomed us like brothers, and soon our explosives evidence technicians were working closely with the local investigators, exchanging ideas, and building relationships.

At the attack site, we could tell that someone had jumped the gun. If the vehicle had been fifty meters closer to the entrance, the destruction would have been far greater. A security guard had approached the driver when he stalled the small truck on the inclined driveway. Someone had panicked, and the crime scene investigators were betting it wasn't the driver. The educated assumption was that the driver, twenty-eight-year-old Asmar Latin Sani, thought he had the detonator stick, but his bosses had actual control. A cell phone had set off the explosion. The JI had again duped a young, uneducated man into being its tool. His head blew through the windshield, careened off a wall of the building, and ended up inside a fifth-floor room.

Within days, the Indonesians reconstructed Sani's head, complete with a glass eye, and posted its gory picture on the front page of the major Jakarta newspaper. His sister identified him the same day. Western societies would not stomach this approach, but it was effective. As an added benefit, it probably dissuaded more than one would-be jihadist from going down the suicide path. There was nothing glorious about the monstrous face staring back from the front page of the *Jakarta Post*.

After about an hour at the crime scene, I heard a distant rumble and saw a wave of humanity off in the distance but headed our way. I began to make out a strident chant and asked one of the Indonesian investigators what was approaching.

"It is a Muslim protest. They are angry because they claim this attack was done by the CIA as an attempt to blame Muslims."

The post-blast JW Marriott in Jakarta. The bomber's head was found inside a fifth-floor room.

Whoa, I thought—talk about taking the offensive! There were only a dozen or so Indonesian police in the area, some crime scene tape, and a few wooden barricades. The crowd appeared to be in the several thousands, if not more, and the chant, led by loudspeakers mounted on vans, was becoming thunderous.

Right about then, Gerald the ALAT bent over and dug sunglasses and a hat out of his equipment bag.

It was definitely time for us Americans to leave, especially since one of our Los Angeles agents decided to start taking pictures of the huge crowd as it decried the CIA. "Hey, Pete, what are you doing? Don't you know what they're angry about?"

He looked at me blankly.

"Come on, we're out of here!"

Now we had to follow the ALAT out the back alley, and he was the only one who had brought along a disguise. It was several blocks to a taxi stand, and when we turned the corner, a phalanx of cameras and reporters lay in wait, snapping photos and demanding interviews.

I cannot imagine the ALAT didn't know what we would be walking into at the crime scene. He was shrewd enough to prepare for it. He got his headline.

The next day the front page of the Jakarta papers declared the FBI had arrived, and there we were, with our ALAT in the lead but well disguised. There had been nowhere to hide, so we had all ended up on the front page of every major newspaper in Indonesia. But at least we didn't have to pay an embassy driver overtime!

For the next several days, wherever we went, someone would point at us and say, "FBI!" I was seething. Whether the ALAT had set us up for an entry in his own photo album or he was still trying to encourage us to leave his territory, I don't know, but it was one of the most unprofessional stunts I experienced during my entire career. Certainly, at the least, our pictures were now in some terrorist's database.

Five days after arriving in Jakarta, we received a phone call from headquarters directing George to fly to another location where, because of his Middle Eastern background and language skills, he could assist the CIA in debriefing a high-level Iraqi defector. George was a great young agent who had been a cop before joining the bureau. His work ethic and manner of questioning subjects reminded me of Ali Soufan. He would be selected months later as the primary interrogator of Iraqi president Saddam Hussein. His performance during those high-pressure months in Iraq was nothing short of amazing.

Other than showing support for Indonesia's counterterrorism effort and our Australian friends, our unit's trip was largely an opportunity for our bomb technicians to study JI's tactics. We also recommended to headquarters that it send more FBI personnel, at least temporarily, to help the Indonesians in their counterterrorism efforts.

Personally, I had already seen enough carnage wrought by large bombs, but I still struggled with the psychology of the suicide bomber. All indications were that this tactic was becoming a worldwide epidemic. I left Indonesia, though, convinced that we had two strong allies in that part of the world.

On October 15, a roadside bomb blasted a UN embassy motorcade in the Gaza Strip. The officials were on their way from the U.S. Embassy in Tel Aviv for a meeting with the Palestine Liberation Organization (PLO). Three security guards died. Since Gaza, in essence, was under the control of Yasser

The setup—walking the phalanx of newsmen outside the blast site of the JW Marriott Hotel, Jakarta. This photo was published on the front page of the Jakarta Post, *among other newspapers, and the original caption identified us as "United States FBI agents."* AP Photo/Tatan Syuflana.

Arafat, the chairman of the Palestinian National Authority, he sent a message through the State Department asking the FBI to help determine who had executed the attack. This request was a major shift in the FBI's relations with the Palestinians. Bill again personally led a Fly Team contingent to Gaza, where the group assisted the PLO in conducting a crime scene investigation. Eventually members of a little-known Palestinian splinter group called the Popular Resistance Committee were arrested and charged with the attack.

I'd only been back in Washington for a month, again choking on bureaucratic red tape and defending the Fly Team concept against FBI inspectors who seemed committed to taking down our fledgling organization, when on November 15, 2003, suicide bombers killed twenty-seven people at two synagogues in Istanbul. Five days later, suicide bombers attacked the Istanbul offices of the HSBC Bank AS and devastated the downtown British consulate, killing consul general Roger Short, who happened to be in a small building near the main gate where the truck bomb exploded. When the explosion occurred, President Bush was meeting in London with Prime Minister Tony Blair. Bill received a call from upstairs telling him to get a Fly Team to Istanbul and see if the U.S. government could offer any assistance.

Bill tapped me on the shoulder, and the next day we left on the bureau's G-5 for Istanbul. My team consisted of William, a Fly Team investigator; Donna, a senior Fly Team analyst; Michael, a Diplomatic Security Service agent recently detailed to us; and Leo West, the explosives unit chief and lead examiner from the embassy bombing's investigation in Dar es Salaam. When we arrived, we learned that all initial indications were that al Qaeda, not some Kurdish separatist group, was behind the attack. Everyone gathered downtown at the old U.S. consulate—an initial command post for the joint Turkish, U.S., and British investigative effort—to make sense out of what had happened.

It was late fall and the leaves were falling in Istanbul, the ancient seat of the eastern Roman and Ottoman empires. We could see the Bosporus, the strait that connects the Black Sea to the Mediterranean, and across on the other side stood Asia. Istanbul was the only major European city that echoed to the Muslim prayer call emanating at sunrise and four other times during the day from dozens of minarets. A heavy fog bank would slink up from the water and blanket most of the eastern part of the city until late morning. Just as in Tashkent, splendid cultures had first collided and then gradually merged into one.

At the first of many intergovernmental meetings, we conveyed our deepest regrets and offered whatever help the FBI could bring. Leo did an exceptional job of assisting and advising the Turkish forensic investigators, who gave us access to the carefully collected and cataloged evidence found at the four attack sites.

We walked the crime scene at the British consulate, where a British evidence response team was sorting through the wreckage. The consulate was in the heart of an ancient part of the city, where cobblestone streets encircled the walled compound. The bomb-laden vehicle had approached the embassy on a twisting, narrow, and congested street. I couldn't imagine how any terrorist would risk driving down to the consulate's entrance unless a lookout

Remains of the consulate vehicle-borne improvised explosive device, an evidence technician's playground. Photo courtesy of Leo West.

called in that the route was clear and that the consulate's steel delta barrier was down. The driver must have waited for a phone call that he could get through; otherwise, he would never have chanced it.

After reviewing surveillance photos showing the bomb vehicle stopping at the consulate gate, guards moving in quickly, and a resulting flash of white, Leo and I walked back to the site. A senior Turkish investigator was waiting for us. I asked, "Colonel, have you collected many cell phones from the crime scene?"

He was curt, "Yes, yes, but we are convinced that this bomb was not activated remotely. We have found no signs of that. The driver set it off."

As tactfully as possible, I told him, "Colonel, I have walked the approach. It would be impossible for the driver to see or know when the way was clear. It is a crowded, winding, narrow street, and the consulate guards regularly raised the delta barrier, which no vehicle could get over when raised. I believe your suicide driver had to have a lookout, which means he had to have a cell phone."

The colonel looked at me, mulling over what I had said. "Hmmm, yes, we did collect many phones." Then he changed the subject.

The site where the British consul died.

Two weeks later, the Turks announced that they had identified the cell phone used by the suicide driver, collected its calling records, and were very busy tracking down his associates. Eventually, seventy-four individuals were charged with having a role in the attack. Seven received life sentences. Two of the leaders had had direct contact at some point with Osama bin Laden. One was killed in Iraq; the whereabouts of the other, Gurcan Bac, are still unknown.

Mike Dorris, the FBI legat in Turkey, was everywhere and could not have been more helpful. His office was in Ankara; however, he was trying to convince headquarters that the situation in Istanbul demanded an FBI presence. He lobbied us for a Fly Team member to cover the location until headquarters would approve a permanent position. The work environment in Istanbul in comparison to Jakarta was as day is to night, thanks to Mike. He was a team player, adept at handling the diplomatic sensitivities and developing solid, trusting relationships with officials and police. Of all the legats I have worked with, he was one of the best. William, one of the Fly Team's rising stars, volunteered to cover Istanbul until a permanent position was approved. He stayed on for months, performing like a seasoned veteran.

I believed we were proving our team's worth. Whether at home in the States or on the other side of the world, we had shown repeatedly that we could respond and adjust unlike other operational units in the FBI's Counterterrorism Division. As the team had expanded, assignments had flowed in.

Domestic missions continued, but clearly the field divisions were beginning to get ahead of the curve. The Fly Team had received requests to surge investigators to Riyadh, Saudi Arabia, after suicide attacks on three residential compounds killed nine Americans; to Charlotte, North Carolina; to Atlanta; to Minneapolis; and even to the Bahamas to assess a growing concern over radicalized Muslim elements in the Caribbean and the tri-border region of South America, where the borders of Argentina, Brazil, and Paraguay intersect. In addition, the U.S. military asked for hardy agents who could be assigned on a long-term basis to special operations units and assist in hunting down terrorists and in preserving evidence for possible prosecutions. Overnight, the Fly Team took on an additional role as trainers to army units deploying to Iraq and Afghanistan.

In February 2004, we were told to prepare a team for deployment to Qatar. The former separatist president of Chechnya, living in exile in Qatar, had been blown up in his car. The government had asked for FBI assistance, and when the U.S. secretary of state asks the FBI director for help, it's usually given whether it makes sense to the troops or not. When I heard Bill announce that we were putting together a team, I said, "Bill, the guy who was killed was a Muslim, and he is hated by the Russians. The assassination was pretty crude. It smells of the Russians. I don't think we need to rush into this one." Bill was too busy to listen, and our team was on the ground little more than a day later.

The Fly Team helped the Qataris set up a crime scene and collect evidence. A fragment of the bomb detonator was located, bearing a Cyrillic inscription. Two days later the United Arab Emirates turned over two Russians to the Qataris. Both had been hastily trying to leave the area and were acknowledged members of Russian special services. All hell broke loose in Moscow. Every Qatari visitor was either threatened or picked up on trumped up charges.

In classic Moscow style, the Russians, who had been caught red-handed, went on the offensive. In the end, they got their agents back, and the Qataris learned a lesson about dealing with Russia. The rumor around headquarters was that Prime Minister Vladimir Putin was upset about our Fly Team's meddling and conveyed his dismay to the White House. He admonished the United States, saying that it and Russia were supposed to be partners in the war against terrorism, not adversaries.

Twenty-One

Blood Diamonds

I recognized some of the regulars in the coffee shop in downtown D.C. A convenient spot, just around the corner from headquarters, it attracted a typical D.C. mix, which was unlike the crowd found in most other American cities. If I were a betting man, I would assume that anyone younger than thirty I'd run into there on any day would be somewhere else in less than five years. Many of them were lawyers, spending a few years at the Department of Justice, honing their trial skills or clerking for some powerful judge as a prelude to signing away their personal lives and making real money in a high-powered law firm.

Then there were the people like me, trying to make it on a government salary in one of the most expensive regions in the nation. Unlike most government employees working downtown, however, I was there by choice, trying to turn a concept into reality. Most everyone else was looking for the way out.

The din in the busy restaurant masked conversations about politics, business, exams, and sports. I was meeting an investigator for the Special Court for Sierra Leone (SCSL), which was established by the United Nations and the government of Sierra Leone. Allen Black was coming by to present his theory. He was sure that al Qaeda had a hand in the blood diamond trade in West Africa. He walked in with the swagger of a good salesman and shook my hand before he sat down. "Did you order yet?"

"Just coffee. I'll get our waitress back."

Black began, "I suppose you have an idea of what I'm here for and what I'd like you to do for me."

"I may have, Allen, but I'd like to hear it from you directly."

"We have little doubt about al Qaeda's role in the civil war that's taking place in Sierra Leone. Charles Taylor is behind it so he can get his hands on the diamond fields, and we're sure al Qaeda is in there too, buying diamonds to fund terrorism. Taylor, the so-called rebels, and al Qaeda—they're all working hand in hand in the mines."

His theory emerged from the SCSL's investigation into war crimes and atrocities committed during the long, brutal civil war in Sierra Leone. The SCSL believed that there were al Qaeda operatives in Monrovia, Liberia; Burkina Faso; and the Kono diamond region in Sierra Leone. The allegations weren't new; however, the SCSL believed that previously unavailable information might be accessible in Monrovia and Sierra Leone now that Taylor's thugs had been ousted and the civil war was over.

I didn't buy into his proposition. I had researched the so-called blood diamond operation and reviewed the classified intelligence. I knew that al Qaeda had a presence in many places, but the facts just didn't support an al Qaeda diamond operation in West Africa. We knew al Qaeda members went into the tanzanite (a blue-purple gemstone discovered in Tanzania) business in Kenya and Tanzania while planning their attacks against the embassies. But other than some speculative investigative reporting by a couple of European roving reporters, there was no evidence that al Qaeda was operating in and around the mining areas of Sierra Leone. Proponents of the blood diamond–al Qaeda link presented as key evidence that diamond field workers in Sierra Leone had positively identified one of the suspects in the African embassy bombings from a Belgian reporter's spread of photos. The photo spread had been faulty. The reporter mixed photos of the embassy bombing suspects with pictures of local men. Of course, the Middle Eastern terrorists looked nothing like the West Africans. That conspicuous difference, coupled with a natural desire for approval and possible reward, made the shrewd natives tell the reporter what they believed he wanted to hear.

As tactfully as I could, I told Black that I had studied many intelligence reports on the blood diamond issue. Although I could find none that proved an al Qaeda connection, I would keep an open mind and help wherever I could.

Black insisted that he had the goods. He claimed that his office had uncovered a number of key witnesses who could confirm the connection between terrorism and the blood diamonds.

I told Black I would have to speak with my bosses and that I would get back to him. I reported to Pat D'Amuro that I didn't think the blood diamond–al Qaeda connection held any water. It didn't make any difference. The real story was that the investigator worked for a powerful congressman who, apart from having strong feelings about helping the brutalized people of West Africa, had substantial influence over the FBI's budget.

Two days later Pat called me up to his office. I arrived as he was heading down the hallway to see the director. "Follow me," was his only comment. We went to the director's inner study. The director wasn't well, still mending from recent surgery, and his head hung down.

When he heard our footsteps, he looked up and did not look happy. "I thought I told you to fix this thing with the congressman."

Pat replied, "We have, sir." Then to my complete surprise, he added, "Agent Holcomb will be taking a team to Africa tomorrow."

"Well, I just received another call from the congressman, and he's angry. It's not fixed yet, so fix it!"

The Office of War Crimes Issues of the State Department worked closely with the UN Office of the Special Prosecutor. That same afternoon, Pat towed me along to a meeting at State Department headquarters. Black was there, grinning. He thought that I was now working for him.

The group discussed a witness who was purportedly critical to any successful prosecution of Taylor. Brig. Gen. John Tarnue, the former commanding general of the Armed Forces of Liberia and the closest thing to a professional soldier Taylor ever had, was in hiding in Ghana. The U.S. Army had trained him, which was one of the reasons Taylor put him in such a highly visible position. Taylor actually had no army. He had some undisciplined and ill-armed groups of soldiers, but he really relied on thugs—the equivalent of Haiti's once feared paramilitary force, the Tonton Macoutes—and a strange collection of rebel groups and children's battalions. He took kids from their parents, fed them drugs and fear, empowered them, and handed them AK-47s. They became perfect little terrorists.

Everyone at the meeting agreed that we should bring Tarnue to the States to testify. He was in hiding because Taylor had sent assassins looking for him, so we had to move quickly. I had to point something out: "What if we go retrieve your general and bring him back to America, then it comes out that he was up to his elbows in blood and slaughter and just as culpable as Taylor himself? Now you have a worthless witness, the media screaming about how stupid we are, and a guy who will claim that he is entitled to political refugee status." If the general was every bit a criminal as his old boss, then the U.S. government agencies involved would collectively look foolish if we brought him to the States.

The Immigration and Naturalization representative responded, "Point well made, agent. How could this guy serve that butcher Taylor for so long without being a criminal himself?"

Black was annoyed again. "Don't you FBI guys always say that you can't catch evil people with priests and nuns?"

"That's true, we do say that," I conceded. "I can bring a good polygrapher, and we can interrogate the hell out of him. I'll report back and let you know what we determine."

Everyone agreed to that plan, and Pat announced again, "Agent Holcomb will be taking a team to Ghana tomorrow."

Everyone in the room was impressed except me. I thought, Does Pat have any idea what it takes to round up a team and get it launched?

Somehow, we got it all together in two days: visas secured, inoculations received, gear packed, and reservations made. This operation was a Fly Team deployment, as would be all our trips regarding blood diamonds. No squad had an open case on the blood diamond matter, since the bureau had already concluded the connection to terrorism was unlikely. We knew we were being sent to West Africa largely to appease the congressman. My team comprised a first-rate polygrapher from Quantico and my two original Fly Team members, Matt and Brad. Our proverbial albatross, Black, came along. We flew into Accra, Ghana, where an unusually helpful embassy regional security officer welcomed us. Unlike on our trip to Jakarta, we had the State Department's strong backing on this mission, so the embassy threw its doors open.

■　　■　　■

John Sarwoquoi Tarnue, former commanding general of the Armed Forces of Liberia, had fallen afoul of his megalomaniac boss, Charles Taylor, the president of Liberia. Taylor was a story in his own right. As a young man, he had moved to the States from Liberia to get an education. After graduating with a degree in economics, he was arrested in 1979 for threatening to take over the Liberian diplomatic mission in New York City. He returned to Liberia and backed Samuel Doe's coup to take over from another in a series of terribly corrupt and inept presidents. As Taylor's reward, he became a minister in the new government and promptly started embezzling from his employer. He fled to the States, where he had secreted close to a million dollars in stolen funds; however, the U.S. government arrested him on an extradition warrant to face charges in Liberia. In September 1985, with his wife's and sister-in-law's help, he escaped from jail and eventually made his way to Libya, leaving his wife and sister-in-law sitting in prison on charges of aiding and abetting.

In Libya, Taylor joined Muammar al-Gadaffi's team and trained in insurgency and terrorism. There he also met numerous soon-to-be-famous terrorists. He eventually, through cunning and brutality, engineered his rise to the presidency of Liberia. Once ensconced in the presidential palace, he needed a front man to be his chief of staff of the military. The only person who remotely could fill that role was John "Ju Ju" Tarnue.

At an early age, John had fallen in with some American Special Forces trainers who had come to help build Liberia's army. Just as any teenage boy, he had found his role model. Bright, outgoing, and with an engaging smile, he wanted to be a spit-and-polish airborne trooper. The military attachés and his own soldiers accepted him readily. Everyone liked him except Taylor, who quickly grew tired of his popularity. After Tarnue challenged Taylor on a number of his absurd policies, Taylor concluded he was a threat. It was time to get rid of him.

Before I left on this mission, I read classified Defense Department reports that detailed how Brigadier General Tarnue was demoted and taken to the presidential palace, where Taylor's son "Chucky" had his thugs brutalize the general. One detail stuck: they had taken knives to his penis.

Lying low in a Ghanaian refugee camp, Tarnue began to receive tips that others were looking for him. Weeks before our arrival, another dissident from Taylor's government, a former senior aide-de-camp, had fled to Ghana and also lived in a refugee camp. Taylor sent an assassination squad there to kill him, and it succeeded. Taylor's killers had hunted down a former senior police officer from Liberia in the Ghana camps as well, so Ju Ju Tarnue had good reason to be concerned.

Tarnue came to the U.S. Embassy, seeking asylum through the State Department. The State Department arranged to have Tarnue hidden until we arrived. When we finally met at the embassy in Accra, I directed the members of my team to wait while I took the general alone into a back room. I wanted to make sure he understood our mission clearly. I was going to explain things in a way that is unfamiliar to a general in any army, and I wasn't going to do it in anyone's presence because I wanted to keep his pride intact. As I turned to face the general, I was startled to see him unbuckle his pants and drop them to the floor. My first thought was that this gesture must be some kind of strange Liberian custom. Then I noticed that his white undershorts were red with fresh blood. He wanted to show me that he was real, that he was not faking his claim to be in mortal danger, and that he should be secreted out of the country.

In an instant, I recalled the detailed report of Tarnue's torture. It revealed that evil little bastard Chucky was in charge of the so-called Anti-Terrorism Unit (ATU), the de facto presidential guard unit. The men, loyal to Taylor, were ruthless murderers. Daddy Taylor had become even more paranoid when he learned that General Tarnue had some unusually secretive meetings with the American defense attaché. He suspected everyone and became particularly angry when he learned that the general alone had been invited to the attaché's farewell party. It didn't really matter what John Tarnue told the little sadist; Chucky was going to have fun. After stabbing his chest with a bayonet, burning his arms and chest with cigarettes and melted plastic, and slicing his genitals, Chucky demanded that the commander of Liberia's Armed Forces grovel at his feet and refer to him as "master." When he refused, John was struck in the face with the muzzle of a weapon and beaten until he passed out. When he awoke he was still bleeding from his eye, his penis, and his chest.

He received some medical treatment for his wounds in Liberia during February and March 2002. Eventually the doctors in Liberia recommended he travel to Ghana, where he could receive better care. Chucky, in some strange change of heart, signed an order permitting Tarnue to leave for Ghana. Maybe

Taylor wanted to keep Tarnue alive a little longer. Perhaps he didn't want it known what he had done to his commanding general. He knew Tarnue had many friends in the U.S. Army, so Taylor wasn't ready to kill him yet. Once Tarnue went into hiding, however, Taylor figured he'd better dispose of him because he had become a liability.

Tarnue and my team took adjoining rooms in a seaside hotel outside of Accra. We were prepared to stay as long as it took to get the answers about the diamond trade and al Qaeda. We had come a long way, and we were going to finish the job. Other than meal breaks and time to sleep, we sequestered ourselves each day in one room and grilled Tarnue for hours on end. He was hard to keep on track, but he was eager to talk about his time as chief of staff of the Liberian army.

Taylor had intentionally decimated the regular army, creating in its place children's units, and he put Tarnue in charge of their training. These units included the Small Boy Unit (SBU), the Yellow Jackets, and the Cobra Unit. The SBU consisted of boys between ten and fifteen years of age, and the Yellow Jackets were girls of the same age range. The Cobra Unit was a group of young men from the Gio tribe of Nimba County. They were largely volunteers who stepped forward because they knew their service would indirectly improve the living conditions of their relatives. These three units were Taylor's most trusted, and their purpose was to accomplish any mission Taylor deemed especially sensitive. Missions that adults might abhor these brainwashed children did with glee.

Tarnue told me that while he was in charge of all the National Patriotic Front of Liberia (NPFL) training, he witnessed the execution of a number of his trainees, who were killed for being members of the Krahn or Mandingo tribes or for their former affiliation with the old Liberian army. It was common for Taylor's brother, Gbatu, and his special security units to arrive at the NPFL training camps when the new recruits were on the parade ground, standing in formation for reveille or retreat ceremonies. Whether his actions were spontaneous or based on some hearsay, Gbatu would always find someone to execute. He would have the recruit pulled from the formation and summarily executed in front of the others, whom he would then order to dig the victim's grave. Tears welled in his eyes as Tarnue explained that to intercede would have meant instant death. He justified his inaction by saying that he alone had any chance of bringing some discipline to the rabble of an army Taylor had assembled. He wanted desperately to build a proud, professional force, while the Taylors wanted nothing but obedient killers.

Some of Taylor's victims had their throats cut in the executive mansion. A number of times during our weeklong interrogation, locked inside the stifling hotel room, Tarnue appeared embarrassed. "I could not stop them. I could not stop them," he muttered. He described how Taylor sometimes carried a silver-plated AK-47 assault rifle and would use it for special executions.

Tarnue provided extensive details of murders, beatings, rapes. He said everyone knew that when Taylor or Chucky said he "did not want to see" someone again, it meant the person was to be killed.

When Taylor moved to a new residence, the SBU cleared away all the surrounding civilians, evicting them from their homes, raping young women, and looting property. Three women who resisted the evictions were later accused of conducting reconnaissance for the rebels opposed to Taylor. They were seized and taken down to a beach, where their throats were cut and their bodies buried in the sand.

There were frequent large-scale murder campaigns. To suppress dissent or to plunder local resources, Taylor ordered his militias to commit atrocities in regions throughout Liberia, including a 1991 raid against a village in the Liberian diamond region, where innocent villagers were murdered and their property destroyed. In 2000 he ordered an attack on a Guinean town so that the ATU could loot and pillage the area, killing villagers and burning their homes, after stealing all the rough diamonds the ATU could find.

We talked about Taylor's support for the Sierra Leonean thug Foday Sankoh, boss of the Revolutionary United Front (RUF). Sankoh was Taylor's tool in the conflict in Sierra Leone. He told me Sankoh's RUF collected diamonds and passed them to Taylor, who, in turn, used two Lebanese businessmen to sell the diamonds and provide Taylor with cash, weapons, and other matériel banned by the UN embargo on Liberia.

I struggled to stay focused in that stifling room, with the curtains pulled taut to block out the blinding light. The stories were sometimes hard to digest. Tarnue swayed between animation and a blasé monotone as he talked about the fear of black magic and voodoo that consumed the region. I would often have Tarnue repeat himself because I thought I might have misheard him. I learned that children often disappeared and were killed, and their body parts—fingers and ears—used in black magic as amulets.

One afternoon, as the general was rambling about a particular region of Liberia, my men's heads began to bob. Then, I thought I heard him say in the most matter-of-fact way, "We would find enemies of the Gio tied to trees, their insides removed. The Gio eat their enemies."

"Whoa, General, could you repeat what you just said?"

Now everyone in the room snapped upright, looking on attentively. "Oh, yes, when you are in the land of the Gio, you'd sometimes come upon people who were crucified, chest cavity split wide open. It was common for them to eat their victim's organs. It gives them power."

I glanced at my men, now wide awake, to see their looks of disbelief.

He also told us of the special amulets that witch doctors imbued with powers so strong that they could turn away bullets. Some of the rebel gangs in Sierra Leone would charge into battle wearing nothing but these amulets. When I asked him whether he believed the amulets worked, he answered, "If you believe strong enough, they will work. I have seen it."

Well after this assignment, I talked to a retired State Department officer who had served in West Africa. The subject of the bullet-defeating amulets came up, and he told me of the time he visited a senior army officer in Liberia who also claimed he was protected by the strong juju of his amulet. When my friend appeared unconvinced, the officer called his guard into the room and ordered the guard to draw his weapon and shoot him.

The guard was terrified to carry out the order, so the colonel yelled at him and threatened, "If you do not shoot me, I will shoot you!" At first, my friend thought it was all a joke. Then he watched aghast as the guard, eyes closed and hand shaking, fired at the colonel who instantly grabbed his shoulder.

A bloodstain appeared on the colonel's shirt. He furiously glared at the guard, "You fool, you were supposed to shoot at my heart! Do it right this time!"

It was then that my friend hurriedly excused himself, not wanting to be a witness to the killing.

Tarnue insisted that Taylor's assassins were operating in the Ghanaian refugee camps. He claimed that he recognized a few of them. Based on what had already happened to two other fugitives who ran afoul of Taylor, I didn't doubt it.

After four days of intensive questioning, I huddled with my team. "He's answered all our questions. Now it's time to put him on the machine. If anyone can think of something else to ask, do it now. Otherwise, let's have him talk to the box."

We left our polygrapher alone with the general for several hours. Tarnue had reasonable answers for all our questions, and we agreed that if what he had told us was true, he had only acted as most anyone else under the circumstances. He claimed he had never executed anyone, although he admitted to standing by while others committed murder. It came down to the polygraph.

Gary the polygrapher finally appeared from the room. "As far as I'm concerned, he passed every question you gave me."

"OK, then, let's have some dinner, and then start preparing our final report for headquarters. If we're directed to bring the general to America, we'll have to come up with a plan."

When we took Tarnue to Ghana's airport for the long flight home, it was teeming. The monsoon-like rain contributed to an oppressive mantle of humidity inside the airport that coalesced with the odors of human sweat and feces. Swarms of mosquitoes buzzed, and an occasional cockroach paraded over the luggage on the carousels.

My danger senses were on full alert as I looked around, trying to identify threats. I was convinced that Taylor's gangsters were watching the airport to prevent Tarnue from slipping away. The general had no passport or identifying papers. It was a big problem. Fortunately, before departing the States we had arranged a contact with an immigration official at the embassy who had a direct line to the top. In spite of this connection, he was still working the phones minutes before our flight was supposed to leave Accra.

I began to wonder whether we'd ever get out of there when Tarnue nudged me and whispered, "That man over there in the white shirt is one of Taylor's people. He is a bad man." I took the general to another corner of the crowded terminal and told Matt and Brad to watch the guy and see if he followed us. I wasn't sure what my next step was going to be, but then the immigration officer came over, his forehead covered in sweat. "OK, they will take care of things on the other end. I drew up an official-looking document before I came here, and hopefully we can bluff our way onto the plane. Follow me."

The Ghanaian customs officers were perplexed, but we overwhelmed them with our FBI badges and a document with a big embossed seal that said we had the right to take Tarnue to America. I have never been so happy to get on board a plane, as congested and dirty as it was. I checked the general's location, then the lights went out and I didn't open my eyes until the intercom announced London Heathrow. Once out of Africa, Tarnue would testify as a prosecution witness in the special court's case against Taylor. Although we members of the Fly Team had rescued what we believed to be a future star witness, we received no pats on the back, not even a "Lads, job well done!"

▪   ▪   ▪

A few weeks later, we were heading back to West Africa to prove or disprove the blood diamond nexus to al Qaeda. The congressman and Allen Black had remained adamant about a connection. It was not easy getting to Sierra Leone. We had a layover in Brussels for a night, and then we flew down to Lungi International Airport on the other side of a huge bay from Freetown, the capital of that small, tortured nation.

The test of nerves began the moment we landed in a torrential monsoon rain. An embassy facilitator ushered us onto a tired, rebuilt Russian helicopter that was overcrowded and crewed by men who looked as if they'd been drinking all day.

It was one of the blackest nights I've ever known, and I have never seen it rain so hard. The overloaded, ancient Hind shuddered so fiercely I was sure we wouldn't make it to the other side of the bay. Approximately six months later a helicopter from the same fleet crashed in the Sierra Leonean jungle, killing twenty-four.

Sierra Leone had been a beautiful place before the Taylor-backed civil war. During its British colonial period and for a short time afterward, the quaint city of Freetown, on a bluff overlooking the Atlantic, comprised well-kept and attractive clapboard houses painted the bright tropical hues that Bermudan and Caribbean homes are famous for today. The fondness for the yellows, pinks, and aqua blues started in places such as Sierra Leone, just as the darker side—the belief in juju and voodoo—and slavery were exported

Tired, rebuilt Russian helicopters moved us over the jungle of Sierra Leone. One crashed several months later, killing twenty-four.

to the Western Hemisphere. During the colonial days, local residents would dress in their finest versions of European attire and stroll the tree-lined boulevards after church, the women wearing bonnets and carrying parasols, the men in top hats, spats, and tail coats. All of that gentility had ended with the long, senseless nightmare brought on by a series of corrupt governments and culminated with the interference of Taylor and his crew.

Eastern Sierra Leone is rich in alluvial diamond fields, an area where millions of years earlier the cooling volcanic magma deposited diamonds over the earth's surface. In that region, mining for diamonds simply took a strong back, shovel, pick, and some type of screen.

We stayed in the only passable hotel, which was owned and operated by a Lebanese expat and his Irish wife. Mamba Point was small but comfortable, with good food. Europeans, Americans, and UN and embassy workers hung out there. A place of loud voices and laughter, cigarette smoke, and a strange, eclectic mix of jazz and African and European contemporary music, it was an oasis in a devastated region that wasn't close to getting back on its knees, much less its feet.

Finding satellite phone service in Sierra Leone.

Our mission was to interview as many people as possible who had had a part in or a front row seat for the brutality. Black and the UN Office of the Special Prosecutor had assured us that they would arrange access to all of the right people. We interviewed former rebel henchmen and men who ran the mining operations for the RUF, which, with Taylor's backing, eventually took over Freetown in an orgy of cruelty and destruction.

One morning we waited in Mamba Point's dining room for a newly minted Sierra Leonean colonel who had been a senior RUF member. He arrived with a bodyguard who stood nearby our table. The colonel—a very dark, fit man in his thirties with a cruel look and feel that was exaggerated by a series of horizontal scars on both cheeks—sat down at our table and grunted. We explained that we were investigating claims of al Qaeda terrorists purchasing diamonds from the RUF or Charles Taylor's people. In decent English and with obvious disdain, he said, "This place was full of terrorists. For a time everyone was a terrorist."

Then I felt someone moving behind me, and I could see the colonel's eyes glance over my shoulder and beyond. My pistol was tucked in the waistband of my pants, in the small of my back and under my shirt. The bodyguard had spotted the bulge and was moving in. I had been lulled by my surroundings and the false sense of security of our comfortable little hotel, but this city was a place where a thin veneer of civility only recently covered murder and mayhem.

I felt the barrel of the guard's weapon in my back. Looking straight into the colonel's eyes, I extended my hands out over the table, very slowly. I met his gaze to convey that I wasn't intimidated. Fortunately, my partners didn't make any foolish moves. The colonel looked up at his man and, with a twitch of the head, sent him away. The interview was uneventful and unproductive. I made a mental note of my mistake.

We went to the Kono diamond region. Our helicopter flew over a winding river for close to an hour. Below was only jungle, and we never saw a craft on the river. Only twice did we see smoke from a fire wafting up through the heavy jungle canopy.

When we landed, several Range Rovers were there, driven by fierce-looking Pakistani troops from the Kashmir region. The United Nations employed them to maintain peace as part of the UN mission in Sierra Leone (UNAMSIL). Bigger than most Pakistanis, they wore heavy beards and glared at us with the same intensity I remembered from the Taliban on the outskirts of Kabul. On our ride to their headquarters, I saw a group of UN peacekeepers helping the locals build a mosque.

The Pakistani colonel was cordial and insisted we have tea with him and dine in his battalion's mess hall. Housed in trailers and refurbished buildings, the compound was immaculate, and I could not complain about the food. After our meal, we climbed aboard the white UN Range Rovers and headed through town to the diamond mines. Dozens of small children begged in the streets as chickens played "chicken" with our speeding trucks.

Even with sunglasses, I had to squint as I looked out over diamond mining fields as far as the eye could see. People in loincloths shoveled muck through sifters. The irregular digging had created an anthill effect, covering the terrain with hundreds of chimney-like mounds interspersed with water-filled gullies. Overseers, better dressed in long African gowns and sporting parasols for shade, stood at various spots on the anthills. Our armed, turbaned security detail was even fiercer looking when juxtaposed against the undernourished and scantily dressed natives. Then, I heard the sound of a radio in the distance and instantly recognized the song, a favorite from my high school days, "You've Lost That Loving Feeling" by the Righteous Brothers. It was about the last thing I expected to hear and it was the only sound other than the slicing of shovels and the click of pickaxes.

When Taylor's RUF allies rampaged through the Kono area, his armed thugs stood on the anthills and played target practice with the workers. If anyone raised a hand above his waist, a furtive movement that might betray an attempt to swallow a diamond, they shot him on the spot.

We drove to the buildings that once housed the RUF overseers, the only place where the workers could "sell" the fruits of their labors when the rebels controlled the region. By prearrangement, the man who had served as an RUF boss in Kono was waiting there. He was young, no more than thirty-five years old, and he willingly described how the mines functioned and how they collected the rough diamonds from the workers. He had received amnesty as part of the peace agreement that resolved the conflict in Sierra Leone, and just like the colonel whose security man had gotten the drop on me back in Freetown, he was now an official of the Sierra Leonean government.

He was pretty convincing when he told me, "I've never seen an Arab anywhere near the diamond fields, and I know what an Arab looks like." He had no reason to lie. He was smart enough to realize that even if he had passed rough diamonds to Arabs, it was not a crime in America, and the likelihood of prosecuting him in the States on some kind of terrorism conspiracy charge was nonexistent. I had no leverage; he didn't even try to work me for money. People we interviewed, people who had been in positions to know, repeated his story. Africans in the Kono region are very dark. An Arab, even an East African, would have stood out. Everyone would have noticed men with strange features and facial hair, had they been there. After a day of interviews, we returned to Freetown.

Next, we arranged interviews with two of the old, established diamond merchants whose families had been dealing in the trade for several generations. They were all Lebanese, descendants of the Phoenicians, the famed original Mediterranean merchants who had dispersed and settled up and down the West African coast. When we arrived at their location, several local

The diamond fields of Sierra Leone, the source of many years of death and suffering for thousands.

thugs with machine guns stood near the entrance. They eyed us closely, and one motioned to the stairs. We entered a small office and saw an older Middle Eastern–looking man with reading glasses perched on the end of his nose. He sat down behind his shabby desk and pushed a set of scales aside so that we could see each other. I was now out of my league. I knew, however, that I had one thing on my side, the aura of the FBI. I could see the wheels churning in his head as he thought, Why would the famous FBI come all the way to this place to interview me? I tried to play his game. Remembering what Ed had taught me back in my first days as an agent in Georgia, I took my time. Smiling, sipping tea, commenting on the weather, I was escalating his curiosity and anxiety.

"Persons in the U.S. government believe that terrorists such as al Qaeda—have you heard of this group?" He nodded his head in acknowledgment. "They may have traded in the diamonds that were mined in eastern Sierra Leone. They may have used these diamonds to finance the murder of many Americans, and that is a very, very serious crime for which my government will stop at nothing to find the people who helped them."

I had his attention, but I didn't expect him to be honest. After he covered his family's history in Sierra Leone and explained how he had managed to survive the RUF terror, I asked him, "What is your annual export, in gross dollars, of diamonds from this region—that is, of course, of those diamonds that are legal and in conformance with the Kimberley Accord?"

Without hesitation, he replied in a much lower tone, hardly above a whisper, "I would say that we export about nine million in diamonds a year."

Damn, I thought, I bet he cut the real figure by two-thirds!

While preparing my interview notes later that evening, I pondered what I had learned. Along with the diamond merchant, there were at least three other families, all Lebanese and all Muslim, down along the coast of central West Africa that were controlling the diamond trade. Multiply by four or five and triple the figure, and you have a more realistic idea of the kind of money that the Lebanese are pulling out of that region. Again, much of this information is derived through confidential sources. Hezbollah controls Lebanon, and no businessman functions in Lebanon without paying off Hezbollah. They all have family back home, so whether they are dedicated Shi'a supporters of Islam or not, they are giving a lot of money to Hezbollah. To date, Hezbollah has not attacked the U.S. homeland. Avowed enemies of Zionism and Israel, its members rely heavily on funds from the hundreds of thousands of Palestinians and their supporters who reside in the West and in the United States. Hezbollah is a much more pragmatic organization than are al Qaeda and its associates. Hezbollah understands capitalism. It has won widespread support owing largely to its efforts to assist Palestinian refugees and Arab victims of the endless conflict with Israel. Its members run hospitals, orphanages, and a rudimentary pension system for their fighters and their families. They don't want to kill the golden goose, but there is little doubt that events could carry them across the line, causing them to unleash their brand of terrorism on U.S. soil.

We returned to the States after several more interviews, and I filed my report. It didn't read the way Investigator Black wanted it to read. Based on our investigation, we concluded that there was no legitimate basis for connecting al Qaeda to the blood diamond trade. What we did learn was that Hezbollah was profiting from a trade controlled by Lebanese Muslims, and we filed that report with the appropriate organizations.

284 ■ Endless Enemies

We also picked up some other valuable information. The new minister of justice for Sierra Leone told us that his organization had uncovered many travelers from Central and South Asia, primarily Pakistan, who had come to Sierra Leone and applied for new passports. His department was struggling just to find pencils, and he had no resources to check the stories or the backgrounds of these people. His point was that these Pakistanis, having hidden their trails, could easily move to the West. Again, we reported this troubling loophole to the new Department of Homeland Security, the people responsible for watching our borders.

I had never been more satisfied that my people had performed in a professional and thorough manner. In the end, though, the congressman, who still wields a budget pen, tore into Director Mueller during a public hearing. After a not-so-subtle threat from Black that our report needed to be "revised," I had tried to warn the director that he might be walking into an ambush during that hearing; however, my repeated calls to the front office were not returned. I understand that the usually calm Director Mueller reached a point during the hearing where he had endured enough of the congressman's tirade and rose and left. I had learned a great deal about the danger on the street after eighteen years as an investigator, but I was still an amateur when it came to Washington politics.

The pressure to connect al Qaeda to West Africa did not abate. Several months later the Fly Team sent Brad and Matt back, this time to Liberia, which was in turmoil. Taylor, under extreme international pressure, had fled to Nigeria, and Black had come up with the names of more people he believed held the keys to the al Qaeda–Taylor–blood diamond connection. But when the "witnesses" were available, they gave unconvincing answers, or their knowledge turned out to be just hearsay. It was another fruitless deployment.

The UN Office of the Special Prosecutor, after building an expensive prison and courthouse with UN funding in the capital of Sierra Leone, relocated the trial of Charles Taylor from Freetown to The Hague in the Netherlands because of civil unrest in Sierra Leone. Incredibly, Taylor still has friends in West Africa.

The prosecution presented ninety-one witnesses at Taylor's trial in The Hague including victims of the conflict in Sierra Leone and former members of his Liberian government, the RUF, and the NPFL. After offering twenty-one witnesses in Taylor's behalf, the defense rested. Taylor denied all charges against him. As of this writing, closing arguments have been made but no verdict has been returned. Meanwhile, in 2008 Taylor's son Chucky was sentenced to ninety-seven years in prison for participating in torture. The Department of Justice handled that case.

Twenty-Two

We Need More Agents

When the U.S. military invaded Afghanistan in October 2001, the FBI provided approximately forty agents to assist the effort. FBI agents were embedded with military special operations groups as well as with the CIA from the beginning of Operation Enduring Freedom. The Taliban and al Qaeda retreated. Many in al Qaeda fled over the border into the Federally Administered Tribal Areas (FATA). While the FATA were ostensibly part of Pakistan, tribes sympathetic to Islamic fundamentalism controlled them. With this operation's success, there were hundreds of prisoners. The military recognized the importance of the FBI's presence, and its demand for more agents became incessant. Director Mueller promised additional support.

The first group of agents was scattered countrywide in Afghanistan, with some going to outlying firebases with little oversight or connectivity. The general idea was that they would help capture high-value targets, process and interrogate prisoners, dispose of land mines, and provide expertise about al Qaeda in general, but nobody knew for sure what these agents were doing, the dangers they were facing, or how they were managing to survive. With this expanding and shifting role, management concluded that it was time to assess the situation. My boss Bill and I accompanied then assistant director Art Cummings to tour Afghanistan and draft a report outlining a future plan. Unlike most of my FBI travels, this time I didn't have to do all the legwork. One of the perks of traveling with an assistant director was that someone else arranged our transportation, housing, and food. It was a routine I could have gotten used to.

We flew over in the bureau's G-5, landing at Bagram Airfield late in the evening, and met with one of the senior officers and his staff the next morning. He was highly complimentary of our agents' work and voiced the same sentiment we would hear all over Afghanistan: "We need more FBI agents."

Our people—both agents and analysts—were showing young soldiers and Marines how to collect evidence from what the military calls a "sensitive site exploitation," which is really just a crime scene. Bags of pocket litter and documents, and the occasional computer, were being dragged back to Bagram after every raid, but there wasn't a system in place to track the evidence. It didn't do much good to have overworked translators dig through piles for days, only to have one suddenly find a critical piece of information but not know its source.

There was a developing awareness and appreciation that this low-intensity conflict was unlike anything we'd faced before. With that realization came the understanding that it would require a traditional task force approach. Cops and investigators had some valuable tools the war fighters would need to employ, particularly if we were going to figure out a way to detain dangerous people for a long time. Human rights advocates around the world were railing against the facility at Guantánamo, and as the specter of 9/11 diminished, the United States was increasingly being portrayed as the bad guy because of the allegations of unlawful renditions and extreme interrogation techniques.

On the battlefield, the agency and every other intelligence-collecting outfit were only concerned with learning the enemy's whereabouts and plans. With the notable exception of the FBI, in the years immediately after 9/11 the last thing on anyone's mind was a police or criminal investigative approach to dealing with al Qaeda. Focused on stopping the next attack, most weren't thinking about what we were going to do with all the people we had incarcerated.

On my second day at Bagram, I met the lieutenant colonel who was in charge of the Document Exploitation (DOCEX) facility, one of several central intelligence collection points throughout the country. He looked weary. He and his staff were working overtime, sleeping next to their desks, and trying to find nuggets in mounds of debris. He motioned to a stack of bags, nearly six feet high, in the corner. "That's prosecution material over there. Stuff we don't have time to translate now."

It was a few months before the 2004 presidential election, and back in the States everyone was working frantically to discover and disrupt terrorist sleeper cells such as the one that had recently bombed trains in Spain. Only a fool would think that terrorists were not planning the same thing for the United States.

I told the colonel, "Sir, we're sure they're getting ready to hit us back home just before the election. There could be information in those bags that would be critical to finding them before it happens."

Until that moment, the DOCEX team had concentrated on one thing: battlefield intelligence. This focus was understandable. The team wanted to locate Osama bin Laden and his crew and engage the scattered, well-hidden enemy. The colonel said, "Well, agent, if you can get me some help, I'll reprioritize what we're trying to translate." From then on, I took my speech wherever people would listen.

Every time the Marines launched from Bagram on an assault in the mountains, I asked to address them. It took little time to convey what we needed and why. "Men, focus on your mission, but when you're clearing huts and buildings, or when you're going through detainees' pockets, remember this: somewhere back home there are evil people planning to attack us again. Your families, moms, dads, brothers and sisters, your girlfriends—everyone is at risk. So if that piece of paper looks like it just might pertain to something in America—it could be a shopping receipt from Kmart in Orlando, doesn't matter—please bag it and tag it. Make a note of who had it or where it was found."

Within two weeks, good material was pouring in. Young Marines would hop off incoming choppers and hand carry information directly to DOCEX and sometimes even straight to the FBI.

Although experienced analysts were in short supply, I requested one from headquarters to help at DOCEX. In the interim, I also briefed the CIA boss in country. He replied, "OK, agent, you tell the colonel that if he'll put that stuff on a truck and send it up here, we'll help him out."

I returned to Bagram, where I conveyed the CIA chief's message to the colonel. He promptly responded, "The chief can kiss my ass." It was obvious that "sharing" still had a long way to go in Afghanistan.

When I returned to the CIA office, I told the boss precisely what the colonel had said. The chief wasn't having a particularly good day. "Agent Holcomb," he said, "if you can't get that material up here for our review, then you are responsible if one day there's another attack back in the States and we later find the critical piece of intelligence in that pile down at DOCEX. I'm putting that in the file."

"Sir, I only represent the FBI here," I responded. "I can't force an army colonel to do anything. It's not my job, but someone needs to take care of this." The CIA boss was frenetic and wound tight. He was a nervous, chain-smoking, working-twenty-hours-a-day kind of person with a hair-trigger temper. He grunted and spun around in his desk chair, turning his back to me.

▪   ▪   ▪

Our work often took us between Kabul and Bagram. The U.S. Embassy, Coalition Headquarters, the fledgling FBI legat's office, and the seat of Hamid Karzai's government were all in Kabul. Before departing from either location, because the route was highly dangerous, we would walk through our counterassault plan and review checklists: so many extra magazines of ammunition, tracking devices, radios that worked or at least a cell phone backup, and a heavy-duty, quick-change jack in every vehicle along with a healthy spare tire.

Many convoys had been struck while moving on the old Kabul road, and we noticed the small holes in roadside embankments where IEDs had exploded. We were playing the odds. We were armed and wore level IV body armor, but some of our vehicles were soft skinned—that is, lacking any armor. Nothing we had, however, would stop a shaped charge (a deadlier version of an IED), the Taliban's latest murderous gift from Iran but by way of the Russians. It was a form of payback. U.S. Stinger missiles had helped the Taliban bring down many Russian helicopters during the Afghan-Soviet War (1979–89).

We would pass Afghanis walking the long, lonely stretch of road, sometimes a lone man with a woman and a camel or two trailing behind. With skin as textured as old leather, without water bottles, in frayed sandals, and with nothing in their hands or on their backs, they were heading out across a waste-

With some of the team in Bagram (author on the left).

land toward nothing but barren, jagged mountains. We saw burned-out Soviet tanks or trucks and still unexploded bombs implanted in the fields, their
winged tail ends protruding at an angle. It was a scene from some doomsday
movie. We took our pistols everywhere, even to the john. Some days the wind
blew the sand so hard, we had to wear goggles to find our way.

In addition to Kandahar in the south, Herat in the west, and Jalalabad in
the east, I flew out to a number of forward bases to check on my men. While
in Kandahar, we met with a seasoned FBI agent who was part of a team that
had bivouacked in Mullah Omar's old compound. Omar, a principal Taliban
leader and supporter of bin Laden's, had been forced to flee into Pakistan
in 2001.

Jalalabad was at the doorstep of the famous Khyber Pass, where the threat
level was high and Afghan irregular troops provided security. With weapons
pointing out of every window, we raced down the country road at almost
blinding speed, trying to outrun the danger.

After Bill and Art left, I stayed on for weeks, living in converted shipping
containers. Fitted with air conditioning, refrigerators, and bunk beds, they

Assessing the bureau's mission in Afghanistan.

weren't bad accommodations even though in Bagram I had to walk a quarter mile across the airport tarmac to reach a bathroom. My hooch was right next to the runway, so every night I would hear aircraft, usually A-10 fighters, take off and land.

After more than a month in Afghanistan, I returned to the States and cowrote a lengthy assessment of the FBI's role in Afghanistan. I recommended that we send more personnel to assist with interviews, intelligence gathering, and the preparation of criminal cases against the worst of the detainees.

Mullah Omar's compound in Kandahar.

Rumors began to circulate that the assistant section chief who oversaw the Fly Team and two other units was moving on to a well-deserved supervisory position in the field. Some encouraged me to compete for the position because the Fly Team, still struggling with critics and sniping from every corner of the bureau, needed someone who understood its purpose and would continue to fight for it. I had had a hand in creating the Fly Team as much as anyone else did. Although I hated to step upstairs, I knew that my days of long-term deployments were nearing an end, so I applied for the job.

While I was waiting for the agonizingly long process to play out, the commanding general in Afghanistan, during a meeting with the FBI executive assistant director (EAD) who had flown into Bagram, asked the FBI to send a team of agents to help interrogate a fast-growing detainee population. The EAD had promised the general he'd send agents, so the Fly Team had to deliver. We called on several of our now-seasoned and over-deployed men to respond. We were one body short, so we accepted a volunteer who had been lobbying hard to be part of the mission. A former operator with the Hostage Rescue Team and a military vet, he pleaded to go to Afghanistan. Although he struck me as a little intense, I consented since Bill, who was also former HRT, wanted him on the deployment. I couldn't deny that he had a good résumé. I tapped one of our best men, Steve, a former army ranger who had been in Afghanistan before, to take the lead.

The military was forming a joint interrogation team for some high-value detainees, people who seemed to deserve some special attention. Several days after our folks arrived in country, I got a call from Steve, who obviously couldn't talk freely. "Ray, this guy you sent with us is getting a little weird about this interrogation assignment. He keeps bringing up Abu Ghraib and all the bad press. We haven't been asked to do an interrogation yet, but he's already assumed that somebody is going to torture somebody. He's a powder keg."

"OK, Steve, we'll try to fix it." I briefed my boss on the looming problem, and he told me to keep him advised. Two days later, on a Friday afternoon, I received an e-mail from our intense volunteer. He was worried that he would be asked to do things that might be illegal. I called him on the phone immediately and asked him if anything had occurred.

"No," he said, "but I sense it's coming."

Although I was now convinced that he was not suited for this assignment and wasn't managing the stress well, I recognized that our agents needed clear guidance.

What had happened at the Abu Ghraib Prison in 2004 was an ugly mess, and more stories were percolating about prisoner abuse in Afghanistan, even cases of murder. We couldn't ignore the reality that FBI agents in the field might have to withstand pressure from another organization to do things that went against FBI protocols. We met with the bureau's lawyers, told them of our unease, and asked them for clear, written guidance that would be blessed at the top.

"That is going to take some time to work through the approval process."

"We can't leave these guys hanging out there without guidance any longer."

"Well, we'll try, but we just can't promise a quick turnaround on this."

"Counselors, doesn't anyone realize we are sitting on a bomb about to go off any minute? We have to give our people some rules."

"Well, if you're that worried, just bring them home, or have them recuse themselves from any activity until they hear from us."

That approach was not viable. We had people embedded throughout the Middle East. They had managed to foster solid relations with the military and the CIA. If we told our agents to remove themselves from interrogations, the message would be that we were passing judgment on our counterparts and that we suspected they were acting illegally or immorally. This behavior would support the suspicions they had about the FBI at the outset—that is, that we were keeping books on them and maybe even building criminal cases against them. That misperception would have been the death knell for cooperation of any kind.

My people were in a precarious place while waiting for direction. Having been there, I thought the situation was unacceptable. I drafted a communication to our embedded agents, and Bill signed off immediately. In essence, the message was, "You will only employ interview techniques and policies that you were taught at the FBI Academy. If you are engaged in a joint interrogation with persons belonging to another government agency, and they employ techniques outside of the scope or guidelines taught at the FBI Academy, you will excuse yourself from that interrogation. Bear in mind that other government agencies may follow guidelines and practice techniques that differ from those followed by the FBI; however, that in and of itself does not make those guidelines or techniques unlawful. If you believe that individuals of another government agency are exceeding their own guidelines, then you will report your concerns to your senior FBI agent on scene, and he will address the matter with his counterpart."

This memo was fundamental and clear. It would permit our agents to work unencumbered. If the voice in the head, the one entrenched after hours of legal training at Quantico, said, "Hey, this isn't right!" the agent could step away and talk to his boss. After that, it was up to the senior agent on site to square away the issue.

We supplied supplementary instructions for each senior FBI agent in charge of a team. He or she was to learn the rules that applied to the other agencies participating in the joint interrogations. Then he or she would know when something was wrong and when it was time to address it. The Fly Team was an operational squad, and our mission was to get the job done. We put together solid direction for our people in one day without waiting for the lawyers or the bureaucrats. Months later, the FBI's Office of General Counsel formalized and approved this policy, which became the rule for every agent deployed overseas.

To date, in spite of a massive effort by the world media, human rights organizations, and U.S. government institutions, including Congress, to find instances of detainee abuse, there is no serious case where anyone can show that an FBI agent stepped over the line. Whether at Guantánamo Bay, Cuba; Bagram, Afghanistan; or any of the detention facilities in Iraq, there is not a single instance of an agent employing questionable interrogation techniques. From Director Mueller on down, FBI decision makers would not allow the FBI to be drawn into the mentality of "anything goes because it's war." To those who profess that the FBI did not acquire solid intelligence out of detainees using traditional law enforcement approaches to an interview, I vehemently disagree. I watched many good agents slowly and adroitly draw good information out of prisoners who didn't even realize they were revealing it.

I am not arguing that there is no conceivable circumstance where "enhanced" interrogation might be required. I can conceive of critical situations where only through such techniques can we stand a chance of averting an imminent, horrific attack. I strongly believe, however, that in the vast majority of cases, such techniques are nonproductive and unnecessary. Abuse and duress, in the absence of an extreme emergency, are nothing more than poor and generally ineffective substitutes for a scarcity of knowledge, cunning, perseverance, and skill on the part of the interrogator.

Twenty-Three

The Next Chapter

Sharing information and connecting the dots have become catchphrases in the law enforcement and intelligence-gathering communities. The walls that once prevented the FBI from talking to the CIA and from revealing information even within its own organization continue to come down.

Within the law enforcement community, on a human level where egos are reality, sharing will always be a challenge. I recognized this situation ever since my early days as a counter-narcotics agent, when I saw how the DEA's interest in statistics and promotions trumped taking the time to go after the people at the top of a drug organization and how the rush to be the first agency to arrest high-profile criminals in order to get those headlines blinded investigators to what really mattered. Later, I saw how anger over losing control of an investigation prompted our SWAT "brothers" to leave us behind in Tanzania without any of the information they had surely gathered during their weeks there. We were working at cross-purposes when the customs agents at Kennedy Airport tore open a pallet of heroin in the presence of a crowd of airport workers—some of whom were possibly implicated in the smuggling operation—in clear disregard of any common sense, just so that the agents could claim the statistic.

I saw a U.S. ambassador bar a brash but effective bureau leader from ever returning to Yemen because of a clash in philosophies and roles. Though they had distinct missions—the nurturing of U.S.-Yemeni relations and the identification of those responsible for the deaths of Americans, respectively—in the final analysis, both the Department of State and the FBI have an ultimate obligation to ensure the security of America. We should have done a better job of working together.

Within the FBI, I also witnessed conflict and short sightedness. Again, the human ego, that thing that makes an investigator track a criminal to the end of the earth, turns the same investigator into a hoarder of information. I had a front row seat to a process that didn't recognize how critical it was to immediately tell the director of the FBI that a couple of investigators on the other side of the world, only days after the 9/11 attacks, had positively identified people responsible for killing over three thousand Americans.

It comes down to what I learned early in my career about being a federal agent and gaining the trust and support of local law enforcement: we all need each other, whether it is the intelligence collection business or the law enforcement business. It doesn't matter who gets the stat when we're talking about the security of the American people. When we aren't competing among ourselves or withholding information, we are a very effective brotherhood.

I did finally get the job I applied for, becoming the assistant section chief in charge of the Fly Team, along with two other units critical in the war against terrorism. This section was designated the Counterterrorism Operational Response Section. I became the consummate bureaucrat, knee deep in the frustrating responsibilities that attend impressive-sounding titles. I had lost the fight to stay on the bottom. With my section chief, Frank, a solid, dedicated man, I worked hard to make these new counterterrorism units productive and to increase the FBI's offensive capacity. We focused on the problem of Islamic radicalization in America, particularly as it seemed to be growing within the American prison system. We took another hard look at FBI operations in Guantánamo Bay and found, once more, that our agents and staff were handling things according to the bureau's guidelines.

I wasn't going on the road anymore, but I took comfort in knowing that my Fly Team was in able hands and that it could now stand on its own. The team had evolved into what I had always hoped for: a highly trained cadre of terrorism first responders—including agents and analysts—based out of the FBI's new counterterrorism facility. Fly Team agents and analysts now had expansive quarters and a ready room where they stored their gear, prepared to roll out to any point on the map with just a few hours' notice. It is a far, far cry from 2002 when the Super Squad consisted of a few dedicated people who had to scratch together their gear and who weren't quite sure how to make it happen but understood what had to happen.

Today, the Fly Team has agents and analysts who, as a group, speak about a dozen languages: Arabic, Spanish, French, Swahili, Dutch, and more. Agents and analysts who apply must have at least five years' experience with the bureau and undergo rigorous tests to qualify for the Fly Team. Then they must complete drills, team-building exercises, and five months of in-depth training, where the recruits are taught everything from advanced post-blast investigative techniques to how to use specialized weapons and handle hazardous materials. They also learn combat medical skills, fingerprinting, hostage survival and resistance, and cultural awareness. Once the team is called on, the members quickly gather intelligence reports and information about the mission, reaching out to their counterparts in the impacted field office or overseas and learning as much as they can about the locale. They assemble the equipment they will need from well-stocked stores, pull together the required situation-specific specialists—evidence experts, bomb technicians, hazardous materials personnel, and others—and then head for a plane. Once on the ground, they integrate, assess, and attack the mission. The team's reputation is now well known, and its talents are in demand.

It is a challenging job, however, and even the most dedicated cannot maintain the deployment rate forever. The graduates of the team have moved on to senior positions throughout the FBI. They bring their invaluable experiences to the field, running squads and units. More important, and as I had always hoped, these veterans are now beginning to return to the team, having come full circle, and are rejuvenated and ready to hit the ground once more. If allowed to continue down this path and if management tampering is limited, this unique and effective weapon in the war against terrorism will spin off benefits to the entire FBI in many, some unforeseen, ways. This development is what we had always envisioned.

I also had oversight of the National Joint Terrorism Task Force (NJTTF). Created after 9/11, it comprises representatives from every entity—federal, state, local, and private sector—that has a role in protecting America from a terrorist attack. They all sit together, exchange information, and connect the leadership of their respective organizations directly with the FBI. It is the culmination of everything that "joint effort" stands for. The NJTTF is directly tied in to every JTTF in America; mirror versions of the national force, they are strategically placed in every state in the nation. Members of the NJTTF can walk next door to the FBI units that oversee every ongoing terrorism investigation in the world. They don't have to worry about red tape or layers of bosses to mull over requests that might have a negative impact on their personal careers. More than any one civilian counterterrorism unit in the U.S. government's arsenal, the JTTF program is the tip of the spear.

Just like the Fly Team, the Military Liaison and Detainee Unit was thrown together immediately after 9/11 amid the chaos at FBI Headquarters. Agents were detailed to military units in Afghanistan and Iraq because the military needed help processing and interrogating prisoners. Soon prisoners would also flow into detention centers from Bagram to Guantánamo Bay. Jeff, a former operator with the Hostage Rescue Team, was put in charge of the MLDU, given the task of overseeing the FBI's new, quickly expanding mission. With the help of a few agents, he did whatever was necessary to make it work. He kept track of dozens of agents in two war zones, sent them supplies, maintained some lines of communication, found replacements, and dealt with hundreds of other issues that no FBI supervisor had ever handled before. The days were particularly long for everyone in headquarters during those months, but no one complained and no one gave less than 100 percent.

Mandatory retirement was looming. I had been so busy that I hardly realized I would have to start looking for a new career. I spent the last months of my FBI career representing the bureau in interagency discussions to create a national plan that would coordinate and synchronize all U.S. government efforts to fight terrorism. An ambitious goal, it was the first ever effort to catalog in detail the role that every federal department and agency has in thwarting and undoing the terrorist threat. After almost twenty-three years I realized how little I knew about our partners in the fight against terrorism and how pervasive the misunderstanding was among most departments and agencies. It was a critical and major first step to make America's counterterrorism effort more effective, but a great deal of work still lay ahead.

The author with former FBI director William Webster and former CIA director Stansfield Turner.

We were writing concepts on a whiteboard when my time ran out and I had to turn in my badge. It was a difficult moment. I walked away quietly.

■   ■   ■

Today, al Qaeda leadership is cornered. It no longer exerts operational or tactical control over the growing number of affiliates that are springing up around the world. This fragmentation is the result of a prodigious effort by our military, the CIA, the NSA, organizations within the departments of Homeland Security and Justice, as well as many other federal organizations. The Base is hiding, reduced to little more than a spiritual concept for its ardent followers. The semiautonomous affiliates are becoming the real danger as they plot spectacular attacks against the U.S. homeland from their havens in Pakistan, Yemen, the Horn of Africa, and Southeast Asia. Al Qaeda–like

cells still exist throughout Europe. However, Western governments have finally begun to empower their security agencies with tougher laws to combat
the terrorists.

As the West becomes more effective at stopping the terrorists, their tactics change. In 2009 the attacks in Little Rock, Arkansas, and Fort Hood,
Texas, and Umar Farouk Abdulmutallab's Christmas Day attempt to bring
down a commercial airliner over Detroit were harbingers of a new, insidious threat. Technology has fueled this new danger; hate-filled imams now
deliver sermons over password-protected, secure websites to self-radicalized
Americans. These days, an American who is so inclined can become a terrorist in the privacy of his own home. The FBI, with limited technical and
linguistic resources, has to adapt and contend with Internet technology that
is ever changing and providing terrorists with new ways to defeat government
monitoring.

Our security can vanish in an instant should we accede to the clamor to
reverse the gains we have made. Our enemies are elated and inspired by the
open airing of American discord. The rancorous debate over how to protect
ourselves, how to deal with the terrorists we capture, and how to protect the
privacy of individuals all fuel the terrorists' belief in their ultimate victory.
They don't understand our democratic values, and they really don't care. Regardless of one's politics, it is a fact that for every terrorist locked up or eliminated, there will be more. Osama bin Laden's son, Omar, has disavowed violent terrorism. In a 2010 televised interview, however, he stated that his father
is the least vicious of the Islamic terrorists and that the upcoming generation
of young terrorists is far more dangerous and brutal. This war—for it still is a
global war against terrorism—will be won by the most patient and the most
durable.

Now we have a National Counterterrorism Center and a director of National Intelligence specifically to ensure that critical intelligence information
is imparted throughout the law enforcement and intelligence communities.
The center made up of many analysts, a good portion of whom are detailed
from other agencies, is tasked by law with reviewing and coordinating the
massive volumes of information that flow into databases every day from every
imaginable source. Databases and hundreds of analysts alone, however, will
not guarantee our security. We will never be allowed the luxury of believing

that we have everything covered. Our enemies are adapting to our methods daily, and we must learn to anticipate and adapt to them. As our new generation of terrorist fighters matures and learns, our agencies will become more effective. We can only hope that we will quickly surmount the steep learning curve.

As for me, it is a serious understatement to say that I'm very proud to have spent almost twenty-three years of my life as a special agent of the FBI. The end came too quickly. I would have changed little. Throughout my career, the sense of accomplishment was fleeting. Most evenings I would think that I could have done more or that I should have done something differently. Yes, I had that occasional sense of closure when the judge would slam his gavel after sentencing or the subject of my investigation would confess to his crimes, but that feeling was always short lived. The next day brought new or unaddressed challenges.

I still feel a strong tie to the FBI. I believe that no organization is more diligently enforcing America's laws within the framework of our Constitution and that no other nation has a law enforcement entity of its caliber. The FBI has many good people who make sacrifices every day, working long hours and traveling treacherous roads. The organization could not exist without the dedication and hard work of every support person and every analyst. Its grit, however, is the corps of street agents who fight against all crime, wanting nothing but the personal satisfaction of a day's work well done on behalf of their country.

▪ ▪ ▪

On August 9, 2006, seven months after my retirement, the National Foreign Intelligence Community, based on the recommendation of the director of the FBI, awarded the Fly Team the National Intelligence Meritorious Unit Citation for the "implementation of innovative strategies targeting terrorism resulting in superior accomplishments" since its inception in June 2002 to December 2004.

Index

Note: Pages numbers in *italics* indicate photographs.

About the Authors

Raymond W. Holcomb is now a strategic planner for the U.S. government's counterterrorism effort. In that position, Holcomb has received numerous awards in recognition of his innovative strategies targeting terrorism.

Holcomb retired from the FBI in 2005 after more than twenty-two years of service, during which he also received numerous citations from the director of the FBI for outstanding performance. His most recent position in the bureau was as assistant section chief of the Counterterrorism Operational Response Section (CORS), with oversight of the National Joint Terrorism Task Force; the Military Liaison and Detainee Unit, which manages FBI agents detailed to the various military commands responsible for the Iraq, Afghanistan, and Horn of Africa theaters of operation; and all FBI operations at the Guantánamo Bay Detention Facility.

CORS also managed the FBI's roles in supporting the Iraqi Regime Crimes Liaison Office, the prison counter-radicalization program, and the FBI's Fly Team (formerly Fly Away/Rapid Deployment Team Unit), which provides a rapid response element of experienced counterterrorism investigators and analysts capable of worldwide deployment on hours' notice. Holcomb was instrumental in the creation of the Fly Team in 2002. In 2006, it was awarded the National Intelligence Meritorious Unit Citation for efforts in the war on terrorism from May 2002 until April 2004.

Holcomb was involved in the arrest of the 1993 World Trade Center garage bombers and was part of the team that investigated the 1998 destruction of the U.S. embassies in Tanzania and Kenya. He served as a member of the Zacarias Moussaoui prosecution team. He was also the FBI's senior agent for numerous FBI counterterrorism deployments, including the terrorist attacks on the JW Marriott Hotel, Jakarta, Indonesia; the British consulate, Istanbul, Turkey; the investigation of terrorist links to West African "blood diamonds"; and numerous terrorist investigations in Yemen, Pakistan, and Afghanistan. He lives in Arlington, Virginia.

■   ■   ■

Lillian S. Weiss is a practicing attorney and a freelance writer, speechwriter, and editorial consultant. She lives in Voorhees, New Jersey.